Damnatio Memoriae

THE SHALL NOT BE FORGOTTEN

A study of the Francoist genocide
of Cordoba 1936-1949

VOLUME II
CRUSHING THE VANQUISHED

Annotated English Translation of
La Victoria Sangrienta by
FRANCISCO MORENO GÓMEZ

by
MAGDALENA GORRELL JAÉN

Towards the retrieval of the Historic Memory of Spain

Damnatio Memoriae Vol. 2 by Magdalena Gorrell Jaén

ISBN 978-1-970072-38-9 (Paperback)
ISBN 978-1-970092-39-6 (Hardback)

This book is written to provide information and motivation to readers. Its purpose is not to render any type of psychological, legal, or professional advice of any kind. The content is the sole opinion and expression of the author, and not necessarily that of the publisher.

Printed in the United States of America.

New Leaf Media, LLC
175 S. 3rd Street, Suite 200
Columbus, OH 43215
www.thenewleafmedia.com

VOLUME II
Crushing the Vanquished

CONTENTS

TABLES

APPENDIXES

Terror does not exist only when violence is being applied; it also exists when the violence has ceased and appears only as a constant threat that hangs over men's heads. The threat of terror creates an atmosphere, where terror is the determinant factor; an ambiance that poisons life even more than the actual root of the terror.

Oscar Steimberg, Buenos Aires
Quoted by Pablo Uriel 1988.

INTRODUCTION

Francoist regulations and repressive legislation stemmed from the illegality of the June 17 1936 military coup, as the dictates of the totalitarian, i.e., anti-democratic, system of governance on which Francoism was rooted.

Francoist justice has been widely described as a farce, devised solely to provide a quasi-legal cover for the regime's criminality, both before and after the creation of the New State.

In addition to the innate vices of its origin, there immediately appeared a multitude of orders, decrees and laws unfettered by any due process guarantees of any kind and with utter contempt for the Rule of Law. As the latter was non-existent, the system understandably spawned hundreds of thousands of extra-judicial sentences. Such is the lingering influence of the Francoist Regime today, that instead of repealing these sentences, Law 52 of 2007 only describes them as being unlawful.

When Francoist criminality is looked at from the viewpoint of International Law, it becomes apparent that the Regime's crimes were considerably more grievous than one had imagined. Today, however, there still is a large sector of the community that pathetically insists on denying or at the very least, repudiating, this criminality.

The oppressive maelstrom that began near the end of the civil war continued throughout the post-war period without any hesitation or pause in the Regime's repressive project. It was an ongoing program superimposed upon the contingencies of war, a continuum, beginning 17 July 1936 that lasted until the early 1950s, at the very earliest, occasionally lingering until Franco's death in 1975. Nothing less than 15 years of harsh, relentless punishment and extermination unleashed against the social base of the Republic, its politicians and its illustrious elite. It was the ruthless annihilation of half of Spain, something that cannot continue to be excused or ignored.

The state of war declared by Franco to have begun 17 July 1936, officially remained in force until 1948. In other words, the first period of post-war repression that actually began before the 1939 Nationalist victory, ran concurrently with the civil war until the end of the 1940s. The transition of the Regime's methods and objectives provided a semblance of unity for a decade and a half of terror, extermination, punishment, ideological and economic repression, starvation, social exclusion, purging, annihilation and forced exile; a multifaceted repressive nightmare.

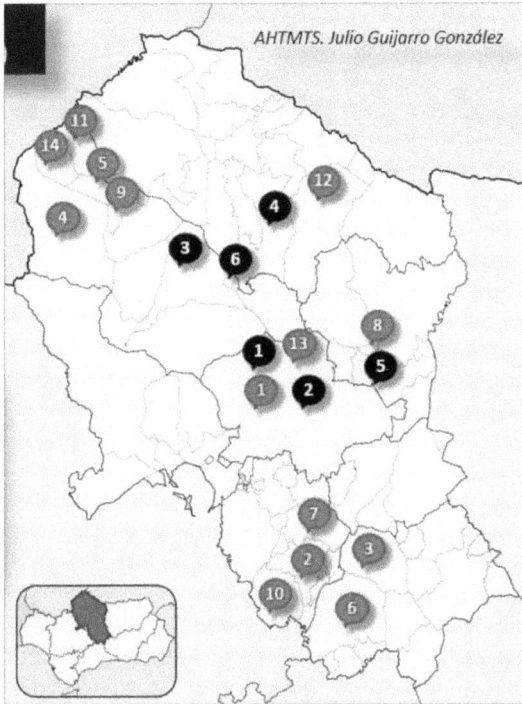

AHTMTS. Julio Guijarro González

Prisoner Concentration Camps and Prisoner-of-War Workers Battalions in Cordoba province (1938-1941)

Second Territorial Military Court Historic Archives - Andalusia

WB – Workers' Battalions	CC – Concentration Camps
1. **WB** nº 59 Cerro Muriano	1. **CC** Cordoba. Cordoba
2. **WB** nº 113 Infanteria de	la Vieja. San Caetano
Granada de Cordoba	2. **CC** Aguilar de la Frontera
3. **WB** nº 208 Espiel	3. **CC** Cabra
4. **WB** nº 203 Pozoblanco	4. **CC** Fuente Obejuna
5. **WB** nº 5 El Carpio	5. **CC** La Granjuela
6. **WB** nº 101 Villaharta	6. **CC** Lucena
	7. **CC** Montilla
	8. **CC** Pedro Abad
	9. **CC** Pueblonovo
	10. **CC** Puente Genil
	11. **CC** Valsequillo
	12. **CC** Villanueva de Cordoba
	13. **CC** Cerro Muriano
	14. **CC** Los Blázquez

I

CRUSHING THE VANQUISHED (D). REPRESSIVE LEGISLATION, DEATH RITES, FIRING SQUADS

FRANCO'S REPRESSIVE LEGISLATION.
EXECUTIONS AND DEATH RITUALS:
1. The *enterado*. 2. The *sacas*. 3. The chapel. 4. The firing squad.
EXECUTIONS IN CORDOBA TOWNS
AND VILLAGES (PART I).

Franco's repressive legislation

All victims of Francoism were persecuted for the crime of military rebellion, a political crime that carried the death penalty. Justification for these assassinations was two-fold: a)sentences sanctioned by wartime edicts; or b) sentences handed down by courts martial, the two faces of the same Francoist criminal coin.

This is the argument frequently advanced by the few magistrates who openly declare their observance of democratic principles, their real independence of thought and judicial understanding, whenever they are confronted with Francoist outrages against human rights. Magistrates such as Javier Moscoso, José A. Martín Pallin, the brothers Carlos and José Jiménez Villarejo and, of course, Judge Baltasar Garzón (recently ousted from office by a Supreme Court hidebound by inherited Francoist practices).

Although it is always worth turning to the Law when attempting to shed some light on historical events, the assumption that today there might be some academic consensus regarding Francoism is inconceivable. The theoretical *corpus* that issues from Academia regarding Francoist criminality is chaotic. For example, when speaking of Francoist criminality, Julio Ponce from Seville distinguishes between 'murdered' and 'executed', thereby attempting to spread the idea that among the victims, some of these acts were simply common criminals. Today in Spain, right-wing members of the judiciary, especially those who prefer to ignore the advances in universal jurisprudence, who disparage and rule in blatant contempt of international treaties (a typical feature of Francoism), are being forced to face reality in the form of occasional cases from outside Spain, such as the current cases arising from the famous 'Argentinian lawsuit' against Francoist crimes.

A noteworthy and instructive feature of the April 14 2010 lawsuit[1] before the National Criminal and Administrative Court, under the generic title of 'Genocide', is that it classified the crimes it claims were committed into five different groups:

- individuals who were seized from their homes or jails to be 'taken for a walk', or *paseo*;
- individuals sentenced to death and shot by firing squad following summary proceedings in which due process of law was notable absent;
- individuals sentenced to long prison sentences in trials equally devoid of due process of law and, furthermore, sometimes condemned to forced labour;
- mothers and fathers from whom children were stolen or made to disappear; and
- others who suffered directly from torture and arbitrary arrest.[2]

Lastly, the most significant feature of Franco's great repressive project was the torrent of wartime edicts, orders, decrees and laws against Republican Spain, the toughest and the most forceful being those that were published in the immediate 1939 post-war period. Faced with this terrible reality, whose effects we have and will continue to examine, no one can say that once the Nationalists claimed victory, Francoism acquired a moderate or benefactory nature, as this is totally false and contrary to the facts.

Francoist Jurisprudence

Franco's wartime jurisprudence began with the extra-legal publication of *bandos de guerra*, or wartime decrees, that the insurgent forces issued in profusion right from the very beginning of the civil war, in 1936 and that ushered in the wave of summary executions.

The initial summary executions were first 'legally' authorized with the publication of National Defence Junta Decree of July 28 1936, the point of reference for the beginning of the extermination. This and subsequent decrees gave real substance to all the so-called «Reserved Instructions» from 'Director' General Emilio Mola, with specific references to *terror, cleansing, extermination* and *exemplary punishments*, all of which are euphemisms for genocide.

This was followed by National Defence Junta Decree 79 of August 31 1936, published during the widespread atrocities committed by the entire Nationalist rear-guard, written in the same spirit as the Director's decrees and as legally farcical, based on directives such as the one that states: "*It is necessary at the present time (…) for speed to be the norm for military judiciary actions…*"

Franco's famous <u>Decree 55 of 1 November 1936</u>, instituted the *emergency summary procedure* that during the first six months was only applied to a few military individuals loyal to the constitutional government, to Republican leaders and to anti-Franco persons of note. With few exceptions, the remainder of the repressed population was prosecuted on a large scale by extra-judicial summary executions, paseos and murder in situ, under the ex-judicial <u>Law of Fugitives</u> during the entire war in all of Spain occupied by Nationalist troops. An excellent example of this are the martyrized towns in Badajoz province, after the fall of the La Serena pocket of Republican resistance in 1938 and during the advance of the Italian-Francoist troops through Catalonia in the autumn of 1938.

Some historians believe, incorrectly, that the extra-judicial summary executions known as *paseos* stopped in March 1937 with the widespread resort to trial by courts martial, despite the fact that Francoists continued to resort to these as late as the early 1950s. Students of Francoism today show an alarming lack of general knowledge of this. With victory in 1939, during April and May, the period that Moreno Gómez calls the Black Spring, the paseos became a terrible reality in the entire Centre-South of Spain, the last region to fall to the insurgents. In 1941, there again was a marked rise in the number of paseos.

Furthermore, during the period that Moreno Gómez calls the Triennium of Terror (1947-1949), the extermination programme rose to unexpected new heights with several thousand extra-legal summary executions under the Law of Fugitives. During this period, Francoist terror fully penetrated the rural world throughout Spain under the leadership of Camilo Alonso Vega, Director General of the Guardia Civil, who received his orders directly from Franco. In 1949, this terror spread without mercy throughout the countryside in the Seville mountains and in 1950, uncountable country people were assassinated in the region of Nerja, Málaga.

Decree 55 reappeared re-cast under the <u>July 12 1940 Ley de Seguridad del Estado</u>,[i] that created 'ordinary summary procedures', which only differed slightly from the 'emergency summary procedures' conceived by Franco in 1936 in that they included the prosecution of those Franco considered would be defeated after the fall of Madrid. Once again, the text of this law was accompanied by a so-called magnanimous slogan that these procedures would guarantee '*the indispensable speed and exemplary actions of military justice*'. The reader can well imagine what the concept of 'exemplary actions' implied…

---

[i]   Law for the Security of the State.

The <u>November 21 1936 Circular from the High Court of Military Justice</u> issued in Valladolid made it almost impossible for anyone to appeal for a revision of sentence because it excluded any appeal following a summary proceeding, which meant, almost every single case that was tried.

Lastly, Franco's <u>Decree 191 of January 26 1937</u>, published in Salamanca extended the application of Decree 55 to the newly occupied territory of Málaga.[3] Decree 191 became the justification for the impending slaughter of the great number of Rojos the Nationalists troops soon expected to capture in Málaga.

Repressive Francoist laws

Soon after the Nationalist victory, the above were followed by the enactment of major legislation under the jurisdiction of Francoist military, directed at fine-tuning and redefining the crime of military rebellion, which encouraged the liberal application of the death penalty. The fact that this repressive legislation began to be forged as the end of the war approached, indicates that the Regime was not interested in lessening or even tempering the repression of the defeated. Quite the contrary. Its purpose was to assist with further planning and developing, from every possible angle, the multi-faceted program against the defeated. It was Franco's great all-embracing project.

Now began the great battery of judicial bazookas against the social base of the Republic and its political and illustrious elite who had already beaten *in pectore* by the <u>Law of Political Responsibilities (LPR)</u> of February 9 1939 (later amended by Law of February 19 1942). The purpose of the LPR was to pull the plug on the defeated's financial system, an economy that had already been battered by multiple seizures of property during the war. This post-war act was both a fiscal punishment and a purifying and disqualifying measure to ensure that the defeated would be left without any means of survival. In actual fact, the total economic destruction of the defeated was not really a result of all these regulations, but of the plundering, the seizures and hands-on theft of property and assets belonging to Rojos during and after the war.

The <u>January 25 1940 Order from the Presidency of the Government</u> regarding the 'Examination of sentences' by provincial committees, established extremely restrictive criteria and a detailed description of those individuals who were prohibited from appealing under this legislation. All the excluded were persons of some political or trade unionist importance of one kind or another. In effect, only individuals of no importance whatsoever could benefit. This feature of the Order is important, if only to correct those persons who have misunderstood its purpose and who believe that this Order was a sign of the longed-for moderation of the Regime, which it definitely was not.

On the other hand, this Order is particularly significant as it reveals the importance of the extermination to Francoists, not so much regarding the extermination of individuals as the destruction of the entire Republican system or Marxism, according to the Nationalists, because of their belief that "The Republic is guilty". This purpose is clearly stated in the preamble that refers the Regime's *"responsibilities regarding the criminal treason against the Fatherland that Marxism was guilty of when it opposed the Revolt of the Army and the National Cause."*

What Francoist military jurisprudence did was to initiate legal proceedings against the entire Republic as a political movement, brandishing the effigy of Marxism, not so much against individual Marxists but against all citizens of the Spanish Republic who in any way participated in the democratic State's opposition to the military coup. This is a clear example of 'reverse justice' the Regime used to justify legal proceedings, whereby it qualified the Republican's constitutional defence of the country as a military rebellion, an all-encompassing crime punishable under 19th century Military Law. In view of this, those who interpret those proceedings as a desire to revenge Nationalist martyrs are speaking nonsense, as Franco had planned the extermination from the onset, regardless of whether there were any martyrs or not.

According to Jiménez Villarejo, the 1940 Order embraced 83 different kinds of military rebellion, including being a Freemason, having held a public office, supporting the Rojo revolution and so forth. In other words, the 'Marxist rebellion' was guilty as charged.

The March 1 1940 Law for the Repression of Freemasonry and Communism had as very specific objectives the ghosts raised by Francoism and the Church, because both Franco and the Church had an obsessive hatred of Freemasonry. As part of the emergency summary procedures against Masons, with the publication of this law all Masons were forced to recant their association with Masonry, an atavistic procedure dating back to the Inquisition. An example of this was the trial of the Mayor of Posadas in 1931 who, as a member of the *Abril* Lodge, was forced to draft and sign the following recantation:

5

"I, Rafael Matencio Muñoz, aged forty-nine years of age, married, profession potter and resident in Posadas, Cordoba, with a view to complying with the stipulations of Article 7 of the Law of March 1, 1940 for the repression of Freemasonry, and in conformity with Article 1 of the Order dated the said month, hereby declare …" [that he first joined a lodge in Seville, sponsored by Antonio Rueda Aguilar; that he was given the symbolic name of 'Galdós' and that he reached grade two; that he was assistant to the Grand Master of the Posadas lodge, Ángel Lara Muñoz] … and "lastly, I formally declare in this recantation, that since the year one thousand nine hundred and twenty-eight, I have repudiated all my obligations to the sect, that I abjure my errors and endorse the above recantation. Cordoba, April 10, year one thousand nine hundred and forty." [4]

Communism was the perceived threat and pretext for repressing all 20th century insurgents. The Court against Communism was based in Madrid and one of its most violent wielders of the judicial gavel against heretics was the sadly infamous Colonel Enrique Eymar, a disabled veteran. Everyone captured during the repression of the guerrillas throughout Spain was tried by this Court.

The July 12 1940 amendment to the Law for the Security of the State, qualified the crime of military rebellion under Article 237 of the Code of Military Justice, thus placing the absolute control of all these cases under military jurisdiction.

The March 29 1941 amendment to the Law for the Security of the State, toughened the repression greatly by adding to the list of crimes punishable by death, crimes such as ordinary theft of which those who had fled to the hills and their connections in the countryside could be accused. Under this law, numerous orders from the Guardia Civil were further directed at extermination. The punitive reaction was so swift that in 1941 there was a marked rise in the number of summary executions and in the application of the Law of Fugitives. (Table 1) Clearly, there was no decline in the repression during this year.

Law of March 2 1943, introduced changes and extended the application of the crime of military rebellion, again adding fuel to the purifying fire, so that *"from now on, nobody will dare stray from a strict social discipline"*. Article 238 expanded the obsessive and neurotic definition of the crime of military rebellion. Military justice understood nothing else.

The new Code of Military Justice of July 17 1945, in which the crime of military rebellion was now brought under article 286, was a way of celebrating July 18 as a national holiday.

During the next couple of years, one could speak of a slight relaxation, or brief parenthesis, of the Francoist repressive furore, a loosening of the noose because of the international situation, the defeat of fascist Europe and the Regime's concern with the Allies' attitude towards the Spanish situation. However, seeing that the Allies were refraining from acting, the Regime gathered its forces and embarked on a new wave of oppression, the Triennium of Terror.

The <u>April 18 1947 Decree-Law on Military Rebellion, Banditry and Terrorism</u> was another of Franco's terrible laws, under which several thousand persons were sent to the grave.

This was not the last piece of Francoist repressive legislation. Once the guerrillas had been exterminated and the hills and the countryside had been subjugated, there remained a scattered clandestine resistance to the Regime that kept breaking out. With a view to suppressing this clandestine but stubborn resistance, particularly by members of the Communist Party, the Regime created the <u>Court of Public Order</u> (TOP – *Tribunal de Orden Publico*) under <u>Law 15/1963.</u>

A great many of these laws were rescinded by the so-called Law of Historic Memory 52/2007, after thirty years of hesitant and timid democracy.

Now is a good time to close this section with a numeric allusion to the hyperbolic magnitude of the Francoist slaughter, enveloped as it was by the Regime in the glitter of extra-legal decrees and laws that were never more than extra-judicial coverage to a maelstrom of crimes against humanity. The data, updated in 2012 by Ángel Viñas,[5] speaks for itself.

Before September 1939, during the year and a half the followed its coming to power, the III Reich had assassinated 473 individuals under the law and a thousand extra-legally. In comparison, in Seville General Queipo de Llano achieved this number in fifteen days in 1936 and by the end of the war in 1939, Franco had already assassinated 100,000 individuals. In fascist Italy, only 9 death sentences were handed out by 1939 and some 3,000 victims fell during the years of the regime. During the entire period of Italian fascism, 13,000 were exiled; in Spain, the number of exiled totalled almost half a million.

Until 1939, Franco was the most bloodthirsty of all the European fascists and he led the list in terms of criminality. Not only did he surpass his 'brother regimes' before that year as he was also some kind of pioneer in setting standards of barbarity for totalitarian Europe. Franco only fell short in that he did not invent gas chambers nor set up soap factories from human fat. As Paul Preston said[6], Franco killed more Spaniards in Spain than Hitler killed Germans in Germany and Mussolini Italians in Italy. (German barbarity occurred outside its borders and the victims were predominantly foreign.) Extermination of fellow countrymen who opposed Franco's Regime was the real purpose of military jurisdiction during Francoism, with its extra-legal decrees and its laws. (Table 1. Estimated Balance of Victims of Francoist Repression in Cordoba Province and Capital.)

Executions and the death ritual

> *"Most of us did not fear death, but we feared the act of dying… I was there when they died. They died with tears in their eyes, begging for help in vain, failing, as men should die. Because dying is a serious matter, and we must not make a drama of it. Pontius Pilate did not say:* Ecce heroes; *he said:* Ecce homo."
>
> Arthur Koestler[7]

The culmination of the extermination ritual was execution by firing squad, but this was not the only way to die, very much not the only way. This was a chapter in the physical elimination of the defeated, essentially those classified as group C (Republican authorities, worker and trade union leaders, senior officers of the defeated Army and eminent individuals, more or less that which is called politically significant people; also eliminated were those in group D (those accused for presumed 'crimes' that were rarely, if ever, proven). According to the classification of prisoners, at the end of 1937 only 2.13% of those executed belonged to group D. Also killed, a great many individuals from group B (Republicans of no political significance, farmers from the country and ordinary townspeople, caught by the witch-hunts and the furore for revenge killings during the first two post-war years). Many thousands of people of all kinds and social classes died, in compliance with the criterion that a 'sufficient extermination' would ensure fear in the present and in the future and help in preventing even weak opposition in the present and the years to come. As the Seville war criminals said: "Thirty years from now, not a soul will be alive."

Regarding the professional occupation of the eliminated, logically the majority belonged to the working class, especially tenant farmers and farmhands. Rural fascism drew its sustenance from the numerous and demanding peasantry. Italian fascist theoreticians defined war as 'the hygiene of the world'; employing pure fascist logic, Francoists believed that the time had come for "cleansing and exterminating, a fundamental principle of the Movement", as they justified the bloodshed they initiated on July 18 1936.

All Moreno Gómez' lists of victims in Cordoba capital and province, indicate their profession, when known, which enable him to confirm that the overwhelming majority were rural labourers and farmhands. Several historians have compiled some percentages. In Toledo, 52% of all executed were workers, according to José Manuel Sabín[8]. In Albacete, of a total 72% of executed individuals, 40.2% were farmhands and 31.9% were general working class, according to Ortiz Heras. In Málaga, 64.27% of those executed in the provincial prison 1939-1942 were farmhands. The percentages are similar for all of Spain, especially in the south. [9] Members of the working class and, most specifically, the rural proletariat, were scapegoats for the fascist extermination, which was the whole purpose of the military coup - to cleanse and force the rebellious proletariat to its knees.

A very important feature that is barely touched upon in many studies, is the tactical use that Francoism made of the great number of death sentences handed down during the first two years after victory, when so many suffered the terror of that period, although later the 'magnanimous Caudillo' accepted *motu proprio* to commute a number of sentences, at his discretion.

What the Regime immediately wanted was a program of great terror that would destroy the dignity of the individual, based on the abundance of death sentences, so that the great possible number of defeated would have to suffer the dreadful experience of having the death penalty hanging over their heads for several months, as long as a year in many cases.

Someone who has endured the anguish of expecting, each night, that his name will be called for the last trip, who cannot rest, who has lived each day as if it were his last, will be forever damaged. After such a terrible experience, the inner psyche of a prisoner can never be the same as before, even though at the end his death sentence is commuted. Many of those whose sentences were commuted remained seriously damaged in terms of their will to fight.

The percentage of sentences that were commuted varies and is difficult to compute. Some studies have come close. According to Matilde Eiroa, of the 800 death sentences handed down in Málaga capital 1939-1942, 710 detainees were executed and only 90 sentences (11.25%) were commuted.[10] In Cartagena, according to Pedro María Egea, there were 176 executions 1939-1945 but he only discovered 20 commutations in 1939. In Monóvar (Alicante), according to Sánchez Recio, of 324 sentences, 38 were death sentences; of these, 21 were executed and 17 were commuted. The figures vary greatly. The possibility of a commutation increased gradually after 1939, inasmuch as the revision of sentences became possible after changes to the law in 1940. In summary, in addition to those who were executed, many prisoners suffered the long-term threat of the death sentence and, once that terror was removed, their minds were irretrievably damaged in one way or another. An example of that is the playwright Antonio Buero Vallejo (whose dossier Moreno Gómez examined), who lost the fighting spirit he was known for before 1939, as he became totally apathetic from the suffering he endured in captivity. Francoism had its methods.

1. The *enterado*

The last step in the humiliation consisted in the manner by which a sentence was confirmed. The annotation *enterado* (meaning 'noted'), written by Franco himself on a sentenced individual's dossier was the ultimate life or death decision. Once a case was tried by a military court, whether permanent or temporary, the dossiers for prisoners who had been condemned to death were sent to the Judge Advocate's Office, first in Cordoba and then in Seville. The Judge Advocate for the Army of the South's mission (two judges in 1939: Ignacio Cuervo and Francisco Bohórquez) was to examine each dossier, approve the death sentence, order the execution of the sentence and send his recommendation to Franco - "His Excellency, the Generalisimo" - for confirmation.[ii] More specifically, the Judge Advocate was responsible for confirming the final ruling on the sentence proposed by the military court.

The case remained with the Advocate's Office until the Legal Advisor to the Ministry of the Army, the woefully infamous Lt. Colonel Lorenzo Martínez Fuset, returned the individual's dossier with Franco's decision. The Legal Advisor would meet daily with Franco and present him with a huge file filled with death sentence recommendations from numerous towns in Spain. It is said that when time came for the coffee break, the dictator would indicate his approval by scribbling «*enterado*» on death sentence after sentence, whilst continuously joking with Martínez Fuset. There is a famous jocose moment when Franco's chaplain, Father José Maria Bulart, called out in his usual macabre voice: "What? You do mean buried?" playing on the Spanish meaning of *enterado* – noted - and *enterrado* – buried. The priest's behaviour reflected National Catholicism's self-satisfied and exultant approach to the "purging" of the 'Godless'.

Every dossier arrived done and dusted on Franco's desk and he would rarely make any changes unless it was to underline the word *garrotte* or *garrotte and crush*, or write C for *conmutado* – commuted. Some proposals for the commutation of a sentence already bore the notice *Ojo!* Take note! A remark by some high-ranking individual. For example, General Varela wrote this on the dossier of Republican Artillery Major Francisco Blanco Pedraza, who had served under Pérez Salas on the Cordoba front. This was the result of the efforts of the Major's mother, who was able to soften Varela's hard soul, pleading that as the Rojos had killed one of her sons who was serving

---

[ii]   Rafael Sánchez Guerra, an eminent Cordovan victim of reprisals, sarcastically nicknamed Franco His Excellency the Criminalisimo, meaning Supreme Criminal, a play on words on the Spanish "Generalissimo" meaning Supreme General.

Franco in Madrid, she couldn't let the Nationalists kill her other son. Franco commuted the sentence.

In 1939, when the Regime launched itself with special urgency on its wave of punishments, revenge and ruthless repression, Franco's *enterado* arrived swiftly by teletype. [iii] For example, Luis Romero Cortés, from Torrecampo, was sentenced to death in Pozoblanco June 15 1939. June 27, the Seville Judge Advocate approved the sentence, the *enterado* arrived quickly by teletype from Burgos, where the Franco was living at the time, and he was executed August 5. In a single month, the death sentences that rained incessantly upon the defeated during the second half of 1939 were processed without appeals or revisions of any kind. Every case was judged to be most summary and most urgent and besides, before January of 1940, there were few regulations allowing for the possibility of appealing or reviewing sentences.

In 1940, there was a kind of slowing down in the processing of Francoist justice, not because the 'Criminalisimo' wished to show any generosity of spirit as such altruism would be unthinkable, but because the overwhelming volume of summary trial actions in all of Spain resulted in a monumental bureaucratic gridlock. This slowdown, which enabled a small minority to escape death, prolonged the suffering of the many thousands of prisoners who had already been condemned and had to endure a year or a year and a half of fear of the pending death threat, in the knowledge that there was no possible escape from the final solution.

When the exterminating bureaucracy came to a virtual standstill whilst Franco moved his headquarters from Burgos to Madrid on October 18 1939, his Generals took matters in their own hands and, from 1940 onwards, dealt directly with the great volume of proposed commutations and appeals to sentences that the condemned sent them. Orders for sentencing piled up in the War Courts as they waited for these proposals and appeals to be processed. In Cordoba capital, the military bureaucracy struggled even further after the summer as the military began emptying the provincial prisons of inmates and sending them all to Cordoba capital where they would be interned[iv] at the end of September and throughout October.

Whilst requests for commutations and appeals in 1940-41 were examined and in most cases, denied, inmates in Cordoba who had been condemned to death were transferred to Burgos prison, where they remained for about one year, until they were again brought back in the so-called "train of

---

[iii] The Advocates always confirmed and approved the sentences, never disagreeing. At least, Moreno Gómez knows of no such case.

[iv] There were two prisons in Cordoba capital. The main one, the *Prisión Provincial*, Plaza del Alcázar, and a new prison, the *Prisión Habilitada*, on the road to Pedroches.

death" for immediate execution by firing squads in Cordoba cemeteries. Few unfortunate individuals, knowing of their fatal destination, were occasionally successful in escaping during that ride.

A case in point illustrating the 1940-1941 delays in carrying out the sentences, is that of Socialist Antonio Baena Moreno, from Pozoblanco, condemned to death by garrotte, April 22 1940. November 7 1941, the dictator had still not given his *enterado* to the order nor had the Military Governor for the 2nd Region approved it. Baena Moreno was finally executed ten days later, November 17. In all, nineteen months' waiting in anguish. The following was written at the end of his dossier:

> "...We thereby pronounce, order and sign our sentence on 05-1940. I, Judge Advocate for the Army of the South hereby rule that the proposed sentence should be approved, that the ruling is final and must be executed, and order that H.E. the Head of State is informed of this capital punishment. H.E. the Commander General of the 2nd Region has approved the sentence and stated that it should not be carried out until the appeal for commutation of the sentence is examined and decided upon at the highest level.
>
> November 7 1941, I, Cirilo Genovés, Head Advocate of the Ministry of the Army, certify that His Excellency was notified of the sentence pronounced by the Pozoblanco Court Martial against Antonio Baena Moreno - case 27.505, and that H.E. gave his approval..."

In yet another case, Pedro Torralbo Gómez from Villanueva de Cordoba was judged and sentenced to death May 1 1940. May 11, the Judge Advocate confirmed his sentence and April 23 1941, the Commander General of the 2nd Region approved it. June 3 1941, thirteen months after he had been condemned, Pedro Torralbo was executed. His dossier shows that:

> ...11 May 11 1940, the Judge Advocate for the Army of the South approved the sentence, declaring that his ruling was final and must be executed. He further ordered that H. E. the Head of State should be informed of this capital punishment and that this case should remain with his Office until His Excellency's reply was received.
>
> April 23 1941, the Commander General of the 2nd Region, in view of the aforementioned sentence and the Judge Advocate's opinion, approved the capital punishment and ordered that this case be sent to the Military Governor for Cordoba so that the latter could appoint a judge for purposes of the notification, carrying out of the sentence, and publishing all other necessary information...

A few more examples of the long wait between the sentencing and the execution: Juan F. Chuán Soto sentenced to death May 1 1940 was executed

November 6 1941; Juan Lorenzo Cantador, tried on the same date was executed September 12 1941; Juan Escoriza Segura, sentenced April 25 1940 was executed November 6 1941. There are many more examples of men who were condemned at the beginning of 1940 but not executed until well into the following year. On the other hand, in 1941 now that all courts martial were operating in Cordoba capital, death sentences were carried out much more swiftly, the same year.

Special note is made that the approval, or *enterado*, could be two-fold. On the one hand, there was Franco's *enterado* issued through the Judge Advocate for the Ministry of War, and on the other hand, the enterado proclaimed by the Commander General of the 2nd Region. In Seville, this post was filled by General Queipo de Llano from July 18 to 20 1939, when he was replaced by General Andrés Saliquet. At the height of the enterados in 1941, the Commander General in Seville was General Miguel Ponte y Manso de Zúñiga.

The final step for the hundreds of enterados that were processed daily by the Seville Judge Advocate and returned to the most remote towns and villages in Andalusia, was the provincial Military Commander's Office, responsible for appointing the judge who would inform the prisoner of the final decision and carrying out the sentence. However, as the Francoist repressive bureaucracy was so overwhelmed during these first years of the Regime, that as many witnesses and data will testify, numerous notices of the commutation of a sentence were received long after the condemned inmate had been executed. A few diaries and letters sent from the jails speak of the dramatic nightmare that each prisoner had to face night after night, month after month, as he waited to hear whether his name was next on the list of those to be executed or not. The real number of those affected by this terrible situation will never be really known.

2. *Sacas* or illegal removals of prisoners for execution

The first step to the gallows was the *saca*, meaning the illegal removal of a prisoner whose sentence had not been commuted, from prison for execution. The sound of metal doors and bolts at midnight, of wardens reading out the names of the doomed; indescribable tension and heart-breaking silence from all the condemned men in every cell. The networks of signs and unusual information that existed in the jails meant that the prisoners often knew several hours beforehand when a saca was about to take place. With the whiff of tragedy, panic swiftly spread from cell to cell. There was a restlessness and continuous suspicion that totally affected the daily lives of the condemned.

An indication that a saca was near, was when the daily lists of commutated sentences arrived at the prison and the 'fortunate' were called to sign their receipt of the news. That night, there inevitably was a saca from among those whose sentences had not been commuted. The condemned only had a break, a slight pause in the tension, on Sundays and holy days because there never were any sacas on those days. Antonio Baena's unpublished diary, an excerpt of which is given in APPENDIX I, gives one an idea of what it was like, an experience that Moreno Gómez described as a *sprawling wave of terror*.[11]

The Francoist repressive program was not just directed at exterminating or physically eliminating the defeated, nor just at tormenting, mistreating and starving them in the jails. Above all, the Francoist repression was a program of terror, both past and present, terror that provided the essential basis for the survival of the Regime. This terror sprawled over all like a wave; in other words, it not only affected the victim, but it spread outwards to affect all his cellmates and also, logically, his fellow prisoners throughout the jail. As we read in Antonio Baena's diary, the next day, in the patio, everyone "looked as if he was just recovering from a serious illness".

The wave of terror did not stop there: it oozed out into the street. First affecting the victim's family, then, all his neighbours, friends and acquaintances, and lastly, to all the public (in the defeated sector, of course), as everyone, everywhere, spoke with horror at what had happened to Tom, Dick or Harry. Each execution terrorized a great many people both inside and outside the jail, in every town and village. That terror was swallowed like a bitter pill by everyone and grew like a painful cyst that silenced all, a silence that continues to this day as hundreds of times relatives of the victims still refuse to speak. It was a Regime of terror that survived by feeding on the hidden panic of its victims. As Koestler wrote:

> "I never thought that the dictatorship of a minority could remain in power through terror alone. I ignored the extent to which those primeval forces that paralyze the majority from within, are living and real."[12]

Preventive terror also was Franco's strategic instrument for inhibiting any possible domestic opposition and for nipping it in the bud if necessary. In Zaragoza, in a Paseo de Ruiseñores bungalow that housed the local Military Police headquarters, the Francoist colonel in charge decided on the lives of hundreds of Nationalist soldiers. These men were culled and removed from the San Gregorio military prison in the Fall of 1936 when 400 of those soldiers and some civilians as well were executed.[13] A military chaplain who was present, Fr. Gómez, made an unprecedented request - he asked the colonel to show some clemency. The Nationalist colonel's reply was as peculiar as it was political:. He stated that he was willing to forgive a poor worker for becoming an anarchist, but Justice must be ruthless with these men, with intellectuals, public servants, all those who betray their class. That it was the Regime's painful legal duty to be implacable in exterminating these vermin. As it upheld the necessary background terror.[14] (…)

Terror would manifest itself in many other ways, the most insidious perhaps being the fear it instilled in inmates condemned to thirty years in prison as they contemplated what the future might bring for their families. This is reflected in a fragment of the diary that Sebastian Blanco Copado, an alderman for the Izquierda Republicana in Pozoblanco, wrote in prison in Puerto de Santa Maria, Cádiz, after he was condemned to 30 years in prison. This excerpt from a letter he wrote to his wife and family illustrates the immense pain of ordinary people who felt the weight of the destruction created by the military coup.

> "Faced with such a cruel and prolonged separation, I could die and never again see you, and that idea made me tremble; to leave you alone in this intemperate world, freezes my blood and I remember our humble home, our home that harboured so many memories.
>
> That home has now been destroyed and broken, left without direction or order, like a fragile sailing ship floating rudderless at the mercy of the waves; this brought tears to my eyes and I thought of you, poor innocent victims of a time that should never have existed; of you, shipwrecked by a storm of human passion, buffered by a whirlwind of hate such as Man has never known. I do not want to die without leaving you some memories…"[15]

This excerpt from Sebastian's letter to his wife was published in the September 1985 issue of *Revista de Feria*, in Pozoblanco, in an article entitled "The Nationalist repression in Pozoblanco", erupted as a major scandal among the right-wing residents of the town. They showered the Municipal Newsletter with letters, accusing the author of being a fanatic, of poisoning the townspeople and demanding that City Hall ban the sale of the magazine, describing it an unwise, lacking in objectivity and that it would only reopen old wounds.

This was typical apocalyptic right-wing rantings, after almost ten years of the return to democracy, clearly reflecting the difference between the French right-wing Gaullists and their clear anti-fascist tradition and the Spanish Right who never had such a tradition.

Pablo Uriel, in his prison diary, described how the life of the prisoner with the threat of death hanging over his head, suffering the anguish of the nightly sacas, the fear that his name will be called for execution, changed his brother's life forever. [16] When his brother was released from the Zaragoza Provincial Prison, the family found him greatly changed, much quieter and withdrawn. He had witnessed the last hours of thousands of persons and because of that he had become totally indifferent as to his own future.

One of the effects of the terror was the mindless resignation that the carnage produced in the victims. As this bacchanalian blood-letting convinced the prisoners of the inevitably fatal outcome of their situation, the men allowed themselves to be led to sacrifice with a disconcerting apathy. There was always such an almost total lack of resistance that the assassins found it much easier to do their odious work. The passivity with which those men accepted that they were going to die, whether they were civilians or had served as soldiers on the battlefield, is impossible to comprehend today. In truth, their minds had been irretrievably damaged.

The expanding wave of terror resulted in what Pablo Uriel, citing Steimberg, described as an *atmosphere of terror*, which had an impact as effective as the terror itself.[17]

Another important factor in the atmosphere of terror is its unpredictability, when the feeling terror is so arbitrary and so irrational that no citizen feels safe, when anybody can become a victim, as it was in Spain during the 1947-1949 Triennium of Terror when the regime concentrated its repressive efforts on persecuting the guerrillas in the mountains and in the countryside.

Returning to the ritual of the sacas, in the prisons, the condemned men survived without really living, as they awaited death. The bureaucracy of the execution began with a telegram from the Military Governor to the Prison Director, listing the names of those who were to be executed and other relevant information. The eve of the execution, the Director would receive another telegram from the regional military commander, instructing him to 'send the condemned to the chapel'. Next, the Military Governor would send another telegram to the Prison Director of the prison, instructing him to hand the condemned over to the Guardia Civil. The head guard on duty had to sign the telegram himself in confirmation that he would take charge of the condemned men whose names were on the list. It took three or four days for all these telegrams to go back and forth.

In Catalonia, the Military Governor's fatal list would be delivered to the prison by car between nine and ten at night. On the San Simón, Pontevedra, penal island, the enterado would arrive at night, in a motor boat, with a prison officer and the chaplain, Fr. Nieto. When the prisoners heard the motor boat, they froze with fear. In Pozoblanco, the sign that a saca was about to be carried out and that there would be executions, was the presence of the Salesian chaplain, Fr. Antonio Do Muiño, whom the prisoners had nicknamed the 'bird of death'. In Villanueva de Cordoba, Fr. Marcial, the parish priest's arrival at the jail the afternoon before an executions to administer the last rites to the condemned. His arrival shook the prisoners like an earthquake.

There are few witness accounts, diaries or memoires referring to the moment of the saca from Cordoba. One such account, however, Arthur Koestler's diary from when he was imprisoned in Malaga and Seville, excerpts of which are published in Volume I, describe in greater detail those terrible experiences the weeks during which he lived in constant panic and his fear that he, too, would be taken to be executed. His descriptions begin in Malaga, February 1937, a couple of days after the fall of that city, and they continued in April, by which time he had been transferred to Seville, as if he were another Anne Frank, describing that which those individuals who persist in erasing the events of the past would like us to ignore.

Each one of the pages in Koestler's diary from the Seville prison are from April 1937 and each one makes shivers run down your back. The truth of the matter was that the terror that afflicted the men and women of defeated Spain was not the fear of death, which many who were tortured may well have welcomed. What terrorized them was the dying itself, the pain, the shots, the blood. Koestler himself said so: "Most of us were not afraid of death; we were afraid of the act of dying."[18]

Moreno Gómez was unable to find more diaries like Baena's and Koestler's, but he was able to obtain a few eyewitness accounts referring to events in the Villanueva de Cordoba prison: April 2 1940, three were taken by saca, one of whom was Manuel Salazar Vilches, a very active communist, who was accused of having used the Guardia Civil horses after the barracks surrendered. One of his fellow prisoners told Moreno Gómez that before leaving his cell, like the rest of the inmates, he refused to confess. He left shouting Viva! the Republic! in a most courageous manner, even in the street, as most of those who were imprisoned were very apathetic when they were taken out." [19]

Juan Escribano Fernández, aged 23, an active member of the JSU was executed at 5 p.m. April 6 1940 in a saca in Villanueva de Cordoba. His family were able to see him before he died and his sister gave Moreno Gómez her eyewitness account at the beginning of the 1980s. (She has since died.)

> "Emilio – *El del Lunar* came to our house to arrest Juan. He was accused of having attacked the barracks. They beat him so severely that the clothes he sent home were covered in blood, with patches of skin sticking to them. He

had hoped that his sentence would be revised, but the terrible Judge Calero intervened and his appeal was not heard.

The day that he was shot (in the afternoon), his clean clothes and the spoon with his name on it were returned to us, as souvenirs. That is how we knew that he was going to be executed. Moments before he was taken out, his brothers and sister arrived to see him. I hugged him non-stop and the sergeant told them to bring me something to drink. I replied that I didn't even want the smell of that place. My brother Juan tried to console us, telling us not to cry, that 'he was not born to live for eternity'. He was rather inattentive and lethargic.

The next day, our father managed to get permission from Judge Calero to exhume him and place his body in a niche in the cemetery. He had been hit by five bullets in the chest and he had a large hole in his forehead."

Judge Calero would frequently grant favours such as allowing a prisoner's family to say their farewells, in exchange for substantial rewards. Juan Escribano's family complained that he accepted many presents, in exchange for saving Juan, which he did not.

One of the first executions carried out in Villanueva de Cordoba November 7 1939 at 5 p.m., was the saca that included Pedro Juan *El Chunga* Martínez from the Fuente Vieja prison. It was a theatrical affair, with armed Guardias Civiles posted on every corner outside the prison. The condemned men were loaded on a truck whilst vast crowds of right-wingers crowded around to see the show. Tearful relatives of the prisoners remained at a distance, behind the guards on the street corners. As Pedro Juan climbed onto the truck, he went mad. Seeing so many people come to watch him die, he lost his head and began shouting: *"Let's go to the bullfight! Come on everybody! Let's party! Let's go and have some fun!"*

The truck then drove down the Calle Alta, the Cruz de Piedra and the street that led to the cemetery, where a huge Falangist crowd had gathered, singing *Cara al sol* and applauding wildly as the victims were mowed down by the gunfire, the last humiliating sounds they took with them to the other world. It is very hard to die, but so much harder to die under absolute humiliation, to the applause and singing of the enemy.

One witness in Cordoba told of the story of a melon and a saca. An unknown farmer from Villa del Río was saving a melon that his family had sent him; an absolute banquet to stave the hunger in the prison. When his name was called for the saca, he asked permission to share the melon with his cellmates. The banquet over, he went calmly to his death. Someone should tackle the impossible task of writing a treatise on the courageous death of Spanish farmers, victims of National Catholicism.

The multiple circumstances of the sacas in the Cordoba prison will remain unknown forever. The fury and the cruelty was such that special dates were set for sacas of working men. This was the case in Cordoba capital in 1941, when 34 men were executed on Labour Day, May 1st. According to Pedro Molinero's eyewitness account, Blas Gómez Medina, a leading communist from Villanueva de Cordoba, was the least prepared of the lot for what was about to happen to them.

June 22 1940, a saca of 22 condemned men from the Cordoba prison included the famous Paco Dios, from Villafranca, who had commanded a company in the Villafranca Battalion and later served as a Militia Major in the 74th Brigade. He was a great leader, born of the people and to whom Pedro Garfias, the poet, dedicated a poem in his wartime anthology *Héroes del Sur*.[20] He is identified as Capitán Paco in an Irish International Brigade volunteer in his book on the Spanish civil war.[21]

Neither author knew how their hero died, but it did not follow the usual ritual. He was a hero in life, a hero in commanding his men, a hero in death. Moreno Gómez was able to interview his brother Juan, who has since died, in Cordoba capital.

> "The night of the saca, he changed his clothes and shared his belongings with his cellmates. Later, there was an incident with the priest who insisted on pressing a crucifix against his chest. Paco pushed him away angrily, which earned him a slap in the face from a Guardia Civil. While the condemned men waited, talking to each other in front of the La Salud cemetery wall, Paco asked for a cigarette and a last wish: he wanted to say a few words, before everybody, before he died.
>
> They say that he spoke valiantly, censuring fascism and rebuking the Regime's executioners, ending with a resounding *Viva la Republica! Long Live the Republic!* When his brother-in-law Antonio Gómez Torres collapsed, in tears, Paco consoled him with words of courage for what was about to happen. The priest, impressed by Paco Dios' speech, asked him what his profession was and he was surprised with his answer – a simple bricklayer."

The ritual and anguish of the sacas is described in Pablo Uriel's excellent book that Moreno Gómez quoted earlier. This young doctor was arrested as a prisoner-of-war in the Autumn of 1936 and imprisoned in the General Military Academy prison at San Gregorio, Zaragoza, where he came very close to death but survived. When reading his account in the APPENDIX, it is important to remember, however, that he is reporting on a military prison where most of the inmates were soldiers who had been sent there from the front lines, based on unproven accusations from Falangists, mainly members of the Spanish fascist party in Zaragoza. Apparently, the Nationalist Army also had to be 'cleansed'.

In that prison, the person immediately responsible for determining who would be executed was the Military Police Colonel at the Paseo de Ruiseñores headquarters in Zaragoza. Above him, all the Francoist and Falangist repressive machinery.

In the case of those who disappeared unrecorded, the Machiavellian nature of these disappearances was apparent in a short directive, sent to the head of the Brigade of the San Gregorio military prison, instructing him to: "Release imprisoned solider ... [name] ..., if he has not been requested by any other authority".

The last part of the instruction was the key word for the *paseo*[v] and the soldier's subsequent disappearance. It was in this extraordinary manner that 400 soldiers and two sergeants 'disappeared' in the Autumn of 1936 from that Zaragoza prison.

3. The *Chapel*

The ritual of the saca was followed, usually but not always, by a period of waiting before the execution, known as «the chapel». Also, after a condemned man was removed from his cell, he was taken elsewhere, also referred to as «the chapel» and where, as he waited, he could write farewell letters to his family, confess to the priest - which many refused to do and resulted in heated arguments, attend Mass and/or take Communion. Mass and Communion were offered to the condemned in Zaragoza, but not in Cordoba or other provincial capitals.

The bureaucratic procedure was simple. The condemned person's dossier was returned to the military court by the Judge Advocate or Commander General, with the annotation enterado as confirmation of his sentence. In the prison, the saca was put into action and the prisoner was taken to an office where he was read the ruling of the court, informed of the sentence, then taken to the chapel.

In Zaragoza prison, because it was a military prison and the condemned were taken directly to the cemetery for execution, there was no chapel. What usually happened in other prisons was that when the saca was scheduled for

---

[v] As a reminder, the *paseo* was the practice of Guardia Civil showing up at an individual's house in the middle of the night, loading him in a truck and taking him 'for a walk' from which he never returned. Once a soldier was released from the jail, he went home as an ordinary citizen, only to be taken on a paseo from his home, never to be heard from again, hence, he just 'disappeared'.

dawn, the condemned had most of the night to let the sentence sink in or to write to their families. In 1939, the time in the chapel was much shorter as the entire process was much quicker in many townships (although not in the capital cities) where sentences were read in the middle of the afternoon and the condemned were executed at 8 p.m. Other times, the executions were carried out even earlier, at 5 p.m. There could be so little time in the chapel that the victims did not even have enough time to write their last letter. Later however, in 1940, most executions were carried out at dawn both in the capital cities and the townships.

The letters that were written in the chapel were very difficult to write and today, continue to make extremely painful reading. They were the last thoughts of an entire generation of Republicans that was exterminated. They express the pain of the Andalusian farmers who were sacrificed by the fascism of the barracks, the Casino and the Church vestry. Moreno Gómez has quite a few of these letters, written by hand by those who wrote them before they died, several of which are reproduced in APPENDIX I.

One of the most moving letters written by the condemned men who were executed in Cordoba capital, is the letter that Captain Paco Dios wrote to his wife and daughter when he was in the chapel awaiting his imminent execution, reproduced here:

"Cordoba Provincial Prison
June 22 1940.
    Dear Lucía: keep these lines until our dear daughter is old enough to understand them. Dear daughter. Just a few words, as if this were my Last Will and Testament, because as I have nothing else to bequeath you, I am going to tell you why they are killing me.
    Ever since I was able to think with reason, I became aware of the injustice that affects a large part of Mankind, and of the inequality that exists between it and those who control the money. Ever since, I fought to correct that evil and, like me, so did many working men. The more united we were, the more the number of grievances we were able to get corrected, as we defended ourselves from the misery that capitalists impressed on us.
    However, those gentlemen, aware of the danger that our union represented to their rich living, rather than share with us part of that which they had left over, chose to launch the most horrible tragedy ever recorded by History, with a view to robbing us of the few rights that we had obtained.
    We defended ourselves and, briefly, were defeated. Immediately, the victors decided that I must die, as they did thousands and thousands of my comrades. That is all. Many died on both sides, although you will be told differently.
    As I am certain that, when you understand all this, you will benefit from something of that which I fought for, others will take care to inform

21

you of what happened, both to you and to all those who, like you, lost their father.

But whatever happens, I have a word of advice that is, at the same time, a mandate: follow the road that I took and if as you travel it, the same thing happens to you that happened to me, how proud you shall be to give your life when you have the satisfaction of having done your duty.

Nothing more. Your father, Paco Dios."

As we saw earlier when Moreno Gómez described Paco Dios' execution, his morale and personal dignity remained intact when he was faced with death, unbroken by the punishments he had suffered, as did others, although not all desired to be heroes. As a military commander, Paco inspired his men and at his death, he caused consternation among his enemies, such as the priest who was astonished that this 'bad man' could express such clear thoughts.

From Villanueva de Cordoba, there are several letters written in the chapel with very different overtones, including several in which the authors clearly ask their relatives to take revenge upon the executioners when the state of affairs changes. May 17 1940 there was a saca of 5 condemned men, the first one scheduled for 6 a.m., a novelty as during the previous six months, these were held at 5 p.m. to provide a show for the townspeople. One of the executed was a renowned local politician who belonged to the Izquierda Republicana, a moderate man, who had been targeted for extermination like all political leaders: Francisco Sánchez Muñoz, known as *Curro Beatas*, past alderman for the Frente Popular. He left two letters written in the chapel, the first one of which was personal.

Curro Beatas wrote a second letter which he most certainly had delivered by a different means, addressed to his family but undated and also written in chapel. In this letter, he denounces the many who tortured him in Villanueva, adding the wish that someday they shall suffer the revenge they deserve.

On their own, publication of the above letters that the family gave Moreno Gómez is a form of historic redress as well as the condemnation of his Francoist torturers. Nine days later, May 26 1940, another eighteen men were executed, among whom Eurgenio Palmera Jurado Pozuelo, renowned leader in Villanueva, considered a Communist stronghold. Eugenio was horribly tortured and beaten. His death was truly a merciful release. He also wrote a letter in the chapel in which he asks his family to revenge him. This letter, also reproduced in the APPENDIX, is now made public for the first time. It was given to Moreno Gómez by his nephew, Miguel Jurado Tintorero, who was visibly moved. All the papers he had came from his uncle

José Palmera's (brother to Eugenio) archives, who was Mayor of Villanueva in 1935, representing the Leroux party.

Several residents of Villanueva de Cordoba were executed elsewhere in Spain, some of whose letters of farewell are also recorded in APPENDIX I.

May 19 1943, Rafael Porras Caballero from Pozoblanco, son of Antonio Porras the Republican poet and politician, at the time living in exile in France, fell victim to Francoism in Madrid. That morning, Rafael wrote two letters whilst he was in chapel: one to his siblings and another to his parents and brothers. Although only the second letter is recorded here, attention is drawn to the extremely unusual note that he wrote on the first one: "*I have been allowed to send these last letters of farewell by the kind favour of the prison priest.*"

This remark confirms other information according to which many condemned men agreed to say confession only to ensure that their last letters would be sent to their families. Some of those who refused confession were even denied the possibility of writing a last letter. Rafael's second farewell letter to the whole family ends with a moving postscript in which he asks his parents to help the widow and children of a fellow prisoner, who were left destitute:

> "José María San Ildefonso dies with me. He leaves a widow and children. Please do as much as possible for them. They live at Carretera de Aragón number 15, Ventas."[22]

As farmers and workers all over Spain and Republicans of all kinds continued to be eliminated by the Regime, they bequeathed short and simple letters of farewell to their families. In his book of memories, Galo Vierge leaves us some heartrending examples from Pamplona, massacred by Falangists and Carlistas, which just shows how the extermination program reached every corner of the country.

> "Elías Sesma, from Sartuguda [known as *village of widows*], was a thirty-year-old man whose great worry when he was incarcerated was, who would harvest the little bit of farmland that he owned in his village. As he didn't know how to read or write, I wrote his letters to his wife Teresa Arpón, and when he dictated what he wanted to say, he always expressed his great concern regarding his beloved vegetables: "Teresa, go to uncle Vicente's house and ask to borrow the cart and go to the field and pick the green peppers and the tomatoes, before they rot". Again, and again, in every single letter. The day that he was executed, 16 November 1936, with sixteen other prisoners from his village, Elías left his cell happily, naively

believing that he was being set free. In his hands, he carried a draw-string bag for bread where he kept some trinkets for his daughter Teresita. That man, in his supreme ignorance and good faith, had the noble and simple soul of those who work in the fields, and even though they had shot two of his brothers, it never entered his mind that men could go as far as to criminalize innocent victims such as he, in order to sow terror among the simple country folk."[23]

That was poor Elías' last wish: to harvest his green peppers. There was a great rush to exterminate the defeated during the last months of 1936. There was no time for the chapel, no time to write letters, no time for anything. Prisoners went from their cells to the grave, without further ado. The prolonged imprisonments of the post-war period were almost a privilege.

The prisoner's stay in the chapel reached its nadir with the priest. Books of memoires frequently refer to how shocked the condemned men were with the priests' impertinence. They mention cases of irate priests who would go so far as to beat an unrepentant inmate and of less fanatic priests who partly respected the voluntary nature of confession.

The most descriptive book of memoires so far, one of the most terrible documents regarding the extermination, is the one written by a Capuchin monk and Basque nationalist, Gumersindo de Estella, who was charged with giving religious solace to the condemned in Zaragoza during the war years.[24] Although we lack such a book for Cordoba, the best documents regarding the Francoist death ritual are by two Zaragoza prison diarists: aforementioned Pablo Uriel for the San Gregório Military Prison and Rev. Gumersindo for the Provincial Prison, above. In the latter prison, the chapel was in the judge's chambers, where an improvised altar had been set up so that Mass could be celebrated during the terrible fatal hours. There is no evidence that any chapel Masses were ever said in the Cordoba prison.

An ominous group of individuals gathered in these chambers at dawn: The Judge Executioner, his secretary, the doctor, one or more priests, several persons dressed in black (members of the Brotherhood of the Blood of Christ, elsewhere known as the Brotherhood of Peace and Charity) who collected the bodies, and some others. The last to arrive at the chapel were the condemned, whose hearts must have sunk at the sight of this melodramatic gathering.

The first thing that enters one's mind is that to most of the Republican condemned, having to face a priest at such a terrible moment must have been a tremendous psychological, moral and intellectual shock. Logic would suggest – although we know it was impossible – that at such a crucial moment in their lives, they might have been comforted by the representative of an ideology they believed in; not by one they did not. Why not a political commissar who might have praised the great honour of giving their lives for freedom and democracy, or some such? Another blow to their ideals, the recognition that the ideology at the base of the military coup that they had fought against, was now responsible for their deaths. Apparently, no authors have commented on this latter aspect, one that surely meant a great deal to the Republicans who were about to die.

Another feature of note is that in addition to the San Gregorio Military Prison, numerous Nationalist soldiers were also executed at the Zaragoza Provincial Prison. This would indicate that the Francoist cleansing of its own ranks was likewise terrible and widespread. Something like this, so minutely planned, so systematic and devastating did not occur in the Republican zone, at least not to any great extent.

Rev. Gumersindo's assistance to the condemned at the Zaragoza Provincial Prison, began June 22 1937. On his first day at work, he began by attempting to give spiritual guidance to a very cultured and highly educated individual, a socialist, Secretary of the Escatrón Municipality, near Caspe. Rev. Gumersindo's diary entries, many of which are reproduced in APPENDIX II, are descriptive, informative, heart-braking and profoundly empathetic. In his diary, Rev. Gumersindo tells how in February 1938, the Zaragoza Provincial Prison alone housed 5,200 men and 800 women, in a prison that was built for 250 inmates. The overcrowding was evident. In July of the same year, a prison doctor's report stated that 2,000 inmates were suffering from scabies.

Two high-ranking Republican prisoners were executed March 17 1938: General José María Enciso and Colonel José María González Tablas, both of whom were taken prisoner in Escarrón, near Caspe, March 12, during the major Francoist offensive in the Lower Aragón province. The morning of their execution, the General Commander of Zaragoza, Francisco Rañoy Carvajal, was present in the chapel as he did not want to miss the great event. General Enciso refused spiritual comfort, whilst Colonel González turned himself with fervour to confession, Mass and Communion. Rev. Gumersindo said that the colonel burst into tears after confessing and that he sobbed as he received Communion.

April 20 1938, a mutilated man was shot in Zaragoza. Thirty-five-year-old Antonio Botela from Gerafe's, leg had been amputated above the knees because of wounds he had received during a Republican bombing on the prison November 5 1937. Not even this amputation saved his life. In the chapel, when he finished confessing, he sobbed incessantly: "My poor children, what is going to happen to them in this world?... My poor children." He then attended Mass and took Communion. Several soldiers had to carry him to his execution. There was a similar case in Cordoba of a mutilated prisoner who was executed by garrotte. One cannot deny that bad things occurred in the Republican zone, but Spanish fascists were solely to blame for this kind of barbarous behaviour.

The May 12 1938 entry in Rev. Gumersindo's diary refers to nine prisoners who were brought to the chapel, one of whom a woman, María de Asis Figueras. They were from Alcañiz, possibly prisoners of war. That morning, the hour in the chapel was an absolute scandal. The woman refused to go to the chapel from the identification room where the sentences were read out. At that moment, a female prison guard shamefully mocked her: "Ay, María, María. Look how the blessed CNT has betrayed you!". Rev. Gumersindo immediately rebuked her. He then noticed that the woman appeared to be pregnant, so he approached the Judge Executioner for clemency, but the judge refused his request and she was tied up like all the others and executed.

Some say that we historians lose ourselves in the angst of the facts and that we neglect the overall legal picture. Not so. If we choose to resurrect these hidden pages of history, it is because we have to make an elemental reconstruction of events that have, until now, been intentionally forgotten. There is always time to analyse the legal aspect. For now, we need to give expression, without excuses or distinctions of any kind, to how the victims of Francoism faced death. We must make known their state of mind, their protestations of innocence, their pain, the way they faced the priests' harassment, as well as the series of cruel punishments to which they were subjected during this colossal genocide. This is not losing oneself in miseries or an obsession with the facts. Historians are well aware of the task that is before them, a job that has been avoided for far too long.

Rev. Gumersindo's diary shows us that many prisoners-of-war from the Teruel front were continuously being shot. One of those prisoners, from Vich, Isídro Franqusa, denied all spiritual comfort. The great majority of the condemned who arrived at Rev. Gumersindo's chapel in Zaragoza Provincial Prison protested their innocence and denounced the injustice – remember, most of them were prisoners-of-war.

This brings us back to the farce of the courts martial. It is as if, with these summary rulings, we are looking for a non-existent legality, an illusion that innocence would somehow shine through and that only the truly guilty would be condemned. To even suggest such a hope, would be to encourage a fantasy and a false mirroring of the truth, to presume that there actually was a state of law in the Francoist Regime and an independent application of justice, something totally impossible.

Everything that took place in the so-called Zaragoza "chapel" and all of Spain was "standard" Francoist "justice", i.e., non-existent justice. This shows, once again, that the courts martial were a farce, a travesty of justice, an absurdity that only served to provide the genocide with a respectable image. The judges, the Jesuit chaplains, prison directors, advocates, General Commanders and the *Criminalissimo* himself, were not interested in justice; they just wanted to kill, and kill and kill some more, the more the better. The distinction between innocent and guilty was impertinent, anecdotal and unthinkable.

Ingenuous Rev. Gumersindo appeared to believe the fantasy and he trusted the presumed existence of a real justice. It was the rare dawn that he was not taken in. October 19, 1938 he attended to four condemned men, one of whom was from Monforte, Teruel:

> " At first, he expressed his indignation saying that the accusations against him were totally false.
> – But man – I said – Why didn't you say all this when you were interrogated...?
> – Because I was never interrogated at my trial. The Prosecutor made many false accusations; almost all of which were lies. I wanted to protest but I was ignored. The defence attorney never visited me."

Nine months later, July 14 1939, when eight prisoners from Alcañiz were taken to the chapel, nothing had changed. Francoist "justice" continued as usual: falsehoods, lack of guarantees of all kinds, lack of evidence, powerless accused, manifest injustices, disrespect for innocence... One of the prisoners, a young well-educated man, told Rev. Gumersindo:

> "I believe that what they are doing to me is a mistake. I was tried in Acañiz, was absolved and set free. I was later again arrested. I have not been interrogated, they have not spoken a single word to me; and when I expected, with some reason, that I was going to be set free, I find that they are going to kill me. Who can explain this to me? Either it is a mistake or manifest injustice."

Francoist military justice was injustice. Injustice is the *per se* definition of a revolutionary, totalitarian and anti-democratic regime. The opposite is the rule of law of a democracy. Moreover, the genocide of an entire social class in Spain could not be perpetrated with justice, only by injustice. It is therefore clear, that all the Francoist extermination practices were likewise unjust and judicially repugnant, both those carried out under the 1936-1937 wartime decrees and those ordered by the courts martial from 1937 onwards, such as those carried out under the Law of Fugitives at various stages of Francoism (1939, 1947, 1948, 1949, 1950 and later). Sadly, as one clearly shows that the Francoist rulings are intrinsically unjust, we are again reminded that today's democratic government has neither dated nor been capable of passing laws to rescind the rulings of the Dictator's courts martial.

A last vivid entry in Rev. Gumersindo's diary in Zaragoza that could apply to all the Spanish prisons, is dated December 13 1937 when a young woman, Nicolasa Aguirrezagala, aged 22, from San Sebastián, was brought into the chapel. One of so many Spanish *Roses,* she cried non-stop *"Ay, mama! Ay, mama!* How far they have brought me to kill me!"

Rev. Gumersindo begged her to calm down.

> – "How can I calm down when everything they read out is false. I didn't denounce anybody. I didn't know the person called Portolés; I never knew him and never heard his name before they read it out in Court. It is all a lie. I cannot resign myself to die because of a lie. He was denounced by a waitress. I was a cook."

Rev. Gumersindo continues:

> "When I heard these reasons, I looked at the Public Defender, who had entered the chapel behind me, and I asked him: Are you listening to what she is saying? How can this be possible?

The Public Defender replied, lowering his head as if in shame:

> – "The country courts can make mistakes…! I thought to myself that they should err by pardoning, not by condemning. We do not have the right play with people's lives… I did everything that I could…" he added.

Nicolasa looked him in the eye and replied: "But you did nothing…" and she continued to protest her innocence.

"But my daughter, didn't you say all this when you were interrogated?"
> – "I was not interrogated, nor was I allowed to speak…"

"But didn't you explain all this to the Public Defender?"
> – "I never spoke with the Public Defender. I didn't even know who he was, nor which one he was."

> I was astonished to hear this and felt confused; I didn't know what to think, how to explain what had happened."

Enough. Having once and for all described the scene for everything that occurred in the chapel when death was imminent, there is no need to go back to the Francoist court martial. The reality is clear from the convictions of the multitude of innocents who were led to the grave. Moreno Gómez again insists that the were not 'mistakes'. It was the implementation of the extermination plan developed by the Director General Mola, months before the military coup actually took place. There were no mistakes.

4. The firing squad

Execution before the firing squad marked the end of the ritual of death; well, almost the end as the Regime would still attack the condemned by post-mortem enforcement of the Law of Political Responsibilities that resulted in the economic ruin of their families.

There is little information regarding this final moment in Cordoba, although Moreno Gómez was able to obtain several testimonies for 1936 in the capital's cemeteries.[25] He could add some more for the post-war period, but this information will never be as complete and detailed as that described for Zaragoza in Rev. Gumersindo's remarkable diary.

The morning of October 22 1936, 41 prisoners were executed in Seville under the war decrees by order and thanks to General Gonzalo Queipo de Llano, who is still honoured today in Macarena Basilica in Seville, where he is buried, as the Church continues to lend a deaf ear to the 5th Commandment. An exchange of letters with relatives of those condemned with José Garcia Márquez, shed light on how the firing squads acted in Seville on those dates. Márquez' information beginning with his examination of files kept at Seville Military Archives, when he was investigating the wounds that a corporal received from a bullet that ricocheted during an execution 25 October, three days after the previous one, and in which 35 prisoners were executed. At the time, the condemned were shot against the right-hand wall of San Fernando cemetery, by firing squads of Moroccan soldiers, who held their rifles under their armpits and were disastrous marksmen. The executions were held between 2 and 3:30 a.m. The condemned were grouped two by two and shot in pairs, while the remaining prisoners watched and waited their turn. This was such a slow affair that the entire procedure lasted about an hour and a half. The wounded corporal's reported:

- "...That early in the morning of the 25th, as he was on duty at the Commissariat of the Watch, Calle Jesús del Gran Poder, he left with the sergeant and five militia as part of the guard for the convoy of trucks bearing the prisoners and the firing squad to the cemetery walls. In preparation for the execution of the prisoners, these were lined up as usual, two by two; in front of the said wall, the firing squad and on their right side, the truck whose lights shone on the place of execution; the guard stood a bit in front of the truck and to its right, to prevent any of the prisoners from escaping on that side. They had been executing prisoners for some fifty minutes, when the declarant felt that he had been hit in the stomach and that the bullet was in his body, which is why he was immediately taken to this Hospital in one of the cars that was there."[vi]

At this point we need to return to Rev. Gumersindo's diary as it contains the most correct description we have so far regarding the Francoist methods of execution by firing squad.

The day (22 June 1937) that Don Tregidio, Secretary of the Escatrón Municipality, near Caspe, was shot in Torrero (Zaragoza) cemetery, Rev. Gumersindo describes the great cruelty towards the two prisoners who were about to be shot:

- "...We had arrived at the cemetery. We drove along the wall to get to that part of the wall at the front, facing the city and neighbourhood of Torrero, from where we had just come. And ... we found a detachment of some one hundred soldiers. They were formed in rows facing the wall, but about fifty metres distant. Sixteen of them were closest to the wall... As we arrived, our truck stopped. We got off and began to walk towards the soldiers. They looked at us with curiosity. I walked next to Don Tregidio. The other prisoner was accompanied by Fr. Victor, who could not contain his roughness. We walked past a Red Cross van, almost touching it... Next to the van, two gurneys that had been prepared to receive the bodies of both men. And they could see it all! What a terribly sad walk! Sixty or seventy bitterly difficult steps for the condemned men and for anyone who had been born with a bit of heart... Nobody asked the prisoners whether they wanted a blindfold. I still did not abandon my friend. I stood at his side, stroking his right arm and neck with my hand, and I repeated the prayer: 'Merciful Jesus, save my soul'. He repeated it and he kissed the crucifix. I offered it to the other prisoner for him to kiss, but he shook his head. The silence was deafening. I realized that the officer who had to give the sign to fire was waiting for me to leave. I walked away and stood behind the advance squad of soldiers. The officer shouted: 'Aim!' Don Tregidio shouted: 'Long live God and Socialism!'. The officer shouted again: 'Fire!'. The fatal shots rang out. Each body was riddled by eight bullets. They fell backwards, onto the ground... Some Guardias Civiles approached to remove the metal handcuffs that bound their hands. I approached to administer extreme unction to one and

---

[vi] Information obtained from postal exchanges between Eva Ruiz and José M. Garcia Márques at the end of september 2006, and filed with the Historic Memory Association

absolution and a prayer. Both bodies were lying in a large pool of blood that had run down their legs and was mixing with the dew… A lieutenant shot them each twice in the head. The doctor approached to confirm their death. The members of the Brotherhood of the Blood of Christ picked them up and placed them on the gurneys…. [vii]

22 September 1937, three women and one man were executed. When they arrived at the place of the execution and saw all the soldiers who had been assembled – an entire company and a squad of 24 soldiers (six for each prisoner), Rev. Gumersindo writes:

- "…We began the slow walk towards the place of execution. It was the most horrible walk of my life. The three women wobbled as they walked, their hands had been tied, their clothes were in disarray, their hair was a mess (the babies of two of the women had been torn from their breasts as they entered the chapel) … One of the women shouted: 'So many men just to kill three women…!"[viii]

Something that occurred when the condemned were shot must be addressed, painful as it is: many of the executions were bungled, the soldiers did not aim properly, the condemned did not die at once, only after horrendous suffering, as Rev. Gumersindo tells us on 5 October 1937, when eight prisoners were shot in Zaragoza, two of whom were French. The execution was a horrible disaster:

- "…Four soldiers were assigned to each prisoner. They stood in a row, two metres apart from each other, between the cemetery wall and the firing squad… I moved away. The silence was deafening. It was 6 a.m. Dawn had just broken. The fatal shots rang out and they all fell to the ground; but the majority were only slightly wounded. The solders always shot reluctantly. Someone shot at the wall. On the ground, almost all the condemned were moving around, all painfully crying out. I began moving down the line, administering extreme unction and absolving their sins. The second was young Doñate. When I reached him, he began to rise very slowly, he looked straight at me and raised his bound wrists in supplication. When he was on his knees and I was holding him up with my left arm as I absolved him with my right, the lieutenant came up and shot him in the head, a couple of inches from my face. Poor Doñate's blood stained my sleeve. When I saw him given the mercy shot, my stomach turned in protest and anger… But I had to continue absolving the remaining prisoners, before they, too, were killed off.

[vii] Rev. Gumersindo, op. cit. pp. 57-58.
[viii] Ibid. p. 65.

— How badly you shot — I told the soldiers. — You made them suffer terribly…"[ix]

1 February 1938, Rev. Gumersindo records the execution of six condemned men, among whom Joaquim Laguna, 18 years old, who was taken prisoner in Sigüenza cathedral. The execution was another great fiasco:

- "Of the six condemned men, only one died instantly from the shots received from the eight rifles aimed at each prisoner. The others, who had fallen to the ground, still lived and screamed with pain. I gave absolution and the extreme unction to all but one, the most rebellious."

It would be very useful today if we could have death statistics for the Cordoba provincial cemeteries and for the prison in Cordoba capital. The carnage in San Rafael or in La Salud, dozens and dozens of men, shot one after the other, tragically waiting their end. The specific cases, what they shouted, their protestations of innocence, firing squads that aimed badly, and so forth. Sadly, we do not have any formal records either from chaplains, from soldiers (these would never dare document their own crimes), from Guardias Civiles (even less likely to do so), or prison guards. We lack this information and the details, as for example, how did Federico Garcia Lorca die, what might he have said before he was shot, how much might he have suffered as he died. This is not anecdotal information, but very important data if we wish to reconstruct the life and death of those men and women.

Another disaster of suffering was the execution 12 May 1938 of nine condemned from Alcañiz, one of whom was Maria Figueras whose passage in the Zaragoza prison chapel was also recorded by Rev. Gumersindo and described earlier [page 36].

- "When arrived at the place of the execution, we placed ourselves between the wall and the firing squad. I suggested that they turn themselves to the wall so that they would not suffer from looking at the soldiers. Old man Andrel (61-year-old Miguel Andrel), seeing the soldiers arrive, spoke to them:
— Men! You are about to kill sons of the people…!
I stood between the wall and the condemned, unceasingly begging them, one by one, to have faith in God… Suddenly, I heard the prison director's voice shouting: 'Rev. Gumersindo! Get out of the way!' He wanted to give the order to fire and I hadn't realized that. In fact, the officer hadn't noticed that I was still talking to the prisoners. There still was very little daylight.

[ix] Ibid. p. 70

Young Maria was twisting and turning in place. She continued to sob and cry: *Ay! padre mío! Ay, padre!* Why are they killing me...?'
The soldiers were excited and I saw their indifference and disgust mirrored in their faces.
No sooner did I get out of the way that the shots rang out. Four rifles for each prisoner. None of them died instantly. They were not mortally wounded. One of the wounded, rolling about on the ground, cried out: 'They have finished us; we only have a minute left to live!'
They all cried out with pain and some begged for the mercy shot. I went up to each one and absolved them. An officer administered the mercy shot, sometimes repeatedly shooting the dying three times in their heads."[x]

14 July 1938, another eight condemned from Alcañiz and another disgraceful execution recorded by Rev. Gumersindo. On this occasion, the firing squad forgot their ammunition.

- "As we approached the soldiers, the truck stopped but we were ordered not to get off. A quarter of an hour later and we still had not been ordered to get off. I jumped down and asked a soldier what was happening and what was the reason for the delay. He told me that the soldiers had not brought their ammunition. Fifteen minutes later, some soldiers arrived in a car... That delay was very harmful to the condemned. Some lost patience and began complaining: 'Why are they keeping us suffering here? How pleased they are to make us suffer! Then they dare say that it is the Rojos who are cruel!... Hurry up and kill us! Please, kill us and be done...!'

But that morning, something else added to the suffering. Rev. Gumersindo continues:

- "Finally, we got there. They made another mistake. After lining the eight condemned in a single row, they decided that they would execute four first, then the other four. Right there, in full view of the last four, the officer gave the order to fire against their companions. They saw the soldiers take aim and fire and they heard the shots. They then watched them lying on the ground, rolling in the pools of blood and crying with pain. Then the same soldiers took their positions in front of the surviving prisoners, who fell next to the first. Looking at the eight wounded lying on the ground, one got the impression that this was a battlefield."[xi]

When faced with such terrible scenes, the historian attempts to determine what occurred the numerous executions in the cemeteries in Cordoba capital,

---

[x] Ibid. p. 121.
[xi] Ibid. p. 143.

for example, 1 May 1941 when 34 were shot one after the other in the La Salud cemetery, what did the condemned do during the pre-dawn hours, how was the saca done, how long did they have in the chapel, did they protest on the way to their death, what were the circumstances surrounding the final act. Knowledge of these details is important to the history of the men and women involved, when one is attempting to reconstruct document the Francoist genocide against the Republicans. Another 34 fell in the San Rafael cemetery 3 May of the same year; 28 fell 3 June. All of this being a spectacular waste to promote the expansion of the wave of terror. And one cannot forget the executions in Cordoba capital in the summer of 1936, which on several occasions involved more than one hundred victims. Very few details of these massacres have come to light and been collected by historians and they are doomed to oblivion.

The Church's unsupportable harassment of the condemned at the supreme moment has been commented on in a proliferate manner. In the general plan of religious propaganda written by the Jesuit priest, Fr. Pérez del Pulgar, S.J., among other things he refers to:

- "...In several executions, we have seen the impressive contrast that, whilst a group of men died kissing the crucifix and saying Viva! Spain, another waited to be executed singing the International and blaspheming and swearing."[xii]

Two last reports regarding the execution debacles and the unerring Calvary of the condemned, from Rev. Gumersindo's diary. 26 July 1938 marked the execution of 7 victims, against the wall of Torrero cemetery, almost all prisoners of war, several from Gelsa and one from Belchite. The procedure was the same as everywhere else. Rev. Gumersindo records:

- "The victims of the 26th suffered a great deal. The soldiers shot badly. They were apathetic. One of the executed fell to the ground shouting 'Hurry up and kill me!' All cried and screamed with pain. A deplorable and sorry spectacle...!"[xiii]

Finally, a few words regarding the four victims who were put to death in Torrero 18 October 1938:

- "The soldiers who on that day had the misfortune of being the executioners or part of the firing squad, shot badly. The unfortunate prisoners rolled

---

[xii] Joé Manuel Sabín, op. cit. p. 116.
[xiii] Rev. Gumersindo, op. cit. p. 144.

around on the ground, with such pitiful cries and screams that tore at my soul. The unfortunate Martín raised his feet and legs, whilst harsh, deep *Ayes*! from his chest, sounding like a death rattle.

The two who refused confession, exclaimed just before they were shot: ''*Viva!* The Republic! You will soon suffer the same fate!".[xiv]

With these notes from the Zaragoza prison chaplain, Rev. Gumersindo de Estella, we get an approximate idea of that which occurred in the prisons and cemeteries all over Spain, both during and after the post-war period regarding the mechanics of the ritual of death and the extermination of all Republicans by the Francoist «New State», the National Catholicism. All the paraphernalia of death responded, without anything more, to the brutality of European fascism of the times. Every obeyed the strict characteristics of fascism, without any doubt. Nothing of such cruelty can be explained without determining the coordinates of the cult of violence, by the Nazi-fascism-Francoism, with all the variations that one must consider, but within this triangle. Without this, one cannot explain such violence and such extermination.

Post-war executions in Cordoba towns and villages (Part I)

"Terror debases everyone… Terror, whenever it is applied with callousness, will produce an abject acceptance by the community, a humiliating feeling of gratitude on the part of those who managed to escape the punishment… The bloody orgies dishonour everyone involved, executioners and victims. Only thus can one explain many of the things that occurred during those months."

Pablo Uriel[xv]

Executions by firing squad were not carried out in every one of the 75 municipalities in Cordoba province. The slaughter was concentrated in the main towns of the province, in whose jails prisoners from neighbouring townships were interned.

These post-war executions were not carried out with the same intensity in the regions of the Sierra as in the countryside, as the latter region had been under Franco's rule since 1936 and continuously subject to the extermination from the start of the war. For all that, the repression continued to hit hard on Puente Genil, Montilla, Castro del Río, Bujalance, Palma del Río and other

---

[xiv] Ibid., op. cit. p. 151.
[xv] Pablo Uriel, op. cit. p. 27.

important towns. Nonetheless, the most terrible extermination was carried out in the Sierra, which remained Republican until the very end.

One's attention is drawn to the fact that Franco planned the first stage of the post-war extermination in the home towns of the defeated prisoners. The entire repression during 1939 and 1940 was carried out in townships, although it was centred in the more important towns. It is not difficult to discern the reasons for concentrating the repressive strategy in the Centre-South region of Spain as this was the last area of the country to be occupied by the Nationalists.

1) First, the Regime implemented the usual 'cleaning operation' in the recently conquered townships. That is how the same Francoists described it: the «military operations» of the occupation, they said, were followed by «cleaning operations. You can imagine what they were referring to with that tragic euphemism, one they bandied during the entire war. This was no «improvised» repression, as some scholars have suggested, merely devised to «shock». It was planned widespread and devastating. It is well known that in Franco's opinion, dominance of the land was much less important than the domination of the people.

2) By staging the first step of the post-war repression in the townships, Franco guaranteed that the most extensive, most profound and greatest amount of violence would be felt in those places where the disaffected defeated were well known by their neighbours, so as to ensure that these remained «affected to the Regime». This context guaranteed the perfect targeting of reprisals and acts of revenge. As a result, all the principle towns in the Centre-South, in our case Cordoba province, became centres of imprisonment with mass incarcerations, beatings and systematic torture and the venue for the courts martial and the first wave of executions.

3) This rattling of rifles in the provincial towns was a matter of some satisfaction, first, for the winners, and of fear for the anonymous mass of disaffected. At atmosphere of terror, exemplariness, and general punishment that would not have been felt in the countryside if the executions had been limited to the provincial capital cities.

4) Lastly, in this way the Regime could ensure the complicity and involvement of its entire social and political base in the great repressive task. Loyalty and connivance from the winning half of Spain, encouraged and programmed for their unwavering support to the Dictator and his punitive undertakings.

The principle townships of Cordoba province, where Franco concentrated the 1939-1940 repression, were [in bold, the centre of imprisonment; lower case, neighbouring townships and villages]: **Baena,** natives of this town and from Albendín, Valenzuela and Luque. **Belalcázar,** this town only. **Belmez**, natives of this town and from Villanueva del Rey, Espiel and some from outside the province because they were miners and railroad workers. **Bujalance**, this town only. **Castro del Río**; in addition to natives of this town, also prisoners from Baena, Espejo, Luque and some from Doña Mencía, Priego, Bujalance and Valenzuela. **Espiel**, during the 1941 slaughter overseen by the genocide Corporal «Pepinillo», disaffected from Espiel, Pozoblanco, Villaralto and one from Peñarroya, were executed here. **Fuenteobejuna**, in addition to natives of neighbouring villages, some from Hinojosa and Villaviciosa. **Hinojosa**, the location of a great many victims, in addition to natives of this town, many from Belalcázar, Santa Eufemia, El Viso, Villaralto and some from Fuenta La Lancha. **Montilla**, natives from this and neighbouring villages, others from Fernán Núñez, Nueva Carteya and Doña Mencía. **Montoro**, in addition to natives of this and neighbouring towns, some from Azuel and Venta del Charco. **Peñarroya**, in addition to natives of that town, the final resting place of disaffected from a great many places: Villaralto, La Granjuela, Fuenteobejuna, Alcaracejos, Añora, Belmez, some from Hinojosa, Los Blázquez, Pozoblanco and a great many from outside the province (such as Badajoz), such was the influence of the mines and the railway on local employment. **Posadas**, natives of this town and from Frente Palmera and Hornachuelos. **Pozoblanco**, a patchwork of local townships, plus El Viso, Villaharta, Villaralto, Torrecampo, Villanueva del Duque, Dos Torres, Alcaracejos, Añora and some from La Granjuela. **Puente Genil**, almost purely local. **Villafranca**, natives of the town and some from Adamuz and Villa del Río. Last, **Villanueva de Cordoba**, in addition to natives of the town, there was a special concentration of prisoners from Pedroche, Torrecampo, Adamuz, El Horajo and some from Conquista and Villaralto.

The towns that were established as centres of imprisonment quickly became poles of attraction for two different groups of Spaniards. On the one hand, Falangists from small towns flocked there with the only purpose of wielding rods and beat up prisoners from their towns. These were the emissaries of the torture. The scene repeated itself in every centre of imprisonment in the province. The other group of travellers from small towns were the relatives of those who were imprisoned. A multitude of women, mothers, wives and sisters, plus old people and children, walked tirelessly carrying small bundles of food for their imprisoned relatives when they visited them. The country roads, especially in the Sierra, were a constant coming and going of people with bundles and sacks to help their kin. The fact of the matter was that the Regime was totally disorganized when it came to feeding its prisoners, so that any prisoners unable to get food from their families had a very bad time of it, often with fatal consequences. During 1939 and 1940, sustenance of the prisoners was, in the most part, left to their close relatives.

The first great food catastrophe came at the end of September and beginning of October 1940 when the mass of prisoners was transferred out of the smaller provincial towns and concentrated in the capitals, well out of the reach of their families and the food that was vital to their survival. This led to that which is known as the "1941 Spanish Auschwitz", when the death rate in Francoist prisons rose to scandalous heights, something that has barely been studied. 1941 was also the year of uncountable mass executions by firing squad in the provincial capital cities and a year of the massive death toll in Francoist prisons for all reasons. It was not a "year of modulation" for the repression as one uninformed individual wrote elsewhere.

We need to keep in mind that the great post-war slaughter was part of Franco's repressive project from 1936 until 1950, at the very least, always subservient to the demands of the war. The executions were not a side effect of a collateral project, they formed a mission in its own right, a structural and strategic project that was characteristic of the Regime. Fifteen years of programmed bloodshed, with different modules, but always directed at the greatest efficiency. If there were times when there appeared to be some lessening of those crimes, it is because other repressive instruments were being implemented more intensely (hunger, social exclusion, humiliating practices, beatings in the barracks, forced labour, economic repression, cleansings, death rate in the prisons, repression and brainwashing of children, imprisonment with banishment, etc.). Do not forget: *Francoism was a land with two rivers: a river of blood for the dead and a river of tears for the living.* If sometimes the flow of blood lessened, the flow of tears increased. It is time to stop glossing over and publishing syrupy sweet interpretations of the events of these years, in respect for the historic truth and the victims. There is another adage: *Negation is inversely proportional to the work of historical research.* In other words: denial and ignorance of the facts go hand in hand. The field work necessary to investigate and document the events in the townships of Cordoba province goes to prove that adage.

In **Almodóvar del Rio**, there is an unusual post-war case whereby the 6 prisoners who were shot 12 November 1939, presumably so sentenced by a court martial, were not recorded in the Civil Registry. This information was obtained from an oral source. The six were leaders of the CNT trade union and some also belonged to the local War Committee.

Blood again flowed in 1939 in **Baena**, one of the martyred cities of Cordoba in 1936. The Civil Registry records 32 victims in the immediate post-war period (and more in Castro del Río and the capital). The executions began at dawn 22 June 1939. The bourgeois olive growers and landowners were in a hurry to carry out the killing, that it had already began terribly in 1936, with the execution of an additional 700 victims.[xvi] 32 more died in the post-war period (and another 10 in the capital). Since then, there has been not a hint of any kind of collective bargaining in Baena. The Regime got what it wanted.

22 June 1939, 13 post-war victims were executed in Baena. The leader of the group was the famous peasant leader José Joaquín Gómez Tienda – *El Transío*, of the CNT. Seven were natives of Baena, one from Albendín, another from Valenzuela, another from Castillo de Locubín and three from Luque. (Appendix 1). They were all court martialled in Baena with great pomp and circumstance, one month earlier, 20 May. The court was presided by Guardia Civil Colonel Evaristo Peñalver. The Prosecutor was the flamboyant fanatic, José Ramón de La Lastra y Hoces, Marquis of Ugena and grandson of the Duke of Hornachuelos. A slimy magistrate from Rute, Bernabé Andrés Pérez Jiménez also participated in the trial. It was all very symbolic: the Guardia Civil, the old landholding aristocracy and the Francoist judiciary, against a handful of peasants, perhaps a couple of revolutionaries, with calloused hands, shirtless and wearing rope sandals. "Peace" had to be restored to the fields by chopping off a few heads. Rural fascism, without a shadow of a doubt. Another Guardia Civil commander also presided over court martials in Baena and Castro del Reí: Lieutenant Colonel Rafael Herrera Doblas. The Guardia Civil had been sent to bring out order in Spanish fields.

ckilled in the Asilo de San Francisco, the night of 28 July 1936. It was proven, however, that on that day *El Transio* was in Castro del Río trying to get reinforcements. He lived the last six months of his life fully aware that the victors wanted his head. At his trial – a great public event attended by all the Baena finest – when the Prosecutor read out the charges against him, he said: "My hands leave this world clean, whilst yours are dripping with blood, especially Don José Cubillo's."[xvii] He was condemned to three death sentences, by garrotte, to make certain that the penalty would not be commuted. The charges against his companions did not go beyond simple arrest.[xviii]

[xvi] Arcángel Bedmar has managed to describe 403 victims in Baena as follows: killed in the war 327 (officially recorded only 206); post-war, 43; in prison and forced labour battalions, 17; in Nazi camps, 15; and guerrilla fighting, 1. *Baena, roja y negra. Guerra civil y represión (1936-1943)*. (Baena, red and black. Civil war and repression (1936-1943). Juan de Mairena, Lucena, 2008, p. 274.

[xvii] Antonio Gómez Tienda. Account regarding his brother. Interviewed by the author in Baena, 6 to 10 January 1982.

[xviii] Further details of this case can be found in Arcángel Bedmar, op. cit. p. 258.

According to what Antonio Gómez, *El Transio*'s brother, told me, he and his twelve companions left at dawn 22 June from the prison that had been opened on the Plaza de Francisco Valverde, in Baena:

- "The day of his execution, my mother found out beforehand from the lady who cleaned the jail. As the execution party had to walk down our street, my mother spent all night in vigil, next to the window. At dawn, my mother heard them approach and heard my brother say, as he walked past our house, "*Salud, padres míos*". My mother stayed there until he heard the shot of mercy, then she broke down unconsolably. Before he died, Joaquim chastised his executioners and others present, including some rural policemen and the great landowner, Manuel Trujillo."

In Baena, the executions continued throughout the summer in 1939. There was a saca of 10 victims 8 November. On the 11th of the same month, a young farmer, Manuel Cañete Tarifa, was killed during the transfer of prisoners, also according to Antonio Gómez Tienda.

- "Prisoners were being transferred in the town when the prison guard, an animal called Palomero, came in and began calling out names. One asked him whether he needed to take his backpack and he replied that he wouldn't need his backpack where he was going. This caused some concern among the prisoners who, nonetheless, were being tied together, two by two. Soon, they heard a shot. One of the prisoners, so-called Cañete, who was tied to *El Mota*, cut the rope with a shaving stick and ran away. Unfortunately, he was hit in the leg and they caught and finished him off in the Marbella arroyo. The prisoners who had remained inside refused to leave, believing that they would be killed in the street. They said that if they were going to kill them outside, they might as well do it indoors. The prison guard explained what had happened but they did not believe him. They then had to bring the prisoners who were already out in the street, back in to the prison so that those who were inside could see for themselves that they were still alive. The transfer of prisoners then was accomplished without further difficulties. The prisoners were marched down the street forced to sing *Cara al Sol* on the way."

Although there was no violence in the Albendín district of Baena in 1936, Diogo Cantero Morales sent me the following account of what he witnessed 1 July 1939:[xix]

[xix] Diego Canteri Morales, native of Albendín. Letter to the author from Asturias, 18 July 1984.

■ "... those who returned bit by bit from the Republican zone at the end of the war, were arrested and put into prison but as there were no serious accusations against them, the Falangists invented the following ploy. They printed out several handwritten flyers with the following sayings: 'Death to Franco! Death to the Guardia Civil! Long Live the Pasionaria!' and other similar declarations. These were distributed 1 July 1939. It was a clear provocation by the Falange, to provide it with an excuse to round up some 40 prisoners whom they tortured. The following 14 August, they took five to Baena. Four were executed and one was saved."

The idea of printing out false anti-Regime leaflets was a type of provocation frequently used in other towns and villages in the province. Summer 1940, another raid was carried out in Villanueva de Cordoba, the excuse being some pamphlets saying: "Viva Negrín, bring him back to Spain", written by a venal municipal policeman nicknamed *Berenguer*. Those who were caught in the raid were cruelly tortured and given severe sentences. The same ploy continued to be used in other townships in the Sierra in 1948, together with another provocation such as lighting firecrackers, as a pretext for the ruthless application of the Law of Fugitives (in Pozoblanco, Villanueva de Cordoba, etc.).

Prisoners from Baena, Albendín, Luque and Valenzuela were transferred in February 1940, to the Castro del Río prison, set up in a Convent of Nuns, which means that executions would continue to be carried out in Castro. Later, September 1940, there was another transfer of prisoners but this time to Cordoba capital, where they were executed. The last execution by firing squad in Baena was 11 April 1940, against Rafael Herenas Espartero, native of Albendín. His was a strange, theatrical judgement (one of his cousins had denounced him), in which he was accused of having shot at Guardias Civiles in Cartagena, other guards in Valencia and against right-wingers in el Grao (Castellón), and for having participated in the attacks against the cathedral in Jaén. In other words, he was supposed to have committed crimes all over Spain, all of which he denied during his trial (in Cordoba October 1939). A witness interviewed by Arcángel Bedmar, in 2008, told that Herena's confession to the Baena Guardia Civil was obtained under torture (all post-war declarations, i.e., confessions, were obtained under torture) and that he had been made to kneel on a board with spikes.[xx]

Belalcázar remained a Republican zone to the bitter end. A town of unionists and very active country people during the Republic, in 1936 it immediately took up arms and fought the Nationalists fiercely. The Republican

---

[xx] Arcángel Bedmar, op. cit. p. 260.

Militia last went to battle 13 and 14 August, killing 170 Nationalists, the largest number in the entire province. They were to pay dearly for their bravery as during the post-war, the victors entered the town like starving dogs. A division of the Legión under General Salvador Bañuls Navarro, was quartered in the town in 1940 with the purpose of sowing terror in the region, which they did to the full as they spread out throughout the Los Pedroches district (Belalcázar, Santa Eufemia, Pozoblanco, Villanueva de Cordoba and Cardeña). Such was the terror, that all the guerrillas in the region, led by *El Francés*, retreated in a long walk towards Cáceres, which they entered during the first days of December 1940 through Alma, Cañamero and Guadalupe.

The Civil Registry has recorded the deaths of 30 residents executed during the immediate post-war period (as well as others in Hinojosa and in the capital). The executions by firing squad in Belalcázar began very early on, 16 May, because of the work of Military Court No. 4. Death sentences fell like heavy rain on those interned in the local prison (set up in the Divina Pastora School) and the executions followed immediately afterwards. In addition to the aforementioned execution, there were several sacas 4 and 20 June. Because of this, the prisoners planned a great escape that they carried out 4 August 1939. Fifteen condemned to death escaped, of which 3 died in the attempt: Benedicto Cabanillas, José Paredes – *El Boche* and Alejandro Gómez – *El Chefe*. The remainder escaped into the shills where they played major roles in the guerrillas (*Palomo, Huevero, El Portugués, Quivicán, El Fiscal, El de la Carmela"* and others who fled a year later from the Hinojosa del Duque prison: *El León, Bellota* and others.

Rather unusually, two women were also executed in Belalcázar: Carmen Rubio Cáceres and Matilde Medina Pizarro (6 and 20 August 1939). They were taken to their death separately and without any men, as customary during the post-war. An example of this was the tragic episode of the "Thirteen Roses" in Madrid. When these young women left Ventas prison, several hoped that they would re-join their companions so they could die together, but when they arrived at the Este cemetery, the men had already been shot.

Francisco Mesa Paredes -*Mesilla* died 1 November. He served as a Lieutenant in the Militia and assistant to Aldo Morandi, an Italian member of the International Brigade. They fought on the Peñarroya front and were quartered with the 63rd Division in Villanueva de Cordoba during the Fall and Winter of 1937. *Mesilla* was accused of presiding over the local War Committee. From Belalcázar, the prisoners were sent to Hinojosa, where the firing squads continued to operate, and then later to Cordoba capital. An eyewitness told us of some natives of Belalcázar who were executed in Hinojosa, apparently at the end of 1939, but their names are not recorded in any Civil Registry. This was the case of young Luis Prat Blanco, local secretary of the PCE, who had lost a leg from gangrene, on the Madrid front. His niece Guadalupe, kindly allowed me to examine the two letters of farewell he wrote to his family – one to his sisters and the other to his parents:

- "To my dear sisters, nephews and brothers-in-law:
  It is with the greatest pain and with tears in my eyes, that I dedicate these words to you so that you may remember me. Sisters, at the last moments, as I am about to be executed, my heart beats with the memory of such dear sisters of mine alone, as you have had no other brother; you who have always been my greatest joy and hopes, you who have been the mirror of my soul, you who were everything to me, my dreams and my joy, who on this tragic day, fate will take me from me. I ask you to be always good, that you look after the girl of my dreams (Guadalupe), that you forgive everyone as I forgive them, that you educate my little niece well, to be truthful and when she grows up, you tell her that she had and she still has, albeit underground, an uncle who loves her with all his heart and soul, that she was my only joy. Sisters, live in peace knowing that your brother was never bad; you know that I always was, as far as I could be, an honest worker. Goodbye dear sisters and brothers-in-law, forever. Goodbye with all my soul, goodbye until eternity, your brother: Luis Prat Branco, 32 years of age."

- "To my dear parents, from prison:
  With pain in my heart and sadness for myself, in the last moments of my life, I dedicate this letter to you, so that you always remember with fondness, the advice from your son Luis. Dear parents: bad luck now that my life is ending, despite the misfortune of my leg, the best time of my life. Father, keep in mind what you [*sic.* both] must do in the years left to you, resign yourself to the calamity and do all the good that you can for everyone, most especially for my sisters and nephews, be truthful and good, forgive everyone as I forgive them in my last hours. I hope that you will live for many years, considering that I in my last and best years of my life, am being separated forever from you; although it pains me, I ask that you do not go into a corner of pity for me, that you try to dry up as much of the pain as you can, in the hope that you may live life as well as possible, because I am going to rest forever, and my sole and only concern is for you, for how much you will suffer for me. Be certain that your son always believed that he was good to you as you always were to me; I beg you to forgive me for anything I might have done to offend you, as I myself I leave without ever having been offended.
  Goodbye dear parents, goodbye forever and for eternity. Goodbye with all my soul. Your son: Luis Prat Blanco, 32 years old, Belalcázar, 1939."

The **Belmez** Civil Registry record 36 executed by firing squad during the immediate post-war period (some more in the capital). Executions by firing squad occurred rather late in this village of the Peñarroya mining district. Only one in 1939; the remainder in 1940, with one exception: 16 of the victims were taken to the Hinojosa cemetery to be shot and the largest saca of the lot was 25 May with 15 inmates. A few days before they also took a woman to be shot there, Leonor Expósito Palomo (one of the post-war «21 roses of Cordoba»). In Belmez, the victims were not farm workers, but miners, railway workers, manufacturers or craftsmen.

Bujalance, one of the great fiefs of Cordovan anarchism since the beginning of the 20th century, was undoubtedly why the local notary, Juan Diaz del Moral, became an icon of social historiography with his book *Historia de las agitaciones campesinas andaluzas* [History of the rural uprisings in Andalusia], a unique book of its kind. This notary's celebrity led to his being elected Deputy to the Constitutional Courts of 1931 where, as a member of the Group at the Service of the Republic, he became a great expert on the Agricultural Reform.

The eight first post-war executed in Bujalance fell 5 June 1939. One of these was Pedro García Cano – *El Cojo*, a member of the UGT and president of the local War Committee in 1936 and another, Pedro Martinez Ortiz, a member of the same union and committee. The remainder of the victims belonged to the very popular CNT in Bujalance. The executions took place at wide intervals throughout 1939. One of the Haro Manzano brothers, noted local union activists, Manuel, was shot 18 November. Two other brothers, Luis and Francisco, were killed several months later. 7 December they shot a historic member of the CNT, Ildefonso Coca Chocero – *El Viejo*, aged 65.

In Bujalance, Francoism specifically targeted the energetic conscience of the Bujalance peasants, part of the Regime's program for cleansing and mercilessly subjugating the Spanish working class. That is why the military coup was planned and what fascism was invented for: to abort, preventively, the alleged revolution of the proletariat. (" There is a phantom over Europe" and it was on the altar of that phantom that Mussolini, Hitler and Franco officiated and immolated their opponents). Fascism was Capital's prophylactic response to the fear of a chimeric revolution.

Because of the great repression, Bujalance was one of the townships of Cordoba that sent many men (twenty) to the mountains to join the guerrillas commanded by the famous *Los Jubiles* guerrilla group which included men from Belalcázar, Hinojosa, Villanueva de Cordoba, Adamuz and other towns.

To the 21 executions in Bujalance in 1939, we must add another 28 in 1940, in small, frequently individual, sacas. Four men were executed 30 March 1940, among whom another famous local anarchist, Francisco García Cabello – *El Niño del Aceite*, aged 56 years, whose name was made popular by the press following the successful workers' uprisings in Bujalance December 1933. Also fell with him the young Luis Haro Manzano. A brother of *Niño Aceite's*, Manuel, was killed 20 May. The last execution in Bujalance, before the new wave of terror in 1941, took place 12 September 1940. Beginning October 1940, the Regime began to concentrate prisoners from the town prisons in the Cordoba Provincial Prison. The great bloodshed that followed this concentration was as one would expect, as were the ensuing tragic consequences of those deaths. (APPENDIX III).

Castro del Río, perhaps the first fief of Cordovan anarchism, was subjected to one of the bloodiest punishments in post-war Cordoba province. Cradle of the old master lay preachers, who published the *La Idea Libre* magazine, such as Benito Cordobés, Castro de Río had earned the unusual fame of having defeated Nationalist General Varela 7 August 1936. Such "audacity" so infuriated General Queipo de Llano, that he exploded with typical gross verbosity and publicly threatened the town, telling it to "begin preparing graves". So it happened.

In truth, it was not only natives of the town who were killed here but also others from Baena and Espejo, before everyone was sent to the capital to be slaughtered. Between 1939 and 1940, 167 victims ended up in the common graves of the Castro del Rio cemetery. A usual feature here was the time set for the executions. These were not all executed at dawn but more often in the afternoon, especially in 1939 and 1940, both in Castro as in other neighbouring towns (Pozoblanco, Villanueva de Cordoba, etc.) We presume that *enterado* may have arrived in the morning and the authorities wanted to get the business over as soon as possible, aside from the fact that this enabled them to take advantage of teaching a lesson and spreading fear as the executions were carried out in the daytime, while they put on a free show for the Falangists who were always so eagerly seeking strong emotions during the hard period of the Regime.

Thus, the first fatal shots rang out at 3 p.m. and at 4 pm., the first on 19 June with eleven victims. Earlier, 11 May, Felipe Aguilera committed suicide in the latrines as he could no longer bear the torture. 3 August, Francisco Recio Roja, a member of the 1936 War Committee, and José Criado – *Taraje*, another local peasant leader, were both executed. The sacas were more numerous as of November 1939 and included some peasants from Espejo. 19 November, six were executed, among them Antonio Márquez Bello – *El Chino*, age 22 years, a fan of flamenco, who is said, that on the road to the cemetery, attempted to raise his companions' spirits by singing the tragic verses: *«Madre, coge tu pañuelo / y vete para la Audiencia / y dile al señor fiscal / que te lea la sentencia, / que a mí me van a matar».*[xxi]

25 November ten were shot, including young José Cañasveras Villatoro, who fulfilled his wish of being married in his cell before he died, *in articulo mortis*. The last execution of the year, seven victims, was 5 December. The leader of this group was a Unión Republicana attorney, Manuel Castro Merino, aged 53 years, a typical example of the so-called attorneys of the poor. He had defended workers at trials with mixed juries and even donated land that he owned for social housing. He had cultivated a comfortable living as a member of the typical Republican bourgeoisie, with its strict customs and considerable knowledge dedicated to altruistic ideals. He first studied at the Seminary in Cordoba then Law, in Granada. He practiced Law in Granada, in Castro del Río and in other courts. He moved in Madrid and Cordoba circles. He was a friend of Fenando de los Ríos, was associated with the *Institución Libre de Enseñanza* [Free Institution of Teaching], presided the Cordoba Alliance of Farmers where, among other activities, he was an advisor to small farmers. Castro Merino was involved in the Republican build-up of 1931. He ran for office in 1933 and soon joined the Unión Republicana party, from which he organized the Castro del Río Frente Popular.

During the war, because of his age he only carried out administrative tasks with the 24th Mobile Brigade and he wrote articles in the press before and during the war. Manuel Castro Merino returned to his home town in May 1939 and was immediately arrested. He was badly beaten during the interrogations. His shirts were sent home bloody and with strips of skin sticking to the cloth. The rancid rural, señoritos and Catholic fascism did not have the least respect either for the poor or the illustrious individuals who had placed their knowledge at the service of the underprivileged. Even worse, to have done so was considered an aggravating factor and these men were considered as traitors who had betrayed their class. (Both attorneys of the poor as the doctors of the poor, such as Cayetano Bolivar, who was also assassinated).

All these victims were accused, as was almost everyone, of belonging to a so-called Revolutionary Committee, which in reality was the Frente Popular Committee. (Especially accused of belonging to the Committee, were Antonio Elias Herencia, Alfonso Nieves Núñez, José Diaz Criado, Juan Gómez Gutiérrez, Manuel Castro Merino, Pedro Calvo Garcia, Francisco Recio Rojano and José Porcel Rivas, although has proved impossible to confirm these accusations. Besides, as a rule, the Regime labelled everyone

---

[xxi] *"Mother, gather your kerchief / and go to the Court / and ask the Prosecutor / to read you the sentence, / because they are going to kill me."*

they wanted to exterminate as belonging to the Committee.) Manuel Castro, because of his intellectual importance and his philanthropy, had been sentenced beforehand[xxii]. From Goebbels to today, Fascism's despised culture, books and intellectuals, was radical and visceral. It was that fury that deprived us of the genial Garcia Lorca.

Two peasants from Espejo were shot with the lawyer of the poor: Luis Cordoba Jiménez and Francisco Cordoba Lucena, regarding whose lives we have no information. At least we were able to save their names from oblivion. All the executed ended up in the same large mass grave that had been dug in a side path in the Castro del Río cemetery. That same morning of 5 December, we do not know whether he was also in the chapel or not, Francisco Torronteras Garcia, aged 37 years appeared dead in the middle of a pool of blood. He had taken his own life during the night by cutting his wrists with a razor.

The number and size of the sacas increased in 1940, and there were also more in Baena, Espejo and elsewhere. Ten victims were executed 18 March. One of the largest sacas of eighteen victims, 10 April, included the young farmer Diego Prados Bracero who also was married in prison before he died (it is not known whether this was of his own free will or because he was pressured to do so by the priest, a frequent occurrence). 13 May, one of the four executed was Alfonso Criado Garrido, son of the leader *Taraje* who had been shot several months earlier. 18 May, the group of seven included the man who had been the soul of the organization of the local Militias in 1936, Rafael Moreno Herencia – *Maruca*, who commanded a Cavalry Squadron in the Andalusia-Extremadura Unit. He died aged 66 years, blinded by a war wound and condemned to several death sentences (seven, it is said). Also shot at the same time, Alfonso Camargo Ortega whose elder brother José had been killed a month earlier.

28 May, another thirteen victims. 4 June, they killed José Porcel – *El Sastre* and José Sánchez Alcántara. It is said that the latter left for the cemetery barely able to walk and that *El Sastre* had to hold him up. Andrés López Luque – *El Colorin*, on his own, a 25-year-old farmer who had prepared his escape but was caught, was shot in the prison patio 1 June. He had hidden in the loft of the building for several days, waiting for the right time to escape, but he was caught; another version says that he gave himself up because he was starving. All the inmates were forced to walk past his body as it lay in the

---

xxii Information provided to the author by his grandson, Manuel Castro Delgado, in several letters, February 2014.

patio.[xxiii] This was the typical barracks discipline that Franco had determined would apply to all of Spain.

29 June, Eugenio Rodríguez – *El Pavero*, from Baena, who had served as Captain of a unit with the 88th Mobile Brigade and was wounded on the Pozoblanco front, was shot with another two prisoners of war.[xxiv] 28 August, there was another suicide in the Castro del Río prison: José Sánchez, aged 30 years, threw himself down a well in the prison patio. 31 August, another of the famous anarchist leaders in Castro del Río, Manuel Mármol Algaba – *Loreto*, was executed. 7 September, 11 executed by firing squad. The last saca in post-war Castro del Río was 12 September, again with 18 victims. (APPENDIX I). Afterwards, the slaughter moved on to the capital.

The repression in **Espejo** was especially handled in Castro del Río and later in Cordoba capital. Despite everything, the repressive tyrants wanted the people of Espejo to hear the bursts of shots from the machine guns, as a reminder of who was in control. 3 August 1939, they shot five men in the cemetery. The settling of accounts then continued in Castro del Río and in the capital. Nonetheless, Francisco Jiménez García, aged 40, who had served as Mayor for the Frente Popular and was being kept as a spoil of war in the municipal jail, was sacrificed in the town as if he were "a Christ". He was barbarously tortured and we do not know whether he attempted to kill himself or whether the "was suicided", because the cause of death entry in the Civil Registry is most peculiar: «asphyxiated due to incomplete hanging». Just what did that mean? The exact circumstances of his death are unknown, but there is no doubt that he was a victim of torture. This was 27 February 1940.

Espejo, like Castro del Río and Bujalance, was anarchist origins during the so-called "Bolshevik triennium" (1918-1920), but little by little, the townspeople turned towards the Communist Party, particularly around

---

[xxiii] The author owes some of the details of the events in Castro del Río to the pioneering work of a grass roots diarist, Francisco Merino Cañasveras, *Castro del Río, del rojo al negro* [Castro del Río, from red to black.] Terrassa, Barcelona, 1979 Second annotated edition, 1989. On the other hand, a booklet published by the University of Cordoba, by Francisco López Villatoro, *Cambios políticos y sociales en Castro del Río, 1923-1979* [Political and social change in Castro del Río, 1923-1979], Baena (Cordoba), 1999, has a fancy title but it says nothing of social changes. The great social landmark in Castro del Río, summer of 1936, is dispatched by the author with only a few lines. Later, as an example of his "objectivity" and "equidistance", he only speaks of the right-wing victims and not a single word about leftists who also fell. A useless and inane piece of work. Nonetheless, Merino Cañasveras pioneering study, by a truck driver who emigrated, has given us all lessons as to how to approach the social aspect of the townships. When this author travelled in the Cordoba countryside, during his research, he often met with Merino Cañasveras at his home in Castro del Río and shared both his experiences and his table.

[xxiv] Arcángel Bedmar, op. cit. p. 249.

1930, following the preaching of Adriano Romero, a political activist from Villanueva de Cordoba who served as PCE deputy for Pontevedra in 1936. The great readership of the *La Idea Libre* magazine in this town had something to do with a charismatic rationalist teacher, Clodoaldo Gracia (like Benito Cordobés in Castro del Río and Montemayor). Don Clodoaldo was saved, already an old man, as he was condemned to thirty years. Not Benito Cordobés of whom we only know that he was exterminated with a batch prisoners in front of Castro, 7 August 1936, on the orders of General Varela, one of the New State's war criminals.[xxv]

4 August 1936, Robert Capa and Gerda Taro arrived in Espejo, where he took his iconic photograph *Death of a militiaman* in the outskirts of Espejo, not in Cerro Muriano as has been reported. It has also been said that Capa arrived in Espejo following the road of anarchism, which is equally incorrect as Espejo was a stronghold of the PCE during the entire Republic. Likewise, one should not associate Capa with the anarchists because there is no basis for that. When 5 August Capa was in Cerro Muriano, this town was not on any anarchist route, and when in May and June Robert and Gerda accompanied the International Brigade in La Granjuela, there was even less anarchism around.

Fuenteobejuna was another of the martyrized cities of Cordoba as it had already lost some 500 residents in 1936. Franco's victory would unleash the final solution on its townspeople who were socialists and active UGT trade unionists with a longstanding tradition of workers and sharecroppers. In reality, Fuenteobejuna never ceased being punished throughout the entire war, as of 1 October 1936. Post-war, executions continued to be carried out in 1938, when there were at least 20 victims, the last one 18 December.

As the bells of victory rang out, the townspeople eagerly awaited the return of their relatives, whether civil employees who had been evacuated or returning soldiers, all whom had been away for three years because of the war. The Municipal jail was immediately filled to burst with captured Rojos, one of whom had been Mayor for the Frente Popular, Agustín León. Courts martial were quickly organized and the first to fall before the firing squad was Obdulio Romero, 2 June, whose file we have been unable to consult. Three more fell 4 August, including Felisario Cidoncha who didn't even make it to the cemetery as he was shot at the church door. It is said that he was totally broken by the barbarous torture he had suffered. He was accused that in 1936

[xxv] This General's bloodshed reached its height during the march from Toledo to Madrid in October 1936, when he ordered the execution of more than 4,000 Republican prisoners of war.

someone had seen him during the saca or on the truck taking Fuenteobejuna right-wingers to La Granja and Azuaga (Badajoz), where 57 were highjacked and killed by anarchist militia from Alanís (Seville), it was supposed in collaboration with some from Fuenteobejuna. Anyhow, the determination of guilt is a vain exercise because at the courts martial the prisoners always paid as the accusations were considered "fair because they were sinners", whilst those above them and responsible almost always found a way to get out of the way.

The serious business of killing began in the Fall of 1939. 14 October Santiago Rodriguez, a 55-year-old worker, was shot. His cellmate, who survived, Ildefonso Sedano, gave his eyewitness report:

- "I remember a night that I was walking with Santiago Rodriguez; a Guardia Civil entered the patio and asked him if he was Santiago Rodriguez. He replied that he was and the guard continued: 'There is no point in beating around the bush: I have come to get you to shoot you.' And he was taken away. This companion belonged to the CNT, from La Cardenchosa."[xxvi]

24 October at 8 p.m., there was a saca of four inmates, one of whom Tomás Gallardo Habas, from a family that had been sorely punished by Francoism, particularly during the persecution of escapees. One of his sons, Tomás Gallardo Medina, escaped to the hills during the post-war and was never heard of again. The Habas family were from La Cardenchosa and they suffered many lost in the guerrillas (brothers Nemesio, Eugenio and Dionisio Habas Rodriguez, the first two killed in 1947 and Dionisio in 1951, in Seville). The Gallardo family also lost relatives among the people from the hills, through the Law of Fugitives during the triennium of terror. In the same saca, the socialist Alejandro Cuadrado who was second assistant Mayor during the last Republican municipality.

30 October, five executed, among which the brothers Romero Agredando, José and Aurelio. For the rest of the year, the executions were held at nightfall, at 8 p.m. or 9 p.m. The custom of executing prisoners in the afternoon, at the usual time for the bullfights, seemed to be the usual practice in 1939, and during the first quarter of 1940, in most Cordoba province towns. We have no explanation for the abandonment of dawn as the time for the executions.

A heavy dose of killing was planned for 6 November, with six victims, led by the last Mayor for the Frente Popular in Fuenteobejuna, Agustin León Sánchez, a socialist. At the end of the war he attempted to live incognito in a

---

[xxvi] Letter from Ildefonso Sedano, from Cordoba, dated 19 November 1985. A witness native of La Posadilla (Fuenteobejuna).

village in Almeria, but he was identified four months afterwards and he was taken to Fuenteobejuna and kept there until he ended up in the cemetery. The officer in charge of the firing squad was a Lieutenant Flores. Several of Agustin's friends, accused of belonging to the War Committee in 1936, were shot t the same time: Teófilo Mateos Rivera, Antonio Murillo, Francisco Zurita and Rafael Gómez Rios.

The tragic moments that were lived then in the Municipal prison are described by a survivor, Ángel Horrillo, from the village of Ojuelos Altos:

- "When I was returned to my village, in May, even before I entered it I was surrounded by armed men and taken to the Falange. I could easily deny the first accusations, because when they met in their committee where they used to determine the accusation, they came up with such a number of false accusations, with the sole purpose of eliminating me. I was tried by a summary court martial, with another nine men, and there were ten death sentences. There were some 80 of us in jail during 1939 and the beginning of 1940. From the patio, we could see the arrival of those who came to sign the list of those who would be executed that night. In this terrible situation we found ourselves at 8 or 9 at night and, arranged in circles, the jailor – *Don Manuel* he was called – made us sing *Cara al Sol,* once or twice. He then gave us five second for all to go through the 70-centimetre door, but before doing so, hit us left, right and centre. A little later, speaking very slowly, he would read out the list and, sarcastically, say: 'To the chop.' Four of my group were shot on four different nights: Antonio Ruiz, Luis Romero, Antonio Múñez and Juan Pedro Hidalgo, the last of whom was my uncle. He and his wife were kept in a separate room, but of the same lot of prisoners and when his name was called, she let out a terribly cry. I found it spectacular as I could not control either my heart or my nerves."[xxvii]

The Fuenteobejuna victims during this first stage of the repression, 1939-1940, recorded at the Civil Registry number 40. The prisoners were transferred to Peñaroya later one, where the shootings continued. Later, in Cordoba capital, where all prisoners in the province were gathered at the beginning of Fall 1940.

Hinojosa del Duque was another of the Sierra townships that were greatly punished. Its Civil Registry record 66 victims, not just from Hinojosa, but also from Belalcázer and some from Santa Eufemia, El Viso and Villaralto. In the fall of 1940, all prisoners left there were transferred, with the rest from the province, to Cordoba capital.

[xxvii] Eyewitness report from Ángel Horrillo, from Peñarroya-Pueblonuevo, sent to the author 1 July 1983. The witness was a native of Ojuelos Altos (Fuenteobejuna).

51

19 April 1939 the Law of Fugitives was applied to three persons at the La Gutierra farm: Sebastián Martinez, Prudencio Garcia Gómes (a retired soldier for whom we have no details) and 18-year-old Pablo Gómez Leal, brother of the famous *Vidal* (three Gómez brothers were executed, Pablo, Antonio and José).

22 June 1939 there was a burst of shootings with a saca of four led by the man who had been Mayor during the war, Eloy Pizarro – *El Barón*. Together with his companions, they were accused of belonging to the 1936 War Committee, rightly or wrongly (Fermin Muñoz, Ramón Navas and Isidro Barbancho). 1 September 1939 there was a three-man saca, which included Luis Ramirez – *El Montillano*, a wealthy individual of a certain social standing. This man, who owned property, who had money in the bank and even a typewriter at home, was killed so they could rob him. He belonged to an interclass ideology and created a so-called Committee Pro Peace in 1936, to try and get arbitration and agreement between contending parties. That work alone and the wish to steal from him, led him to his grave. 14 August a single woman was taken to be shot, Carmen Aranda Caballero, who left 6 orphan children. This family's history is terrible. Her husband, Lázaro Leal Martínez – *El Perdigón*, fled to the hills where he died on an unknown date. One of their sons, Francisco Leal Aranda also fled to the hills where he died in 1949, between Belmez and Hinojosa. There were 30 executions in Hinojosa up to the end of 1939, plus two who were not recorded in the Civil Registry (Luís Prats Blanco, local secretary of the PCE and Alfonso Vélez, both from Belalcázar). The largest saca of the year was 7 victims on 1 November.

There were executions in Hinojosa throughout 1940, but rather irregularly. The 8 March saca of 5 victims included Pedro Rubio Cáceres, a 28-year-old baker from Belalcázar, whose sister Carmen had been shot the year before in their home town. 8 May they killed Dionisio Bláquez Forgas, accused of having belonged to the War Committee, as was Alfonso Arrellano Muños, shot 25 May.

The great number of condemned to death can be explained by the plan for a great escape from the Concepcionista Convent-Prison, at dawn between the 31 August and 1 September, the last market day. The master bricklayer, Lázaro Leal Martínez – *El Perdigón* (who wife Carmen Aranda was shot the previous 14 August), made a hole in the wall that led to the church vestry and to the convent patio. Some twenty man ran out running through that hole in the middle of the night, and they were chased by the guards through the streets of the town. 15 men managed to make it to the open fields and they became famous in the guerrilla fighting (Pedro Diaz Monje – *El Francês* (who commanded the guerrilla in Cáceres), Manuel Hidalgo Medina – *Bellota*, Lázaro Leal – *El Perdigón* and his son Francisco, Demetrio Morales – *Cuatete*,

Francisco Vigara Mesa – *El Léon* (from Belalcázar), Francisco Corchado Silveira – *Lazarete* (from El Viso), among others. Of those who died when escaping through the streets, four are recorded in the Civil Registry at Hinojosa (Antonio Ramos and Miguel Jiménez of Hinojosa; Pedro Molero and Rafael Herrero, of Belalcázar). Another two from Belalcázar are not recorded: Manuel Paredes and Francisco Cáceres Calderón. There were many such great Fugitives from prisons all over Spain, such was the great despair caused by the tremendous repression that was launched, beyond anything that all the defeated could ever have imagined.

The last person shot in Hinojosa, before the general transfer of prisoners to Cordoba, was Manuel Garcia Blanco, 18 September 1940, a native of Villaralto. He was accused by the *Causa General* as a "eminent revolutionary" in this village, which does not appear to be quite correct as he was an elderly worker.

Lastly, in 1941, the Hinojosa Civil Registry records two peculiar deaths, unidentified, due to "hanging" or "suicide" in the Guardia Civil barracks (an odd place to commit suicide), which is no more than a euphemism for death due to torture, under the aegis of the very hard Law of Safety of the State of 29 March 1941 that led to a great rise in Francoist terror that year in a dozen townships. This was the same year that more than 500 prisoners died in the Cordoba city prison.

Montilla was sorely punished, without explanation, because its extensive Republican neighbourhood, more socialist than communist, the only thing they did was to flee the town in 1936. Already in this year of the military coup, Francoists eliminated at least 200 persons.[xxviii] Despite this genocidal punishment, the Regime looked for another punishment in the post-war, shooting 15 natives in the Montilla cemetery plus 8 out-of-towners (Fernán Nuñez, Castro del Río, Nueva Carteya and Doña Mencia).

The slaughter in post-war Montilla began 7 November 1939, with a saca of 7 victims, headed by the local leader Antonio Cordoba Gálvez – *Arroba* and both Taper Ruiz brothers – Antonio and Francisco. Some of Montilla's most valuable republicans fell in the 1940 sacas. 16 May, in addition to some out-of-towners, a noted representative of Montillano antifascism, Juan Cordoba Zafra, who reached the rank of Militia commander in 1938. He

---

[xxviii] This figure was estimated thus in my book of 2008, *1936: el genocidio franquista en Cordoba* (1936: the Francoist genocide in Cordoba). Crítica, Barcelona, p. 282. Arcángel Bedmar , the great historian researcher of the Cordovan countryside, arrived at the same value in *Los puños y las pistolas. La repressión en Montilla (1936-1944)* (Fists and pistols. The repression in Montilla (1936-1944). Ayuntamiento Montilla, 2009, p. 2004. However, we were only able to identify 116 of the dead.

had been a member of the board of the *Casa del Pueblo* community centre, secretary of the Socialist Youth Movements, alderman for the Frente Popular and, following the coup, organizer of a military unit in Bujalance, of which he was the captain, later integrated in the Jaén Militias and in the 92nd Mobile Brigade. In 1939, he attempted to be saved in the port of Alicante, at the head of his unit.[xxix] He was captured there and brought to Montilla, to the great delight of the local landowners. His great qualifications as a politician and as a Republican soldier led to his death.

Another Republican heavyweight from Montilla fell with the saca of 25 May, Manuel García Espejo – *Chicuelo*, aged 30 years. He had been a member of the board of the *Casa del Pueblo,* secretary of the Young Socialists in 1934, and Militia captain, founder of the Montilla Company in the summer of 1936, that became integrated in the Garcés Battalion and in the 73rd Mobile Brigade, under the orders of Antonio Ortiz, from Espejo. They fought for the Republic to the bitter end and there could be no other end to this undertaking than the firing squad. *Chicuelo*, a brilliant and good-looking man, went to his death 25 May 1940, in his native Montilla, that *Munda* for which Caesar and Pompey fought two millennia earlier. He was only accompanied in his tragic end by a young local communist, José de la Torre Requena, whose appeal for mercy arrived a few days later. That was how Francoism killed in Spain.

The Montilla and neighbouring prison inmates were transferred between 17 and 19 October 1940, to the Cordoba Provincial Prison. The executions continued in Cordoba and ait is there that he who had been the Frente Popular Mayor of Montilla, Manuel Sánchez Ruiz – *El Perla* and who had reached the position of national vice-president of the FNTT, died. Yet another great personalities of Montilla sacrificed by a mad, reactionary and tridentate Spain as they had already done in 1936 with another historic leader of Cordovan socialism from Montilla, Francisco Zafra Contreras, member of Parliament and first Republican Mayor, one of the national founders of the FNTT, whom the troops under Sáenz de Buruaga dragged to Baena where he was murdered by pistol shots in the public square 28 July 1936. In Montilla, the only ones left were the elderly and senile, represented by the Carlist group of the Count of La Cortina Francisco de Alvear, president of the National Catholic Farmers Confederation. All very catholic, such as archpriest Luis Fernández Casado, responsible for "saving the souls" of those murdered, but not their bodies.

Montoro suffered 11 shot in 1939 and 10 in 1940, in addition to those executed later in the capital. We know there were executions on Christmas

---

[xxix] Arcángel Bedmar, Ibid., pp. 109 et al.

Day 1936 when the Nationalists occupied the town. although there is no mention of them in the local Civil Registry. We know that 9 of the executed belonged to the international brigade and several were public servants. The number of victims in 1936 is estimated at 40.[xxx] When the post-war arrived, the Francoists of Montoro received the returnees with loaded rifles. This was a continuation of the same repressive program that lasted fifteen years (1936-1950), in its harshest expression, with its various modifications, all conceived to ensures the greatest effectiveness and application.

The slaughter began with the application of the Law of Fugitives of 29 April 1939, to Miguel Cañuelo Lozano, a baker. 28 November was the first proper execution, with 10 victims, who consisted of: one from Azuel (a village in which nothing had happened in 1936), four others from the village of Venta del Charo (Cardeña) whom the *Causa General* accused of two deaths in 1936, on what basis we do not know; José Antonio Romero, Falangist, and Bartolomé Coleto, landowner from Villanueva de Cordoba. From Montora: Fernando Ruiz Zorro and Francisco Cepas, accused of an attack against a prison full of right-wingers, 22 July 1936, with axes, weapons and dynamite, causing 50 victims, a popular uprising in turn motivated by another killing that the Francoists had just committed in neighbouring Pedro Abad. The accusation of the attack on the Montoro prison was generally applied to everyone they wanted to eliminate, both in the countryside and in the capital. It is now impossible to determine which of these accusations were well based and which were not. Whatever, it is known that the Francoists systematically eliminated everyone with any standing in the labour movement, trade unions, Republican army (first of all, officers and non-commissioned officers) and Republican authorities (Members of Parliament, Mayors, etc. without exception) and all this, whether there had been right-winger victims in the town or not. If in any doubt, look at the killings in provinces such as Navarra, Zamora, Galicia, Castilla-León, Canarias, Ceuta, Melilla, and so forth.

The 1940 executions in Montoro were mainly carried out in September. They began the 4th with the shooting of a local communist: Juan Barbado Zamora, bricklayer aged 52 years, father of a national leader of the PCE, Francisco Barbado, who was commander of the 5th Regiment and played an important role in Andalucía with the restauration of Democracy. He told me the following:[xxxi]

[xxx] Francisco Moreno Gómez, Idem, p. 582.
[xxxi] Francisco Barbado. Interview with the author in Cordoba, 26 March 1983.

- "My father was a communist and they accused him of having participated in the famous attack on the prison in 1936. He was imprisoned in Montoro for a year and the infamous Sergeant Arenas, of such sad memories in the town, destroyed him with beatings. He would go and have breakfast at the Casino with the Señoritos and when he finished said: 'OK. I am now off to give them their breakfast'. And the beatings would begin in the jail. On another occasion, the señoritos in the Casino said, referring to my father: 'Either you kill him or we will.' And they shot him. He had become blind from the torture he was given."

7 September, fell young Francisco Caballero Majuelos, whom the *Causa General* accused of killing a retired soldier, Pedro Arroyo, in July 1936, always it was impossible to confirm the veracity of this. 11 September, there was a larger saca of 6 victims, also accused of the assault on the jail in 1936. Finally, 20 September they killed a woman, Patrocinio Purificación Juárez Pareja, aged 39 years, for whom we were unable to get any information.

Palma del Río, another which suffered terribly in 1936, with several hundred assassinated in "Don Félix's yard", at the hands of this landowner and breeder of fighting bulls (today, the Moreno de la Cova cattle ranch). When I first visited Palma del Río, around 1980, I went to look at the tragic yard, which was very rundown and overgrown.[xxxii] It is located next to the church. Today, it has been renovated and fenced in, to keep the curious away. This is without a doubt, one of the Places of Memory in Andalusia.

During the post-war, there were 32 victims in 1939, 8 in 1940, and more in the capital. The executions began 7 November (this date is interesting as it was chosen in many Cordoba townships for the first executions, as it is the anniversary of the Russian Revolution and the defence of Madrid). Right away, November 1939 was the most tragic, both for Cordoba province and for all of Spain. On this occasion, 16 workers and farmers were taken in a saca (most of them anarchists and members of the JSU). 16 November, another saca, at 2 a.m., with 15 victims, among which the Díaz León brothers – Julio and José, workers.

29 March 1940 there was a peculiar execution of an individual: Gumersindo Santiago Páez, a 59-year-old worker, member of the *Luz y Prosperidad* Masonic lodge that existed in Palma del Río from 1913 to 1936, in whose foundation he had participated and held important positions. It seems that the "crime of being a Mason" was what led to his death, or perhaps because the Francoists of Palma del Río were unable to capture the Grand

---

[xxxii] I published the photograph of the "Corralón de don Félix", as the yard is known, in my book *La Guerra Civil en Cordoba (1936-1939)*, op. cit., p. 376.

Master of that lodge, Antonio España Ocaña, father of the young member of the JSU who organized the militia from this town and their resistance to the military coup, José España Algarrada.

At the beginning of Spring, the executions in Palma were held at 8 p.m. 30 March, 6 more victims, most of them workers. The last execution in Palma was 15 May at 11 p.m.: Francisco Jiménez Ordóñez, a 24-year-old chauffeur. The remaining inmates, natives of Palma, killed were executed in Cordoba capital.

Pedro Abad, on the banks of the Guadalquivir, a small farming town (pop. 4,143 in 1926), suffered an equally merciless repression. There is nothing more enlightening than reading local writings to understand what Francoism was, particularly during the first stage of its development (1936-1943) when the Regime itself classified itself as totalitarian and adopted the Nazi-type salute that even Bishops displayed with remarkable dexterity.

The infernal microhistory of how the townspeople suffered in Pedro Abad (as in countless unknown towns and villages) we owe to a local essay by the Adán Gaitán brothers: Félix and Juan Manuel, *Mártires de una esperanza* [Martyrs of Hope].[xxxiii] The section that is reproduced here, written in a difficult prose, is truly astounding. The tortures, the humiliations, the suicides, aggressions of all kind, even cases of lynching, by the «victorious Catholics», were the order of the day. In anticipation of some conclusions regarding the inflexibility of the Francoist extermination, here is a fact: according to these authors, in Pedro Abad 150 were condemned to various sentences by the courts martial. Of these, 50 were executed, that is, one third.

Implementation of the extermination program began early during the war, 22 July 1936, when a column of Nationalist fighters from Cordoba (artillery soldiers, Falangists and some peasants) appeared that morning in the town with a view to carrying the typical 'punishment sortie', as they called it them. They arrived, ready to kill with a vengeance. As they got off their trucks, the first people they saw was several farmworkers who were working a vegetable patch, the Teviño Nieto brothers, whom they shot and left where they fell. They did the same with another young man who was tending his goats, Salvador Aguilar. As they arrived at the first houses, they saw and shot Nicolás Alonso who was cleaning something; they did the same to José Escobar – *El Gorrilla*, who was selling sunflower seeds on the streets. Seeing what was going on, a 50-year-old man, Francisco Arena tried to save himself

---

[xxxiii] Félix and Juan Manuel Adán Gaitán. *Mártires de una esperanza. República, guerra civil y represión en Pedro Abad.* (Martyrs of hope. Republic, civil war and repression in Pedro Abad) Lopera (Jaén), 2009.

by climbing up a tree. They saw him and shot him down. His sister Ana (mother of *Gato Negro*), finding out about the death of her brother, killed herself by throwing herself down a well. They saw a car on the street being driven by a young disabled man and ordered him to Stop! At that point, Juan Lora Escobar, the village schoolmaster, a man of order who had nothing to do with anything political, called out from the door of his house where he had gone to see what was happening: "Leave him alone; can't you see he is mentally disabled!" A local Falangist, turned around and, without a word, shot the schoolmaster in the head and left him for dead. That is how the «Saviours of Spain» behaved.

(A similar mad crime was committed about the same dates in Aguilar de la Frontera: a poor farmer was leading his donkey laden with water casks, when down the road he met up with a truck full of young Fascists, *Señoritos* from Aguilar. For fun, they shot and killed the poor man, shouting "for God and for Spain" as they drove off roaring with laughter. Their targets were: farmworkers, shepherds, shirtless and poor people wearing rope sandals. This is how the people of order enjoyed themselves. Pure and hard Fascism, very much like the Italian blackshirts during the 1920s, as depicted by Bertolucci in the first part of his movie *Ninehundred*.)

The tragic incursion of the Fascists from Cordoba in Pedro Abad left bitter memories. They went from house to house asking, "Where is the owner of the house?", randomly killing townspeople right left and centre. One of those who opened his door was Pedro Parilla, a 70-year-old, whom they shot dead in the entrance hall. This same tactic of entering and leaving the houses we saw in Villafranca (when the Moorish troops were leading the fighting), in Baena, etc.[xxxiv] That was 1936 in the villages in Andalusia. The consequence of the schizophrenic incursions in Pedro Abad, was the hasty retreat of the Nationalist militia who, as they left the town, shot into the windows of houses as they went, killing 12 and wounding 17 civilians, in protest against the arrest of right-wingers in Casa Olaya. To these, we add another 5 or 6 (including a 17-year-old) dead the Fascists had already killed on the streets, plus several more townspeople who, before the Fascist returned to Cordoba, they took with them as they left town and killed them in the outskirts and then burnt their bodies with gasoline. The morning ended with another 16 murdered by the Fascists, plus another 11 whom they took with them to Cordoba and later killed. I was able to confirm at least 30 victims in Pedro Abad during the war.

[xxxiv] Francisco Moreno Gomes, *El genocidio franquista en Cordoba*, op. cit.

There were 39 executions in Pedro Abad in the post-war period, plus an additional 14 natives of the town executed in the capital and 8 who died from starvation in the Provincial Prison, a total 61.

Seven of those executed during the post-war period fell 2 November. The Military Judge was Francisco Iglesias. The firing squad consisted of an officer and soldiers from the 3rd Falange Brigade of Cordoba. Taken in this saca: Antonio Arenas – *Graniaino*, who had been a socialist Mayor of the town; Francisco Garcia Lara was killed because he was on guard at the Casa Olaya, when right-wing prisoners were shot. In reality, they accused everyone in the town of this crime, indiscriminately; Juan Pulido Canales – *El Zorro* was accused of one death, something that he forcefully denied during his trial; Juan Ruiz López, a 45 year-old tradesman, father of 7 children, only acknowledged at his trial that he had taken prisoners to Casa Olaya but that he did nothing else; Rafael Jurado Castillam, a member of the Libertarian Youth, was also accused of belonging to Self-Defence Group, as were almost everybody, of the attack on the barracks and the Casa Olaya episode; José Fernández of the CNT was accused of being a member of the War Committee and other crimes including that "he bore arms in 1918"; Lastly, Juan Gaitán Valderramas – *Maura*, a tavern owner belonging to the Izquierda Republicana, accused of nothing specifically except that during the war he was living in Villanueva de Cordoba, where he was Treasurer of the Committee for Refugees. From the onset, the Dark World of the accusations under Francoist 'justice' displays its clearly apparent nature as a sovereign, totally untrustworthy farce.

5 November (The Adán brothers say it was the 6th), there was a three-man saca in Pedro Abad: Alfonso Carcelé Galán, a socialist, having seen the cadavers of the priest Antonio Pérez and the retired Guardia Civil Manuel Ortega who had been executed earlier, it occurred to him he should take them to be buried. This act of compassion was turned against him, he was arrested and accused of having taken parts of the statue of Christ when statues of the saints were damaged in the church; Juan Aguilar Cailla was accused of presumably having belonged to a Self-Defence Group. I earlier described how his brother Salvador, who had a pronounced limp, was shot 22-7-1936 when he was watching the goats outside the town limits; lastly, Matías Prieto Castilla, father of five, was also accused of belonging to a Self-Defence Group and of being a communist.

8 November 1939, a 4-man saca: Antonio Rojas Arenas was accused of having shot against his cousin, the priest Alfonso Canales. They said he handed him to the War Committee of Villa del Río, who ordered that he should be taken for a walk, or *paseo*. It is impossible to determine the authenticity of all of this; regarding Fernando Triviño – *El Gordito*, there was

no accusation, unless that he was a member of the Farming Committee and that he was put in charge of the right-wing women who were made to work in the fields and that he belonged to the UGT; there were no accusations against Juan Martín Carcelé Rojas. There was a surprising circumstance indicative of the revengeful post-war rage and the Fascists' ability to invest wicked acts, in Juan´s brothers, who played the drums in processions, were forced to be present when their brother was executed and made to play the drums; there was no specific accusation against Rodrigo Arenas Durán, other than that he belonged to the UGT and to a Self-Defence Group.

20 November a single individual was executed: Rafael García Cambronero – *El del Centro*, who had been a Municipal Judge. As a member of the War Committee, he was a negotiator in the surrender of the barracks and did not advocate any excessive intervention, just attempting to put some order into the middle of all the chaos. Before he was killed, he was so brutally tortured and beaten so badly that they had to take him urgently to Cordoba hospital, to heal his wounds until he was well enough to be executed. He was visited by María Muñoz, his wife, in hospital, and he told her: "I will soon be taken back to Pedro Abad so they can finish their work". He was 52 years old and the father of Rafael Garcia Contreras, who had been a PCE Senator under the Republic. The latter writes, in his book of memories: "What they did in the barracks to my father was unbelievable. Beating after beating, he was tortured until he had a large wound in his back... On one of the 'walks' from the barracks to the prison, my aunt carried me in her arms, so that I could see my father... He was dripping blood all over his body."[xxxv]

24 November 1939 was the last execution of the year, with the death of Alfonso Valcarreras Arenas who was repeatedly accused of belonging to a Self-Defence Group and of having shot against two right-wingers. Frequently, the accused signed confessions through torture, which is why we cannot always trust what is written in their dossiers.

The executions in Pedro Abad recommenced 7 March 1940, this time against a single person, Andrés Lara Gaitlán, aged 49. He had a long experience as an alderman and was famous as a speaker at meetings. He belonged to the War Committee and he participated in arrests. When the town was evacuated at the end of December 1936 he moved to Villanueva de Cordoba where he worked with the Refugees Committee.

5 April, three men were executed: Domingo Ruiz López, a member of the CNT, who was killed because he knocked the image of the Sacred Heart of Jesus that was attached to the façade of the City Hall building, to the

---

[xxxv]   Rafael Garcia Contreras. *Susurros de libertad. Memorias.* (Whispers of Freedom. Memories.) El Páramo, Cordoba, 2009, p. 22.

ground. When these men were being taken away in the truck, on the way to the cemetery, they drove past the prison that housed their companions. Domingo called out to them to keep their spirits up, while the soldiers kicked him in the butt. His brother-in-law, Nieto the Mayor, was executed some days later; Juan Cerdá Moreno was accused of almost the same crimes as all others, i.e., of belonging to a Self-Defence Group and of having been a guard at the Casa Olaya. Two more of his brothers (Miguel and Melchor) were later also executed and another one, Bartolomé, was condemned to a long prison sentence; Regarding Rafael Arjona Hernández, there were no accusations of importance, only that he was a communist and that he bore arms against the «Movement to Save Spain».

This brings us to the great 11 May 1940 scandal in Pedro Abad, the so-called Casa Barcos Case, the description of which is a bit confused in the Adán Gaitán brothers' book (p. 524 et al.). There was some kind of hold-up 5 May, planned by several individuals from Morente, apparently members of the *Los Jubiles* guerrillas. Pistols in hands, they entered the house of the wealthy Fernando Cerezo Barcos and accidently shot off a gun that mortally wounded 14 year-old Francisco Cerezo. Six townspeople from Pedro Abad were arrested as charged by Manuel Albendea Ribas, Captain of the Guardia Civil from Montoro. Urgent charges were filed against all although it was not clear that they were all accomplices to the robbery as they were accused of carrying (non-existent) pistols. Amongst the arrested was the presumed head of the gang, Juan Gallardo, from Morente, whom they beat to death 9 May. That same day, another prisoner, Jerónimo Grande - *Jeromo*, 19 years old, from Pedro Abad, unable to bear the torture, committed suicide by throwing himself down a well[xxxvi]. The four remaining prisoners were subjected to the identical Calvary and were executed on the 11th.

The Emergency Summary Court was set up in two days and it ended stating: "The execution of the condemned will take place at 7 a.m. tomorrow", which was not correct. The execution of the four presumed accomplices to the robbery, which was not at all proven, took place in full daylight, at noon, and it was a public execution, much closer to a lynching.

The Adán Gaitán authors say that the four prisoners were taken from the jail at 12:30 a.m. 11 May, to be executed in the cemetery. The Francoist population prepared itself for a great party. The prisoners were taken from the Old City Hall building with a great excitement from the people, while calls were made to invite all the neighbours into the street, including the school

---

[xxxvi] The Grande family was another massacred by Francoism: two of Jerónimo's brothers were executed in 1936 and his father was imprisoned.

children. They were marched down the street, between insults and shoves from the Francoist pack of dogs.

The executioners cut rods as they reached the outskirts of Pedro Abad and with them they poked and beat the condemned, pulled them by their hair and their moustaches. The poor victims begged: "*Kill us once and for all. Stop this!*". No sooner said than done, right there, before they got to the cemetery, they placed them for a public firing squad. Earlier, the Francoists had brought two of Alfonso Lópes Salinas' young brothers, one of the condemned, for them to watch the shooting. Their bodies were left where they fell for 24 hours, for the general public to jeer and laugh at.

Juan Martinez's mother and fiancée, who were from Morente, came to see him. A soldier told the victim's mother that she would be allowed to give him a kiss, on the condition that she did not cry; if she cried, she would be arrested. The two women somehow held back their tears and complied with the ritual, but when they moved away, amongst the olive tree, one could hear their cries throughout the entire Cordovan countryside. Only one of the detained was temporarily saved, although condemned to twenty years in prison; Bartolomé Regalón, died of starvation in Cordoba Provincial Prison the following year, 25 February 1941.

The bloody events in post-war Pedro Abad were not over, not in the very least. 16 May, five days after the terrible *Casa Barcos* episode, there remained a last coup, a saca of 6 presumed victims who were to be shot to be shot that day at dawn in the cemetery, an event that proved to be even more tragic than usual. The victims were put on the truck, in the middle with soldiers on either side – a corporal and a sergeant. However, two of the *morituri* who were tied to each other, had a desperate plan in mind: José Garcia Yeste – *El Porcelano*, 23-year-old anarchist, and Francisco Cambronero Rodriguez – *El Fraile*, aged 41 years. At a given moment on their way, having managed to free themselves from each other, they jumped off the truck, one on either side. The soldiers, in the middle of the following confusion, started shooting wildly and one of them, corporal José Alonso, was shot in the head. As to the fugitives, *El Fraile* was caught on a street and he died there. *El Porcelano* managed to reach the Guadalquivir River, which he swam across but he was unable to move from the other bank as he was paralyzed with cold because the freezing water. Half of the soldiers found him there (the other half remained guarding the prisoners on the truck). The unfortunate *Porcelano* was beaten, kicked in the butt and punched in an authentic *via crucis,* then taken to a place called Santo Cristo, where they finished off in a true lynching, kicking and hitting him with machetes; a horrendous death.

The remaining four prisoners were executed by firing squad in the cemetery. Rafael Mejias Rivera, a 30-year-old bricklayer, was accused of nothing special other than that he had arrested right-wingers, which he denied, had belonged to the UGT, had attended leftist meetings and had belonged to a Self-Defence Group; José Gallego Olanda, a communist had belonged to a Self-Defence Group. It had been discovered that he had killed his cousin Bartlomé Olanda and that he had gone to the cemetery to bury him. This discovery sent off a furious persecution by his relatives on his mother's side, who did not rest until they had killed him; as to Francisco Arenas, it is only known that his brother Rodrigo had also been executed the previous November.

The Civil Registry for 22 May 1940 records a death due to 'collapse' in prison of Pedro Alcaraz, difficult to clear up. The Adán Gaitán authors mention someone nicknamed *Pardito* who died of a heart attack when he heard his name called for execution.

24 May was the execution of another past Republican Mayor, Francisco Nieto Romero, a socialist and a very moderate person. A member of the War Committee, he was savagely tortured – they pulled his teeth out with pliers, tore off his moustache and beat him so much that he couldn't take off his shirt because it was stuck to his bloody body. This was Franco's justice. His companion in this saca, Antonio Castilla Canalejo, had belonged to the UGT and was an active recruiter for the guerrillas in neighbouring villages.

4 June they only shot Francisco Luque Arenas, of the CNT, accused of belonging to a Self-Defence Group and of signing sentences as a member of the War Committee, which was false, because he belonged to the Committee in November 1926 when there was no longer any violence against right-wingers. There were so many accusations, it was impossible to determine which were true and which were false. Besides, as the Francoist plan was total cleansing, it did not matter as all means were sacrificed to this end.

The last execution of men in Pedro Abad was 13 June, with three victims: Diego Arenas Garcia, 50 years old and father of seven children, was accused of seizures and guarding. He had belonged to the War Committee and to make matters worse, was a communist, everything necessary to ensure that he would be exterminated; Miguel Cerdá Moreno was another longstanding communist, member of the *Nueva Aurora* Society. During the war he served as provincial delegate for Agricultural Reform in Ciudad Real. There was little foundation to his accusations. It was his longstanding militancy that led him to the cemetery wall, just like two of his brothers – Juan and Melchor, as I already mentioned. Francoism exterminated entire families without second thoughts; Pedro Gomáriz Castilla, also a communist, was accused of the usual: belonging to the War Committee and a Self-Defence Group. Although it is believed that the War Committees everywhere usually were comprised only of five or six people, the Francoists used this as an accusation right left and centre. It was the most fruitful accusation for doing away with somebody.

Lastly, the local Pedro Abad Francoists had prepared a last major coup before all the prisoners were transferred to Cordoba capital. This was the execution of a woman, Josefa Ortega Egea, aged 37 years, a widow with five children. When at the end of 1936 Pedro Abad was evacuated, she got separated from her husband Manuel Abajo, whom she never saw again because he was killed in a bombing. When she returned to the village, she had to face the accusations of her neighbour across the street, a fanatic right-winger, who never stopped until she got Josefa killed, which she did 3 October 1940, after waiting for her to give birth to a child. Josefa Ortega was the typical woman who does not shut up before anything or anybody. One could say that her crime was a crime of the tongue and nothing else. Already under arrest, her accuser, no doubt a 'person of good standing' in Francoist eyes, arranged for her to get one beating after another, even though she was pregnant, whilst they called out: "Hurry up and give birth because we have to kill you." One of the accusations against her was as stupid as the following: "She was noted for her communist ideas and she took part in public acts and in spreading revolutionary propaganda. During the Rojo regime, she headed groups of women who persecuted people belong to the Right." These and other absurd accusations were supported by the Pedro Abad Military Judge, Francisco Iglesias Sánchez, and she ended up facing the firing squad.

This last judicial aberration did not mark the end of the repression in Pedro Abad; just the end of executions by firing squad in the town, as the second half of the repression was still to come in the Cordoba cemeteries. Fortunately, I have been able to consult the microhistory of this village written by the Adán Gaítán brothers, which helped me Fcountryside. Everywhere it was the same thing: an inhuman and unbearable punishment, but there are very few detailed studies of these. Thus, when the investigations are generalized, the profiles of the repression thin out and get lost, giving food for present-day negationists who, in generalizing everything, have found their perfect habitat.

Endnotes for Chapter I

1.   Lawsuit filed 14 April 2010 before the National Criminal and Administrative Court, Federal Criminal Correctional Court 1, Case 4591/19, under the generic title of 'Genocide'.

2.   Ana Messuti. *La querella argentina: La aplicación del principio de justicia universal al caso de las desapariciones forzadas*. (The Agentinian lawsuit: The application of the principle of universal justice to the case of the forced disappearances.). In Rafael Escudero Alday and Carmen Pérez González *Desapariciones forzadas, represión política y crímenes del franquiso* (Forced disappearances, political repression and crimes of Francoism.) Madrid, Trotta, 2013, p. 129.

3.   Carlos Jiménez Villarejo and Antonio Doñate Martín. *Jueces, pero parciales. La pervivencia del franquismo en el poder judicial.* (Judges, but partly so. The survival of Francoism in the Fala

4.   Summary Emergency Procedure nº 12.720/1939 against Rafael Matencio Muñoz, Territorial Military Archives II, Seville. Courtesy of Joaquín Casado.

5.   Ángel Viñas. *En el combate por la historia*. Idem, pp. 20, citing Richard J. Evans and Bosworth.

6.   Paul Preston. *El gran manipulador. La mentira otidiana de Franco*. (The great manipulator. Franco's daily lies.), Barcelona, Ediciones B., 2008.

7.   Arthur Koestler. *Diálogo con la muerte. (Un testamento español)* (Dialogue with death. A Spanish testimony.) Madrid, Amarante, 2004.

8.   José Manuel Sabín Rodrigues. *La dictatura franquista (1936-1975). Textos y documentos*. (The Francoist dictatorship (1936-1975). Texts and documents.) Madrid, Akal 1997.

9.   Francisco Moreno Gomes: 'La represión en la posguerra' (The postwar repression), in *Víctimas de la guerra civil* (Victims of the civil war). Idem, p. 330.

10.   Matilde Eiroa. Recent article in the online newspaper *Hispania Nova*, number 10, 2012, available at: http://hispanianova.rediris.es/

11.   Antonio Baena. Pozoblanco. Unpublished personal Diary.

12.   Arthur Koestler. Idem, p. 183.

13.   Pablo Uriel. *Mi guerra civil*. (My civil war.) Self-Published. Valencia, 1988, pp. 83 et al.

14.   Ibid, p. 94.

15.   Sebastián Blanco Copado. Letter to his wife, excerpt published by García de Consuegra in an article entitled "The Nationalist repression in Pozoblanco", *Revista de Feria,* Pozoblanco, September 1985.

16.   Pablo Uriel. Idem. p. 97.

17.   Ibid., p. 30.

18.   Arthur Koestler. Ibid., p. 261.

19.   Juan Gutierrez Romer- Bruno. Interviewed several times by Moreno Gómez in Villanueva de Cordoba.

20.   Pedro Garfias. *Heroes del Sur*. (Heroes of the South). Mexico, 1941.

21.   Joe Monks. *Con los rojos en Andalucía* (With the Reds in Andalucia). Seville, Renacimiento, 2012. pp. 110 et al.

22 Letter kindly given to Moreno Gómez by Floriano Sánchez Bermuda, from Pozoblanco.
23 Galo Vierge. *Los culpables Pamplona, 1936* (The guilty. Pamplona 1936). Pamiela, Pampna, 2006, p. 101.
24 Gumersindo de Estella. *Fusilados en Zaragoza, 1938-1939* (Executed in Zaragoza 1938-1939). Mira Editores, Zaragoza, 2003.
25 Francisco Moreno Gomes. *El genocidio franquista en Cordoba* (The Francoist Genocide in Cordoba). Crítica, Barcelona, 2008.

II

CRUSHING THE VANQUISHED (E). WIDESPREAD EXECUTIONS AND OTHER KINDS OF TERROR. THE *CAUSA GENERAL*. TAKING STOCK OF THE RESULTS

POST-WAR EXECUTIONS IN CORDOBA TOWNS
AND VILLAGES (PART II). THE TERROR OF THE
SPANISH LEGION. UPSURGE OF LAW OF FUGITIVES.
CAUSA GENERAL RAIDS. THE 21 ROSES OF CORDOBA.
EXECUTIONS IN CORDOBA CAPITAL.
SOME CLANDESTINE REORGANIZATION.

> *"Do not let my name be erased from the History books"*
> Julia Conesa, one of the *13 Roses*, Madrid

> *"Do not cry; what you must do is never forget us."*
> The Orozco sisters in Ventas prison, Madrid,
> as they were about to face the firing squad.

Post-war executions in Cordoba towns and villages (Part II)

Having concluded our recovery of the facts in the previous chapter with a detailed description of that which occurred in Pedro Abad, a small village where 150 individuals were indicted, of which 50 were executed, the time has now come to focus on the three major targets of the repression in the Cordoba mountains: Peñarroya, Pozoblanco and Villanueva de Cordoba.

1. Peñarroya-Pueblonuevo, the virtual capital of a large mining basin in the northern part of Cordoba province, served as a Nationalist Headquarters during the war. In the early days of the Republic, Peñarroya stood out as an important Socialist stronghold although with time, its members gradually became more subdued, as opposed to Puente Genil and Palma del Río where the JSU was increasingly more forceful and active.

With the outbreak of war, the Peñarroya Socialists, led by the moderate Eduardo Blanco Fernández, Member of Parliament for the Frente Popular, formed a Militia Battalion known as the *Batallón del Terrible*, but they were unable to launch a defence of **Cordoba, down the Pedroches road.** The miners from Peñarroya were not sufficiently powerful to defend their district, which was captured by the Nationalists October 13 1936. All future attempts to recover their homeland were unfruitful and cost them rivers of blood throughout the war. Apparently, the Peñarroya miners may have been less combative than others from Linares, La Carolina or Puertollano who were also more active from a syndicalist viewpoint. The Terrible Battalion ended up merging with the Garcés Battalion.

When the time came for the Nationalists to celebrate the «**Victory of Revenge», the** Francoists filled Peñarroya with prisoners from all over the North of Cordoba and many other places in Spain. If you look at the list of victims, you see that few were natives of Peñarroya-Pueblonuevo. Most those murdered by Francoist 'justice' beginning in 1939 were prisoners of war - soldiers and militia - who had been imprisoned in Peñarroya or had been sent there from the neighbouring concentration camps of Valsequillo, La Granjuela and Los Blázquez, with the declaration of victory or just before, following the Republic's last battle January 1939.

The first sentenced to death by Courts Martial 1, 2 and 3 in Peñarroya, were shot by firing squads June 20, at the unusual hour of 9 p.m. Hermenegildo Estévez Ferrer, a soldier from Valencia, was shot August 2. Emilio Soligo Molino, a sergeant from Lerida, was shot September 5. Little or nothing is known of all those who fell, soldiers in the service of the Army of the Republic, the «Dignified Army».

These executions were soon followed by those of prisoners from villages in the Los Pedroches district (Villaralto, Pedroche, La Granjuela, Los Blázquez) who had been imprisoned in Peñarroya. Florentino Cubero Aranda from La Granjuela, whose brother Rafael *El Manco de La Granjuela* became a famous guerrilla fighter in the region, was executed November 8; and December 11, and two men and one woman, Martina Alcántara, aged 53. A few days later, according to the Judge Advocate, another woman, Dionisia Alcántara Calvo, was said to have 'collapsed and died', presumably under suspicious circumstances.

During this first stage of the post-war repression in the provincial towns and villages – the 1939 and 1940 biennial – 88 residents of Peñarroya were executed in a first bloody tribute to the victorious Nationalists.

Julio Perea Peña, whose brother Felipe had been a leading Socialist in the mining region before the Republic and an alderman in 1931, was executed January 11 1940. Another active Republican, Fermín Pradera Nieto, was shot February 27 at the same time as the Mayor of Los Blázquez, Honorio Esquinas Benavente, a peaceful man who had sought to prevent any kind of violence in his town. They were followed by another active Republican, Alfonso Rodíguez Imbernón, from Alcoy, April 8. There was a large saca of 12 victims March 16, most of them from Alcaracejos, such as brothers Nereo and José Mansilla Moreno. A third brother, Juan de Dios, was executed elsewhere. All the prisoners from Alcaracejos were accused, en bloc, by the Causa General, in a totally bigoted indictment of minimal historiographic value.

October 30 1939 marked a saca of six prisoners in Peñarroya-Pueblonuevo, one of whom was Gabriel González Godoy, famous Commander of the Stalin Battalion and of the 25th Mixed Brigade (MB). A miner from Linares, he was the local secretary of the UGT. When war broke out, he was charged with organizing the Militia from Linares, with the rank of sergeant. Later, in Baeza, he created the famous Stalin Battalion that became part of the 25th MB as the 99th Battalion. He held the rank of Captain on the Pozoblanco front March 1937, with the 25th MB and his invaluable Battalion, as he led the Republican attack against the Nationalist troops in Villanueva del Duque. He was promoted to Commander[i] in May and spent the rest of the war on the North Cordoba frontlines.

Like many other Republican officers, Gabriel González was taken prisoner in Peñarroya-Pueblonuevo. His trial was based on a mountain of accusations sent to the Court by telegram from the Linares Guardia Civil, describing him as of 'bad past behaviour and having participated in numerous outrages'. He submitted appeal after appeal disputing these accusations, to no avail as a militia Commander could not expect clemency from a Francoist court. His death sentence, dated July 6 1939, was approved by the Judge Advocate for the Army of the South in Seville on August 8 and his dossier with Franco's *enterado* arrived in Peñarroya on the very day of the saca. The Court met at 5 p.m. to read out the death sentences to the sentenced men, after which they were taken to the chapel where they remained for a very short time as the execution was set for 8 p.m. According to the little his family knows, Gabriel's body ended up in the mass grave in Pueblonuevo cemetery. He wrote no letter of farewell, or if he did, his family never received it.[ii]

---

[i]   The rank of Commander in the Spanish Army is equivalent to the rank of Major in the British or American army.

[ii]   Moreno Gómez owes much of this information to the kindness of Juan Peralta, the victim's grandson, who sent him Gabriel González' dossier 24-2-2014.

Some political leaders and ex-Mayors managed to evade the death penalty as they fought for survival through the great labyrinth of death. The ex-Mayor of Peñarroya, Fernando Carrión, also Republican Governor for a short time in August 1936, was sentenced to death but some benevolent hand saved him. The same occurred with the Socialist Ex-Member of Parliament, Eduardo Blanco Fernández, who had also served in the past as Civil Governor during the Republic. He was arrested in Ciudad Real and in April 1940 was brought to the improvised Peñarroya prison that had been created in the old UGT Trade Union Building built by the miners. He appeared before a court martial in Cordoba June 11 1943 and was sentenced to *only* thirty years in jail, because "despite his extremely leftist ideas, he always appeared to have protected persons belonging to the right". His salvation, like that of others, was that he was tried four years after the end of the war. Had he been tried in 1939, at the height of the Francoist thirst for vengeance, he would never have escaped the firing squad. Others like him, who had protected right-wing individuals, were less fortunate. Antonio Baena from Pozoblanco was sentenced to death by garrotte, Joaquim Pérez Salas, a well-known community benefactor, was executed in Murcia, as were the aforementioned ex-Mayor of Los Blázquez and so many others.

April 1940, both Peñarroya prisons (Municipal and Trade Union Building) received inmates from the entire Fuenteobejuna region. From there, they executed Manuel Caballero, accused of belonging to the War Committee. As mentioned earlier, the Causa General regularly accused 15 to 20 persons of belonging to this Committee, to ensure that nobody escaped its grasp, when these local Committees never consisted of more than four, five or at the most, six individuals.

The post-war slaughter was just beginning. When Constanza de la Mora (wife of Hidalgo de Cisneros) wrote the finale to her book of memoires, in New York, July 1939, she concluded with these words:

> "Franco has murdered thousands of Spaniards. As I write these words, the firing squads continue to kill men and women... Hundreds of thousands more are living lives of continuous torture and humiliation in Franco's prisons and concentration camps."[1]

2. Pozoblanco was another Cordoba district martyred by Francoism. The thirst for blood here was one of the worst in the entire province, as we shall see in Villanueva de Cordoba, which had been the regional Republican capital during the war. Both townships were symbols of resistance to the coup on the frontlines in the North of the province. Pozoblanco was particularly vulnerable to Nationalist violence because in the early summer of 1936 the local right-wing and all the Guardias Civiles from a dozen towns in the Los Pedroches district gathered in the town to stage an armed uprising against the Republic. The Republican Government had to send part of the Miaja Column to take control of the town. The rebels surrendered August 15 with the understanding that no Militia would enter the town, just regular army, and that the Guardias Civiles and right-wingers would be evacuated to Valencia. That same day, two trains filled with the Pozoblanco rebels left for Valencia. They were interned in the harbour, on the steamship *Legazpi*. The People's Court began working in September. Largo Caballero's government refused to accept any commutation of the sentences. Consequently, more than 300 Pozoblanco rebels, civilians and Guardias Civiles, were executed in Paterna cemetery. To make matters worse, when the Militia later entered the town August 15-16, they took another 50 right-wingers. It was to be expected that the Pozoblanco right wing would wait until the time was right for them to take their revenge.

That opportunity came with Franco's victory. Even though the residents of Pozoblanco had little or nothing to do with the People's Court in Valencia nor with the activities of local militia groups. Be it as it may, there was no excuse for the imminent bloodbath that could be expected with the victory celebrations. In the previous chapter, Moreno Gómez described the explosion of burning terror that fell upon the town during April and May 1939, in the form of summary executions and the Law of Fugitives in Pozoblanco and neighbouring towns and villages where at least 101 victims were «taken for walks», the infamous paseos. This phenomenon of immediate terror, devoid of all legality, was applied to the entire recently-conquered Centre-South of the country. A terrible reality that has barely been addressed in all the studies of the war.

Now follows Moreno Gómez' study of the application, in Pozoblanco, of Francoist 'military justice' properly speaking, at the hands of Courts Martial 9 and 13, whose sentences began to be executed June 22. That day, they only shot Alfonso de la Cruz (María *La Posadera's* son).

This marked the first frequent use, so typical of totalitarian regimes, of the euphemisms entered as the cause of death in the official death certificates to cover up the real reason for so many 'disappearances': traumatic shock, internal haemorrhage, etc. The Judge Advocate sent the death certificates to the Municipal judge who then sent them to the Civil Registry office where they were recorded.

When examining the death certificates, researchers have to be especially astute in determining which expressed causes of death are actually factual or simply euphemisms, especially when it is known that the prisoners were tortured, considering the widespread use of torture and its frequently fatal outcome. The following certificate from the Pozoblanco Civil Registry, for example, leads one to suspect death under torture:

"War Judge Advocate – Military Court No. 13 – Pozoblanco. Please register the death of JUAN ÁLVAREZ POZO, resident of Villanueva del Duque, born in Honojosa… age 37 years, married to Valeriana Rubio, with two children, who died yesterday from cardiac asystole, as certified by the Coroner. Pozoblanco, 15 October 1939."

In this case, that the prisoner, a healthy young man, died from torture is very plausible. However, unless the historian speaks to relatives of the deceased or to witnesses, he cannot confirm his suspicions.[iii]

The courts martial in Pozoblanco began May 26 1939, according to Bartolomé *Pérez Salas* Cabrera Peralbo, who was one of the accused.[2] This first trial against eight accused resulted in twenty death sentences. The second trial was held May 27, with another eight accused sentenced to 18 death sentences. Of the first trial, only Miguel Arroyo García, secretary of the Socialist Party and secretary of the Workers Agricultural Cooperative, escaped execution. The remainder were shot.

Of the second trial, only Francisco Rodríguez Arroyo and Bartolomé Pérez Salas were saved. As he left the council, Mario Cabrera Amor, who was present, looked straight at him as he told the Public Defender of the terrible situations of some of the men who were being tried. The Defender replied: 'Of this lot, the only one who will be saved is the one they call *Pérez Salas*." And so it was. All the others were shot. In those days, executions were in the afternoon and some Señoritos went to the cemetery to watch.

During the first two years of the repression (1939 and 1940), there were 209 victims in Pozoblanco (not including guerrillas and *paseados*), the highest number in the province during the post-war, not including Cordoba capital, followed by Castro del Rio (167) and Villanueva de Cordoba (102). None of these and other data include the number of residents of the provincial towns and villages who later died in Cordoba capital.

Executions in Pozoblanco continued to be held in full daylight at the end of the day, around tea time. Almost nobody escaped the death sentence in the 1939 trials. Franco's approval, the enterado, arrived within a few days of the trial, by teletype, almost by return mail.

[iii] In Tables 1,2 and 3, when Moreno Gómez was able to confirm that the euphimistic official cause of death was actually torture, this is indicated in brackets (tortured).

Six prisoners were executed August 5, among whom Luís Romero Cortés, from Torrecampo, whose dossier Moreno Gómez was able to obtain. He was accused of the usual crimes: he was a communist, had participated in the attack on the town, belonged to the War Committee, he was a political leader in the Republican zone, and had arrested members of the right wing. Despite the lack of an accusation of a blood crime, he was sentenced to death June 15.

One of the executions that had a major impact on the residents of Pozoblanco occurred October 28 when at 7 p.m., Tomasa Diaz Moreno was taken out to be shot. Aged only 21 years and in the flower of youth, she was a Los Pedroches 'Rose' and a leader in the local JSU, just like the Thirteen Roses of Madrid[iv]. Poor Tomasa was taken to her death both physically and morally crushed by the National Catholic victors. She was tortured, they shaved her head, she was forced to drink castor oil and to walk up and down the town streets with a sign hanging from her neck.

When the Catholics decided to kill, they did so in a refined manner, with the torture and fires they learned to perfection during the Inquisition and many other momentous occasions throughout History. Tomasa died in full of emotional pain as her father, Antonio Diaz Jurado, had been executed the day before. Her fiancé, Gaspar Jiménez Cebrián was executed earlier, April 11. In Tomasa's case, the victorious tripartite (barracks, casino and church vestry) treated her family with special cruelty. Why? For the sole reason that they owned a newspaper kiosque on the main street where her family sold copies of the workers' trade union newspaper. This was a case of killing the messengers.

Cesáreo Romero, a local Socialist leader and Mayor of Torrecampo for the Frente Popular, was executed November 3 in Pozoblanco. It so happened that he was out of town July 25 when the militia entered Torrecampo and he was only able to return many weeks later. Nevertheless, the records of his trial that Moreno Gómez consulted show that he was sentenced to death on clearly futile charges. His wife went to Pozoblanco to visit him on the day he was shot, without knowing that this was about to happen. Because there had been a saca, she was not allowed to enter the prison. As the truck with the sentenced drove away, she recognized her husband among them. She ran to the cemetery. When she got there, the firing squad had done its job; still, she was allowed to go to his body and wipe the blood from his face. She was refused his body and they threw him into the mass grave with the others.

[iv] *Treze Rosas* was the name given to thirteen very young women, seven who were still teenagers, members of the left-wine JSU, who were arrested in Madrid at the end of the civil war, imprisoned, tortured and shot. One of the most tragic early examples of Francoist repression against the defeated.

Socialist Cesáreo's death is important in that it shows how Franco did not shoot his victims as punishment for their crimes, but because of their ideas. The beliefs that were at the base of proletarian *IDEA* philosophy that representatives of the working classes preached the length and breadth of the Andalusia countryside during the 19th and 20th centuries. The IDEA that Franco's rural and Catholic Fascists put before the firing squads.

As he wrote this, Moreno Gómez was reminded of an occasion from his childhood. One day, he asked my mother why someone in the town had been killed. "Because he had ideas", she replied. In retrospect, this was an unforgettable answer from an apolitical, country woman, who was able to summarize, without knowing it, the essence of Fascism: *to eliminate all proletarian and syndicalist IDEAS*, by means of a campaign of enraged destruction that was nothing more than preventive violence against the ghost of a 'revolution', a theoretical nightmare that in the 1930s haunted the Right more than it did the Left.

More words of wisdom from his mother: "Never sign up for anything." Another magnificent motto: never sign up, never get involved, in other words, do not become an activist. She knew that those who were executed since 1936 were those whose names were on Lists. That was Francoism: elimination of all those who were committed to an ideal, those who stood out, who formed the social and political base of the Republic. His mother never told him that people were being killed because of their crimes; only because *they had ideas*. As child, he never paid much attention to her sayings, but today, he finds that they were brilliant words from a simple woman who never belonged to a trade union, never held a job, never worked for any public department. The fact is that ordinary people are prone to giving magnificent lessons that put fancy-pants scholars who promote violence to shame.

The elimination of all Republicans with positions of authority of any kind at every level of society, was the Eleventh Francoist Commandment. Acisclo *El Fraile* Garcia Dueñas, an ex-seminarian Secondary School Latin teacher, was executed November 21 1939. Nothing more political is known of him other than that he served as the Health Officer for the 7th Mixed Brigade. Francisco Diaz Pastor, ex-alderman for the Frente Popular and Manuel Fernández Contreras, member of the Izquierda Republicana, were also taken in that saca. The last one of these was involved in a most unfortunate incident as it was he who helped the notorious Juan Calero Rubio, one of the most bloodthirsty Francoist judges in post-war Los Pedroches, to escape imprisonment by the Republicans before the war. Judge Calero acknowledged Manuel's help but he "could not forgive him for not having also helped his son-in-law to escape". At the end of the war, Manuel

Fernández, who had refused to go into exile because he considered that he was innocent of any blood crime, was interned in the Valsequillo concentration camp, followed by an additional seven months in Pozoblanco prison. At his trial, several individuals falsely alleged that he organized crimes and looting, and he was sentenced to death. His wife begged Judge Calero to be merciful, in recognition for past favours, to no avail. Manuel was executed the next day.

We must not forget the thousands who died from torture, 'those who were left in our hands' (Francoist slang for prisoners), a terrible iceberg of which only the tip is known. These were such as Juan Álvarez Pozo, from Hinojosa but resident near Villanueva del Duque, who was mentioned earlier, a healthy 37-year-old who died October 14 1939 from 'cardiac asystole', according to the Coroner. Another one whose heart failed him, David Cuello Amadeo, from Alcaracejos, died from 'acute endocarditis' December 17 1939, according to the Judge Advocate. Others who 'were left in their hands' include Gervasio Martínez Hidalgo, who died from 'epileptic seizures' September 3 1939, according to the note from the Military Police. November 13 1939, Rafael Bueno Roldán, a 53-year-old physician, was allowed to die in prison from 'septicaemia', considered a suicide apparently because he refused medication for a wound on his knee. One of those executed November 29, Severo García Gonzalbo, arrived before the firing squad on his knees, unable to stand because of the beatings and torture he had been subjected to. How many more cases like these were there?

Antonio Márquez Jurado, ex-Socialist Mayor of Pozoblanco during the last part of the war and who had absolutely nothing at all to do with the fighting, was executed November 29. His political sympathies, as was the case with so many others, led to his death.

The great sacas in Pozoblanco took place during 1940, especially in May. The executed came from this and neighbouring towns: Añora, Dos Torres, Alcaracejos and El Viso. April 11 there was a particularly tragic execution, that of the Head Postmaster, Enrique Ramirez Dópido. It appears that his great misfortune was that the Pozoblanco Falangists hated his father-in-law, Antonio Varo Granados, with a passion. Varo, a Public Prosecutor from Aguilar de la Frontera, was in Madrid when war broke out. Even so, he was accused by omission, because 'instead of coming back to the town to prevent excesses, he remained in Madrid'. This, of course, was a farce, but Francoist 'justice' was like that. Varo was also accused of being 'a prominent member of the Left and effective propagandist of its ideas', also absurd, but because of all of this, he was considered: 'the supreme responsible for all the crimes committed in Pozoblanco'. The rage directed against this man was uncontrollable. He was sentenced to death by garrotte but, fortunately for Varo, a Nationalist

Captain that Varo had hidden in his house in Madrid, spoke in his defence (which was most unusual) and his sentence was commuted.

Not so his unfortunate son-in-law, Enrique Ramírez Dópido, who was executed April 11 1940, on the false grounds 'that he was the link between those who besieged the town', when during the whole time that Pozoblanco was under siege, Enrique was imprisoned in the barracks and was only released after the town had surrendered. To add to both these families' miseries, there were ulterior motives to their arrests, namely that father and son-in-law both owned a Flour Factory in Fuentes de Andalucía that was seized by Falangists. Also, Enrique Dópido owned a valuable market garden at the outskirts of the town that was expropriated by the local leader of the Falange.

There is another interesting case where a prisoner was sentenced to death although his sentence was later commuted, José Madueño, a veteran socialist, who, when war began, travelled to Elche, to Santa Pola and then to Madrid. Nevertheless, when Moreno Gómez was able to consult his dossier he noticed that José was charged with 'by leaving town he did not avoid excesses and crimes' and also was 'considered to be conceited'. Such a list of absurdities were used to send Republicans to their deaths. Madueño escaped on this occasion, but very few others did.

As mentioned earlier, almost nobody accused of belonging to the local War Committee escaped. For this reason, May 11 they executed one of the few leading communists in Pozoblanco, Bautista Herruzo de la Cruz, ex-Captain of the Pedroches Battalion, ex-alderman for the Frente Popular. The Calvary suffered by this man is still spoken of in Pozoblanco because he was savagely tortured and almost beaten to death. He was accused of having sent information to the People's Court in Valencia.

Another member of the Pozoblanco War Committee, Samuel Romero Estrella, was executed May 28 1940 and another, Miguel Justo *el Policial* Sánchez Garrido, June 12. It is said that he was dispatched with three coups de grâce. Miguel was captured in the mountains where he had fled at the end of the war with his father, Justo Sánchez, who was also executed. His brother-in-law Juan Guijo died in Mauthausen Nazi concentration camp, his sister Josefa and her husband Juan Serrano suffered many years imprisonment and all their property was seized. Another family destroyed by Francoism.

On previous pages, Moreno Gómez spoke of the expansive wave of terror, that is, the impact that the executions of inmates had, first on their fellow prisoners in their cells, then on their families, then on left-wing supporters and finally, on the townspeople as a whole, and I quoted some extracts from the diary of one of the prisoners from Pozoblanco, Antonio Baena (later executed in Cordoba capital). (APPENDIX I. Farewell letters from Prisoners.) This was the last execution in Pozoblanco, September 12, before all the prisoners were transferred to Cordoba capital, and to read of the panic felt by all the imprisoned chills one's blood.[3]

Repression by summary execution ceased in Pozoblanco after September 20 1940 when all the prisoners in the province were transferred from the local jails to the Cordoba Provincial Prison in the capital, where 'military justice' continued to implement Franco's program of extermination. (Table 2. Individuals executed post-war by firing squad in Cordoba capital 1939-1945).

There was a curious incident in Pozoblanco in 1986, regarding recognition of the historic memory of the victims of the Francoist repression. Today, the Historic Memory Movement is directed at putting an end to the victors' uncompromising refusal to pay the minimum attention to the memory of the defeated Republicans. Known as the 'pact of silence', this is nothing else than the stubborn official denial of the existence of Republican victims, a *conditio sine qua non* for the restoration of Democracy in 1977.

Gabriel Garcia de Consuegra, the local historian, ignited the controversy around this subject when he published his extensive study of the Francoist repression in Pozoblanco in the September 1986 issue of *Revista de Feria*, the magazine published annually in celebration of the principle town fair. All of Pozoblanco rushed to read his article which included a list of 220 Republican victims (not including guerrillas). The ensuing scandal exploded and right-wing protests rained on City Hall, to be published in the Municipal Bulletin, demanding the seizure of the issue that dared to address the 'other memory', the one that was not about 'their caidos'.

Clearly, the Right felt that they were the only ones with the right to publish the names of their fallen and that those of the Left had no right to a memorial of any kind, an opinion that is still reflected today. The local assembly of the Alianza Popular political party and several private individuals wrote letters of protest.

One protestor wrote:

> "We totally condemn this, because it is neither the time nor the place to set the populace to fighting over four useless and mediocre individuals, who furthermore knew nothing about anything. Pozoblanco does not deserve what has been done to it, on such an important occasion, the celebration of our annual fair."

Another protestor stoked the scandal:

> "How is it possible that, in these times and days, so much is said about peace, which is what all of us want, that a nobody has thought to waste his time writing this article, unless he is an authentic fanatic, in which case he can be considered guilty of everything, except of being a democrat... ... with articles such as this one... the only thing that the author has achieved is an attempt to rekindle the fire and upset the peace."

The October 1986 issue of the Municipal Bulletin published a petition signed by 40 right-wing individuals, containing incredible statements as:

> "...the unfortunate article's lack of objectivity has caused great discomfort and indignation amongst most of the population of Pozoblanco. What will the people think of us? Is Pozoblanco reviving a subject that has already been forgotten? It is revitalizing an aftermath; whose fire began some fifty years ago and has been extinguished for most of the inhabitants."

The above group of 40 did not let matters rest. As Garcia de Consuegra had received the coveted municipal Ginés de Sepúlveda[v] prize for this article and since it was rumoured that what was published was just an extract of his work. The group of 40 vociferously demanded that he be stripped of the prize and that the rest of his work should not be published. Furthermore, they insinuated that as the author belonged to the monied class in Pozoblanco, he was betraying his class, pointing out that relatives of his had also been victims of the Rojos in 1936. All in all, a reactionary hecatomb in Pozoblanco, in September 1986, not long before the 50th anniversary of the beginning of the civil war. All because a list of left-wing victims had been made public.

The great scandal did not end there. The Socialist Municipality lost its nerve and rather than standing firm and remaining consistent with its party ideals, it made a public apology on the local Radio and ordered the seizure of the relevant issue of the *Revista da Feria,* even though it had already been distributed and sold out. Such anxiety on the part of the local socialists was neither more nor less than a reflection of the position of the Spanish Left during the period of transition.

After this skirmish with the Right in Pozoblanco in 1986, Garcia de Consuegra, a secondary school teacher with whom Moreno Gómez had exchanged data and information, asked to be transferred and he disappeared

---

[v] Juan *Ginés de Sepúlveda (1490 - 1573)* was born in Pozoblanco. A great humanist, philosopher and Greek scholar, he was the royal chronicler of Charles V and tutor to Philip II. He wrote numerous books on philosophy and ethics, theology, law, history, and political theory.

from Pozoblanco. The proposal to build a monument to the victims of Francoism in Pozoblanco, hopefully in the cemetery where so many were executed, disappeared.

A similar initiative in Villanueva de Cordoba, long before the one in Pozoblanco, had a totally different result. In April 1981, Moreno Gómez had already spoken in public and published the list of 'the other fallen' (provisional number, 134) in the town in the local press.[4] Nobody protested, although Moreno Gómez knew that the opposition could not get over their amazement at his temerity. However, this was when the UCD was in power and the right-wing was still marching to a different tune. Not content with the List, he and the other members of the Historic Memory group were encouraged to push for a monument to the defeated in the cemetery. UCD City Hall, much more open-minded than others that followed it, did not deny their request. There was, however, a caveat. The inscription on the monument must read: 'To those who died for their ideals.' They, the organizing committee, refused. It had to read: 'To those who died for freedom.'

This was followed by several months of wrangling, during which the Historic Memory Group published a manifesto and collected the signatures of notable and distinguished individuals from Madrid. Today, when he re-read their manifesto, Moreno Gómez is amazed at the list of signatories: José Luis Aranguren, Buero Vallejo, Castilla del Pino, Carmen Conde, Antonio Gala, Gibson, Bishop Iniesta, Rev. Gómez Cafarena and Rev. Llanos, Lain Entralgo, Daniel Sueiro, Antonio Tovar, Tuñón de Lara, Francisco Umbral and a few more.[5] The effect of the manifesto was to demolish the ancestral administrative immobility. The monument 'To those who died for Freedom' was duly inaugurated in Villanueva cemetery on All Saint's Day, November 1 1982. It may even be the first such monument in the province. The local Marching Band entertained the townspeople by playing *The International*, which they rehearsed from the score Moreno Gómez previously obtained from the Madrid Marching Band. Small successes in the fight for the Democratic Memory, before this concept had become a national by-word.

3. Puente Genil follows next in our retrieval of tragic events. After Cordoba capital, it was here that the province was subjected to the most extensive genocide, almost a thousand civilian victims following General Castejón's troops entrance in the town August 1 1936. The slaughter in Puente Genil reached historic levels throughout the remainder of that year and in 1937. This town was one of the birthplaces of several Cordovan trade union movements, boasting a youthful socialism that began in 1936 with very dynamic JSU groups. In 1921, Puente Genil also was one of the places at the heart of the birth of the PCE in the province, at the same time as Villanueva de Cordoba, which explains why the rebel military had decided to crush this stronghold of the workers' movements.

The post-war eradication was led by Jaime García del Val, who arrived in Montilla as Judge Advocate. He was notorious for his cruelty, which was written in blood, and for his licentious behaviour with a courtesan whom the people nicknamed *the Judge's Anita*. Many of the courts martial in Puente Genil and in many other towns in the province, were presided by Guardia Civil Lt. Evaristo Peñalvar, with the infamous Ramón de La Lastra y Hoces, Marquis of Ugena and grandson of the Duke of Hornachuelos, as Prosecutor. Both were examples of the rancid aristocracy that Francoism brought out from behind their glass cabinets to serve as its executioners. On one of the court's visits to Puente Genil, Peñalvar's court tried the eminent elderly Republican Antonio Romero Jiménez, a highly-respected individual, past Republican Mayor, Freemason. Despite the fact that he held the title of Honorary Captain of the Army of Africa from when he served with Franco in Morocco in the past, this did not work in his favour as an Order came from the highest to ensure that the strictest sanctions were applied to him, the only person to Moreno Gomés' knowledge who was executed by garrotte, October 24 1939. One of his sons was taken on a paseo in 1936.

A similar case of Francoist cruelty affected two sets of father and son, November 2 1939. The reason for their execution is unknown but on that day, they executed Francisco Villar and his son José, and Francisco Reyes and his son, also named José. Meanwhile, torture was being liberally applied in the several Puente Genil jails, as described earlier. Francisco *Jesús* Preso Delgado was executed November 6. Broken by torture, he attempted to take his life in prison by slashing his wrists, but he was treated then shot.

The terror reached such heights in Puente Genil that November 16 there occurred an incident that could have been taken from a movie. When two municipal policemen (José Palos Ramírez and Juan Mendoza), accompanied by Jesús Aguilar, the Falangist Mayor, went to Francisco Palos Gálvez's house to arrest him, he was waiting for them in his living room. He lashed out against the policemen with a steel bar, killing them both, and only stopped when the Mayor shot him.

At this time, many notable individuals fled forever from this village of berserk genocides, such as the poet Juan Rejano (a celebrated intellectual who died in Mexico) and the great Socialist leader and Freemason Gabriel Morón Díaz (who joined the PCE at the end of his life and who also died in Mexico).

The April 24 1940 saca of six prisoners included the socialist railway worker José Mora Valencia who appeared to have been President of the War Committee, had been so cruelly tortured that he almost did not survive for his execution. Also, Rafael Reina Hidalgo whose brother Juan was executed a few months earlier.

The last execution in Puente Genil was held June 11 1940 (October 20, the remaining prisoners were transferred to Cordoba where many were executed). Of the three victims of this saca, Emilio *Palomo* López Arisbal was executed despite having been promised his safety in exchange for rendering some confidential services. It is said that when he was taken from prison, a lieutenant called him 'criminal' and Emílio shouted back: "You are the criminals... Murdering wolves! Who in reprisal for a hundred of yours killed by the Left, you have already slaughtered several thousand patriots".[6] In all, twenty-nine were executed in Puente Genil during the immediate post-war period. If to this number, we add those who later died in Cordoba capital and those who were executed in 1936, we note that this town sacrificed 900 victims in homage to Franco.

4. Santa Eufemia is a town in the extreme north of Cordoba province, on the road to Almadén, in the Los Pedroches District. The town's resistance to the military coup was organized by the famous Dr. Pedro Vallina, whose anarchist beliefs were shared by most of the townspeople. Santa Eufemia suffered its own dose of terror during the post-war, with 21 executed in the town, other natives of the town shot in Hinojosa del Duque and in a neighbouring village, and still more later, in Cordoba capital. In 1940, the Spanish Legion, under the command of General Salvador Bañuls, arrived in Los Pedroches to begin its reign of terror in the region, centring its operations in Pozoblanco as well as Belalcázer, Villanueva de Cordoba, Cardeña and Santa Eufemia.

With the onset of this terror, large numbers of men (guerrillas) from the North of Cordoba began to flee towards Cáceres which was becoming a guerrilla centre. In Santa Eufemia, a dozen townspeople fled to the hills, such as Manuel *El Secretario* Fernández and Norberto *Veneno* Castillejo. The Legion was merciless in its pursuit of escapees in the Los Pedroches district, throughout the Summer and Fall of 1940. In Santa Eufemia, legionnaires poured boiling oil into the ears of Norberto Castillejo, the fugitive guerrilla's father, to force him to tell them where he son was hiding. In Villanueva, they beat four men to death with sticks, another one in Belalcázer and yet another in Cardeña.

The notorious Causa General accused all the left Santa Eufemia left-wing sympathizers, en bloc, of crimes and of belonging to the War Committee. Seven men were first executed July 4 1939 and eight more on the 24th of the same month. Later, they executed a few more. It is said that the Francoists also executed a group of townspeople in the La Parraga mine, Agudo, Ciudad Real, supposedly because it was there that a band of Republican militia had executed 35 right-wingers from Santa Eufemia earlier during the war. Moreno Gómez was unable to confirm this.

5. Villafranca. A few words regarding a small town that, contrary to what usually happened in villages, suffered eight post-war executions. Villafranca had been a strong supporter of workers' rights since the dawn of the Republic: it was one of the only four towns in the province (with Villa del Rio, Doña Mencia and Villanueva de Cordoba) that elected Communist aldermen in 1931. A typical town of farmers and laborers, it always was a source of trade union leaders. In 1936, it became the general headquarters of the Andalusian Militia, later the famous Villafranca Battalion, under the command of Francisco del Castillo and his assistant Pedro Garfias. One of the Militia Captains of the Battalion, Paco Dios, was executed in Cordoba.

Francisco Jurado Fernández, who had gained much fame for his bravery as a member of the Villafranca Battalion, was killed June 9 1939. After returning to his hometown at the end of the war, he was arrested and forced to present himself to the military headquarters every day, where he was sorely beaten. The day he died, he was again taken to the barracks and he flatly refused to go. He ran way to force them to apply the Law of Fugitives and end his torment, which they did at 11 a.m. November 25 they executed Antonio Serroche Ramos, whose brother Juan had been the first Communist alderman, in 1931. The last execution in the town that year was December 12 1939, when they shot four men – three from Adamuz and one from Villa del Rio.

This was not the end of the bloodshed in Villafranca. November 1948, the Guardia Civil applied the Law of Fugitives to two sexagenarian brothers, Andrés and Diego González Fernández, simply because they were the brothers of a guerrilla fighter, Juan *El Álvarez* González Fernández, who had been hiding in the mountains since 1941 when he escaped from the 'train of death' that was taking the condemned from Burgos to Cordoba to be shot. Ripping off some slats in the side of the cattle wagon in which the prisoners were travelling, Juan jumped off the moving train. He survived eight years in the mountains until he was again caught, and later executed in Montoro, November 1949.

6. Villanueva de Cordoba. We now enter another of the iconic towns of Cordovan workers' movements, Villanueva de Cordoba, to which Moreno Gómez dedicated an earlier book that is frequently quoted herein. In 1931, the Republican Ministry of Government declared that this town was one of the greatest centres of Communism in Andalusia. The townspeople fought heart and soul against the 1936 military coup, so it is no surprise that the post-war repression fell on the town with all the force of a hurricane, with 102 executions. To this number we must add 36 executed later in Cordoba capital, 20 guerrillas killed, 22 paseados in 1948, 23 townspeople who starved to death in Cordoba prison, and 4 who died in Mauthausen concentration camp to which they were sent.

To this is added the widespread application of torture, the 1940 wave of terror by the Legion, starvation, exclusion, repression of all kind, the Law of Fugitives in 1948, military justice under the most cruel of Franco's executioners such as Judge Juan Calero, Lieutenant *Pepinillo* (Juan Moreno Sevillano, from Osuna), Captain Fernández (from Bailén), Commander Felipe Martínez Machado and Captain Aznar, all who followed the Nero-like dictates of the Regime. Today, all the energetic and forceful syndicalism of the 1930s in this town, one of the main reasons for the military coup, has been erased from the map. The following is a brief step-by-step reconstruction of the post-war extermination, from different viewpoints.

The slaughter in Villanueva de Cordoba began in the early hours of April 19-20 1939, when the Law of Fugitives was applied to six prisoners near the municipal water tanks at the beginning of the road to Conquista. They were buried in the fields where they fell, and their bodies remain there to this day. During April, several temporary jails in the town were packed with prisoners (the Refugio, Romo's house on Calle Herradores, the Municipal Depot and Juan Herrero's house on Calle Conquista). Later, they were all taken to the larger improvised Fuente Vieja Schools jail. The centres of torture were the Military Headquarters in Los Laurianos house on the main square and the Guardia Civil temporary barracks and SIPM [Military Police] headquarters in Malagón house on La Preturilla square. Everyone who was arrested passed through both these centres; some left their skin, others, their lives.

The murderous master of ceremonies of the great local repression was Judge Juan Calero Rubio, from Pozoblanco, who presided over Military Court No. 11 and whose inflicted cruelty and moral torment could fill an entire encyclopaedia. Mentally imbalanced, he ended his homicidal career by committing suicide in his home in Pozoblanco at the end of August 1940. The court martials over which he presided were held in the Torres Hall, Calle Concejo, on the days that the military court arrived in town from Cordoba city.

The Francoists launched the bloodbath in Villanueva de Cordoba on All Soul's Day, November 2 1939. That day, at 5 p.m., a truck went to the door of the Fuente Vieja Schools jail to collect the first five victims, all from Pedroche. As the executions were to be carried out in daylight, many supporters of the regime or just curious public, crowded in front of the

Fuente Vieja. Others went to the cemetery: Falangists, some upper-class bourgeois ladies and several well-known accusers – where they vociferously insulted the condemned, calling them criminals and other names. As soon as the first round of shots was heard, the Francoist public, as usual in the rest of Spain, burst out with applause and sang the *Cara al Sol*, as the condemned men breathed their last amid so much hostility, hatred and humiliation. This was the so-called 'Christian' behaviour of the victors whose idea of 'giving psychological support' to the relatives of the fallen consisted of shaving the women's heads, stripping them naked and forcing them to drink castor oil, to sweep the streets, the Church and Falangist meeting halls.

A few days later, November 7, the anniversary of the Russian revolution and of the first day of the battle of Madrid, a second execution of three victims: Marcial Cobos, from Torrecampo and a member of the Committee on Communities, and two from Villanueva: Pedro *El Chunga* Juan Martínez Capitán and Francisco *Villaralteño* Rubio Gómez. As reported earlier, the latter's family was almost totally exterminated: several months later they executed his father-in-law (Juan Gómez, aged 67) and two brothers-in-law (Manuel and Juan Gómez Luna, aged 27). A third brother-in-law, Hilario Gómez, committed suicide when, upon his release from jail in 1946, he discovered the family tragedy. All the men in the family were eliminated and only two women whom Moreno Gómez visited in Calle Torrecampo at the beginning of the 1980s, were left to mourn.

As to El Chunga, who was very well-known in Villanueva, not because of his politics but because he was some kind of local hero, he is still remembered for inviting everyone "Come to the party in the bullring" as he left for the cemetery, as Moreno Gómez also recounted elsewhere. The infamous bloodthirsty Lieutenant Pepinillo, who ended up taking his own life in Espiel July 18 1941 after killing fifteen farmworkers, was officer in charge of the firing squad and of administering the coup de grâce. Still today, the general public knows nothing of these and similar barbaric acts that took place throughout victorious Spain.

Zacarias Romero Regalón, from Pedroche, was executed November 30. According to eye witnesses, he was arrested for the simple reason that they had found a razor in his backpack, for which he was also cruelly beaten.

1939 ended with the first 20 victims; more than 80 would fall in the town the following year. As 1940 dawned, returned townspeople continued to be forced to make declarations, to receive beatings and be tried by courts martial, ending with the shooting of those who had been 'duly sentenced'.

30 January was the date of the execution of a prisoner who had been sentenced to death by Judge Juan Calero: Misael López, the Head Postmaster,

whose reprieve, obtained by a relative of his, a high-ranking Nationalist military officer, the Judge had hidden in a drawer. Although it cannot be proven, this may have been the 'serious administrative mistake' that led the Judge to commit suicide later that same year, August 28.

Leap year was celebrated with a numerous saca of 14 men at 5 p.m. February 29, almost all from Pedroche and Torrecampo, and one from Villanueva: Lope *El Dinamitero* Ibáñez. A native of the mining region of El Horcajo, he was an explosives expert and apparently fought the coup in 1936. He was arrested in Almodóvar del Campo in 1939, from where he was taken on orders from members of the Villanueva Casino who received him with beating after beating, until he was executed. Several individuals from Torrecampo died with him, namely Sebastián Luque (whose son Juan had been taken for a paseo right after the Francoist victory); Cesário Serrano (because he had belonged to the Rojo Red Cross); young Manuel Luque Herrero, who was cruelly tortured by El Colodro, the Torrecampo gravedigger. Another four were from Pedroche, among whom the famous Francisco *El Pindolo* Tirado, a farmer who had been very active in the revolutionary days of Pedroche, and others from that town whose charges are unknown: (*El Princeso*, Pedro – *El Asentero*, Francisco – *El de la Rosa*, David – *El Cabezón*, Diego – *El de la Zorra*, etc.) El Pindodo was tried in Villanueva September 7 1939 at the court martial presided by Commander Ramón Navarro, on unknown charges, and sentenced to death by garrotte, he was actually shot.

Ten more victims were executed at 5 p.m. March 5 1940. One, Pedro Amil Cuadrado, had been Socialist Mayor of Adamuz, took refuge in Villanueva in 1937 and served as leader of the Committee of the Evacuated from Adamuz. He held various positions behind the Republican lines. Arrested after the end of the war, he was unable to recover from the usual terrible beatings and torture he endured.

Fructuoso Prieto Arévalo was part of that same saca. The AVC newspaper of 1931 printed his photograph as President of a committee in the famous October 1931 strike in Villanueva that was repressed in a scandalous manner. He was arrested by Falangist Diego El Chunga, who was famous for torturing Pepe Delgado, Juan Lucío and others.

Another leading activist for workers' rights died that same day, communist Diego Ranchal Plazuelo, brother of the well-known socialist Miguel Ranchal who had served as Mayor of Villanueva del Duque and was executed in Barcelona by the infamous Campo da Bota firing squad. Diego's 'crime' was that he had been a member of a street band during Carnival, in 1936, whose jingles strongly criticized the local landowners: «*Vote for Tolico, a very reputable man, he who buys votes with cuddles from…*», they sang. Several members of the street band who participated in that event ended up facing the firing squad. Diego was forced to sing that ditty as he was being tortured. Diego Majuelos was also part of that saca, falsely accused by the widow of a Guardia Civil for something he denied. One of his brothers, Mateo, was later executed in Cordoba.

The March 26 saca included Antonio Rubio Cobos, from Pedroche, father of Moreno Gómes' secondary school teacher. Many of the children of those who were shot by the National Catholics were made to attend religious schools and encouraged to follow a religious career, as a form of penitence and reparation for the 'sins' of their fathers. Manuel Rubio was one of those children who was sent to the Salesian seminary. As a young man, he abandoned his religious studies in the early 1950s and moved to Villanueva where he turned to teaching.

One of the four executed April 2, the elderly socialist Ramón Ruiz Hernán, had frequently represented his party in agricultural meetings and committees, which is why landowners hated him. He was accused of having insulted Franco in a letter he wrote during the war and which they found. Also executed that day, Manuel Salazar Vilches was a very active communist. Both men were also accused of having taken the horses belonging to the Guardia Civil after they surrendered their barracks in July 1936. Vilches died shouting Viva! La Republica. "It was one of the most valiant deaths that I witnessed."[7]

Juan Escribano Fernández, son of Juan *El Pedrocheño*, a member of the JSU, was executed at 5 p.m. April 6. He was accused of having been present at the unproven execution of 'the 21' right-wingers August 6 1936. Judge Juan Calero had accepted numerous gifts from his family in exchange for saving their son, but he kept the gifts and sentenced the young man to death. His family was allowed to say farewell to him. The scene was a vale of tears, as the boy tried to console his parents by telling them that he "was not born to live for eternity."

The first early morning execution took place at 6 a.m. May 17, with five victims. Prisciliano Orellana was accused of having gone to arrest a right-winger, Victoriano Muñoz, who was later executed by a person called Rojas. Despite the fact that everyone in the town knew this, everyone who was in the arresting party was exterminated, whilst the only truly guilty person escaped to go into exile. Also executed at the same time, Matías Villarreal (whose brother Basilio, member of the War Committee, was in the mountains with the guerrillas) and Francisco *Curro Beatas* Sánchez Muñoz, whose interesting letters he wrote in the chapel are reproduced in APPENDIX I. Curro Beatas was a member of the War Committee, a leader of the Izquierda Republicana, First Assistant Mayor in 1936, and during the war, joined the PCE. He was always a moderate leader and avoided all possible excesses. Two individuals he 'saved' from Republican action, the Pedraza brothers (Matías and Gregorio, the latter the Francoist Mayor), were both landowners and his principle accusers. In his farewell letters to his family, Curro Beatas asks his family to revenge him and gives name after name of his accusers and executioners. Little did he imagine that the dictatorship would last for forty years, followed by another forty years of forced amnesia.

The most infamous execution in the town during those days occurred May 26, when the saca took the largest number of victims – 18. It was exceptionally held on a Sunday, precisely on *Holy Sunday*, when the religious procession took twice to the streets. It is said that each time, when the procession walked past the Fuente Vieja Schools prison, the hooded members of the religious brotherhoods shouted: "Kill them all! Don't leave a single man alive!"

Historically, religions have been at the root of the most violent movements worldwide. The largest bloodbaths have always occurred in the name of religion and Catholics have always been leaders when it came to exterminating heretics. As proof that nothing in this book is an exaggeration of this, here is a brief extract of that which a priest from a church in Rota, Cádiz, had to say in 1936:

> "The most guilty and ungodly have already answered to God for their actions; they are now paying for their guilt in having infiltrated the Marxist poison in the town, distancing themselves from God. But there still remain some who intend to deceive us. We shall discover them all: everyone shall get what he deserves; no-one shall escape; mark my words. Nobody! We must go even deeper with the cleansing until we have destroyed all the rot that Russia has introduced into this town..."[8]

This was the Church under Franco. Moreno Gómez recently received a letter from Jaén informing him that a local priest, Tomás de la Torre Lendínez, is currently travelling all around the province collecting signatures (he already has more than a thousand) for a petition to abolish or revoke the Historic Memory Law. This is an example of what he writes in his blog:

> "During the many years of the Zapatero Government, we were forced to swallow some disgusting legislation. One of those filthy laws is the ill-named law for the historic memory, the source of vindictive conflicts and hatred..."[9]

Clearly, the Church continues to go its way 0without pain in the heart, nor any desire to change, without confessing its sins or doing any penance.' *Plus ça change, plus c'est la même chose.*

Leading the victims in the unholy Easter saca, was a moderate Communist leader, Eugenio *Palmera* Jurado Pozuelo, an educated man who was a violinist with the Municipal Orchestra and who had represented the local PCE at several meetings in Andalusia during the 1930s. Occasionally in the jail, other prisoners asked him to play his violin, but those sessions were always interrupted by a drunken subaltern from the regular army, with kicks and slaps and shouts that: "Obviously, wild animals also like music."

All the members of the Palmera family were involved in politics. His brother José who had served as Mayor in 1935 for the Leroux Party, did what he could for Eugenio, writing letters and trying to pull influential strings, to no avail. To make matters worse, another brother, Zacharias, was a rabid Falangist who wanted nothing to do with his brother Eugenio. The latter's main accuser was Pepe Delgado whose brother had been tried in Jaén and he accused Eugenio and his wife Florentina of having gone to the People's Court in Jaén to depose against him. The letter Eugenio wrote from the chapel, naming his torturers and asking his family to revenge him, is also included in APPENDIX I. It is said that he died raising his fist high and shouting Viva! La Republica.

Others included in the same saca were a father and son: Juan Gómez and his son Juan, of the aforementioned Los Villaralteños family; Alfonso Leal, a member of the Zamora family, secretary of the Committee of Communities, whom the casino Señoritos accused of having stolen their land; Avelino *Campana* Ayala, because it was alleged that he had been present at the execution of some right-wingers; Antonio *Casillas* Pedraza, saddle maker, socialist, because Pedro *Sargento Chicorro* Muñoz hated him; Fernando Fernandez de Haro, because he was a socialist, private tutor and seller of trade union newspapers , and also because it was alleged that he had 'entered the town at the head of two thousand riflemen', which was absurd. His family insisted that he was executed after he received a reprieve but that it was hidden by Judge Calero; Sebastián *Figurillas* Santofimia, because he had been involved in the Carnival marches; Francisco López Justos, uncle of the famous Mojea (Maria Josefa López Garrido, a member of Julián Caballero's group of guerrillas; and Blás *Catalán* Arévalo, where everything conspired against his survival.

Blás Arévalo's brother-in-law was the great Communist leader, Nemesio *El Floro* Pozuelo, of Jaén where he was Secretary of the PCE, Civil Governor during the war and a member of the party's National Board of Directors.

Nemesio went into exile in the USSR where he became quite famous.[10] Blás married Nemesio's sister Juana *La Flora*, who was sentenced to 20 years in jail for having sheltered the wives and children of the Guardias Civiles who had surrendered their barracks in her house on Calle Cañada Baja, an act of Good Samaritan kindness that was, nonetheless, held against her. One of their sons-in-law, Antonio Pérez de la Riva, was beaten to death in Burgos prison. To make matters worse, when Blás Arévalo was on guard duty at the famous Guerrilla Headquarters at Calle Conquista 14, in Villanueva, at the end of 1937, he did not prevent a commando from removing a right-winger who had been arrested, Francisco Díaz, and made him disappear.

Pedro Amil Ruiz, from Adamuz, was executed in the May 26 saca and his brother Juan, the following saca, June 3. Both were elderly. Of the four men executed June 3, one was a past Mayor of Pedroche, Tomás Rodríguez de la Fuente. From Villanueva, they executed Juan J. *El Conejero* Mohedano Sánchez, a well-known socialist whose only accusation was that he had stood guard over right-wing prisoners at the Regajito Schools. He was a past alderman for the Frente Popular and held several positions during the war, including that of Mayor during the last few days, a position that was cut short at the end of the war because of the Casado coup.

The June 12 dawn saca took three victims, one of whom was the communist Juan Antonio Bustos Casado, son of Gaspar *Legañas* Bustos, both of whom worked for the great landowner Torrico. Juan Antonio Bustos, a member of the PCE, was an alderman during the war and Treasurer of the Local Trade Unions Federation. He played no part in the anti-coup fighting in July 1936 because some miners from Puertollano mistakenly shot him in an arm and he spent considerable time in hospital. His father, Gaspar went to Torrico, his employer, begging for his son's life, to no effect. To make matters worse, Juan Antonio and his wife Antonia had owned a tavern across the street from City Hall that was a favourite haunt of left-wing townspeople and the Communist Mayor, Julián Caballero.

Juan Antonio Bustos was one of those who confessed in chapel before he died, perhaps hoping to ask the parish priest, Rev. Don Marcial, to look after his two sons. One of them, Gaspar, was pushed towards the church and he became a priest in Cordoba, where he remains to this date. Moreno Gómez attended classes he taught at the Seminary.

Also executed with the same saca, Juan Luna Enríquez, communist, brother of the first Republican Mayor in 1931, Andrés Luna, a member of the Leroux Party. His last letter to his family, written in the chapel, is also recorded in APPENDIX I.

There were only two more executions in Villanueva. June 15 they executed 55-year-old socialist Cecilio *El Vinatero* Ruiz, accused only of having stood guard over right-wing prisoners. The last individual executed, September 12, was Alfonso *El de La Loma* Sánchez Pozuela, a communist, because Diego López alleged, on no apparent grounds, that he took part in the 1936 revolt. One of his brothers was later shot in Cordoba capital. Both were sons of Maria La Loma, the head of another local family that was almost exterminated.

On September 26, all the prisoners in the town were transferred to Cordoba Provincial Prison where they would join the hundreds of men who would die during 1941, at the height of the mass Francoist extermination that curiously appeared to coincide with the exterminations in the Nazi concentration camps.

This tragic description of so much that Villanueva de Cordoba suffered during the post-war period, ends with a brief reference to three eminent natives of the town who were executed by Francoists in Valencia and in Barcelona.

Francisco Copado Sánchez was first cousin of the notorious Jesuit Rev. Bernabé Copado S.J., chaplain to the Carlist unit under Colonel Luís Redondo, and whose humane and Christian qualities are best described by the fact that he let his cousin Francisco be executed on the basis of Juan Fernández and Manuel Rodríguez Moreno's clearly false allegations. Both swore that he was a dynamiter and the leader of numerous mobs, when he actually was a truck driver and belonged to the War Committee. Everything else was false. The end of the war found him in Valencia where, with others, he took refuge in the Panamanian Embassy. The Embassy, however, was attacked by Francoists who arrested all the occupants. Copado was sentenced to death with other Republican officers, June 12 1939. Copado was taken at dawn from the Modelo Prison in Valencia November 1 and executed by firing squad in the Paterna cemetery. In his cell, he left a lock of his hair for his wife María and several farewell letters, extracts of which are quoted earlier or reproduced in APPENDIX I.

Another tragic story was that of Miguel Ranchal Plazuelo, also resident in Villanueva de Cordoba and later in Villanueva del Duque where he was a famous Socialist Mayor during the Republic and part of the war. He was married to Maria Josefa Luna, sister of the aforementioned Bartolomé Luna, Socialist Mayor of Villanueva de Cordoba in 1932. When in 1921, the PCE was founded in Villanueva and joined by all the members of the Socialist Youth and a great many local working men, he and his brother-in-law strove to maintain the essence of the PSOE in the town.

Miguel Ranchal was frequently mentioned in the trade union press during the Republic because of his defence of the miners in the El Soldado,

Villanueva del Duque, mines as a truly dedicated Mayor should. Within the PSOE, Ranchal, a *Prietista*,[vi] opposed the faction led by Francisco Largo Caballero. When war broke out July 18, the party was profoundly divided. Ranchal, as Mayor, did his utmost to prevent the outbreak of violence in his town, which he was generally successful at achieving. For example, several times he prevented the Jaén Militia from attacking the local prison where right-wingers were being held. During the war, he held leading positions in the Cordoba PSOE and he argued strongly with the PCE against unifying the two parties and on the frontlines, he served as a political commissar. At the end of the war, he was arrested in Albatera, Alicante. From there he was taken first, to Valencia, then to Barcelona, where he was executed June 13 1940 at the tragic Campo de la Bota,[vii] despite numerous appeals to leading Francoists whose lives Ranchal had saved. One, Demetrio Carvajal Arrieta who was a Judge Advocate, cynically told his wife not to worry that at the utmost, her husband would only receive a more or less lengthy prison sentence.[11] Ranchal's letter of farewell to his family is also reproduced in APPENDIX I.

José Cantador Huertos was another eminent socialist from Villanueva de Cordoba executed in the Paterna, Valencia, cemetery, August 29 1940. A bank employee, in 1933 he moved to Játiva where he was an alderman for the Frente Popular, director of the UGT and the local branch of the PSOE. He had previously served as Municipal Secretary in La Carlota, Cordoba. At the end of the war, he was taken prisoner in Albatera, then taken to the Játiva jail where he was sentenced to death by Military Judge Eusebio González on false allegations by a fellow bank worker, Ricardo Diego Ruiz, for whom he had done some favours in 1936. This was a situation that repeated itself time and time again, when members of the right-wing who had been favoured in one way or another by Republicans, became furious accusers against them after the end of the war. Cantador's letter of farewell to his family, reproduced in APPENDIX I, was found hidden in his pillow in his cell.

[vi] Supporters of Indalecio Prieto, right-wing leader of the Spanish Socialist Party during the Republic.

[vii] The *Campo de la Bota*, a shooting range for French troops under Napoleon, was a Barcelona neighbourhood and military installation on the outskirts of the town, by the sea. Between 1939 and 1952, Francoists shot and killed 1717 persons sentenced by summary trials and executions. Eye-witnesses describe truck after truck laden with prisoners and so many killed as they fled towards the shore, attempting to escape the firing squads, that the sea was stained red with blood. Description downloaded from: http://www.barcelonarutas.com/el-campo-de-la-bota-de-triste-recuerdo/.

7. Miscellaneous other small towns and villages.

Natives of **Villaralto** were executed in various places in the Los Pedroches district (Pozoblanco, Peñarroya, Hinojosa, and others) and after September 1940, in Cordoba capital. The Civil Register lists eight executed; six of these obits also indicate Pozoblanco as the place of death and one Peñarroya, which is why only one name is given for this town. Likewise in **El Viso**, where of eight dead, two are recorded as having died in Pozoblanco, which is why only six names are given. In **Almodóvar del Rio**, there is no entry for death by firing squad in the Civil Register, although we know from eye-witness accounts, that six residents were shot there November 12 1939, which is why there are six names for that town.

In **Cañete de las Torres**, there were only three executions: one, October 18 and two November 7 1939. Other residents died in Baena, Castro del Rio and Cordoba capital. The **Espejo** Civil Register only records five victims in the cemetery, August 3 1939. Others from Espejo died in Castro del Rio and in Cordoba capital. It is also here that the record for Francisco Jiménez Garcia states that he died February 27 1940 by 'incomplete hanging', a euphemism for torture. Just how is one to interpret what is described as 'incomplete'? In **Hornachuelos**, there are eight victims, two in 1939 and two in 1940 and four in 1941, for whom there is no additional information. Five more from Hornachuelos died in Posadas and more in Cordoba capital. There was a single execution in **Montalbán**, Juan Río Jiménez, a shoemaker aged 33, August 10 1939, with no further information. This village appears to have been overlooked by the bloody storm that devastated the region beginning in 1936, although recent information from an eye witness, Alfonso Vaquero Zamorano, indicates there are quite a few more than are included herein.[12]

Moreno Gómez reminds the reader that the data regarding the victims that are given in the Appendixes and Tables, town by town, refer only to the official entries in the respective Civil Registry Offices, and that we cannot lose sight of the possibility that the number of victims for each town and village may be considerably greater as many unrecorded executions were held in the more important towns. *Vide* Table 1.

The terror of the Spanish Legion in the District of Pedroches

"No Government has any right to refute a fundamental right of the victims...
The truth! There has been no truth. If this is contained in the archives, it
still remains hidden from us. During the period of transition, it was not for
nothing that Francoists committed crimes. These have been forgotten. There
has not been even a single debate... And what about the reconciliation? Where
is that reconciliation? In Spain, suffice to even bring up the subject of the civil
war for people to begin to panic. Where is the reconciliation? Lastly, when is
Justice going to ask forgiveness for never having done anything more..."

Baltasar Garzón, University of Sevilla, 13 January 2014.

None of the many historians who write about the Francoist repression,
appear to have addressed the distribution of the Spanish Foreign Legion at
different places in Spain with express repressive intentions. The Legion went
to extreme repressive lengths in many Francoist towns and villages, especially
in 1940.

In 1940, the New State used the African Foreign Legion troops to add
an extra touch of terror in the regions that sheltered those who had fled to
the mountains, that is, a large section of the country. In 1939, part of that
mission was entrusted to several battalions (*tabores*) of regular troops, but the
Moroccan mercenaries who had been useful during the war in the forefront
of Franco's army proved unable to act in the rear-guard during 'peacetime'.

The Cordovan district of Los Pedroches, the last one to fall into the
hands of the Nationalists and a very mountainous region that sheltered
fugitives in abundance, was especially suited for repression by the Legion. The
legionnaires were sent to the North of Cordoba province at the beginning of
April 1940 in the shape of the 3rd *Bandera* of the First *Tercio*[viii] of the Legion,
under General Salvador Bañuls Navarro, who at the same time was appointed
local military commander, first in Villanueva and then in Pozoblanco. The
Legion replaced the Military Police (SIPM) units that had been the first to
act in the recently-conquered villages, indiscriminately applying the Law of
Fugitives,[ix] setting up headquarters in all the buildings that the SIPM had
occupied in the towns and villages. In Villanueva de Cordoba, this was in the

---

viii 3rd battalion of the 1st *Tercio* (i.e., Third - Spanish infantry organization consisting of several companies.)

ix SIPM Lieutenant Leopoldo Mena was notorious for the amount of blood he shed in this manner in Villanueva de Cordoba.

Los Laurianos house on the main square, where many of the defeated had already been cruelly beaten and some killed.

Commanding sections under General Bañuls' orders, we find Lieutenant San Antón, 2nd Lieutenant Barcieiro, Physician Lieutenant Segovia, and others. One section, in **Santa Eufemia**, was infamous for the atrocity of its actions, such as the boiling oil incident, a form of torture that so horrified the people in Los Pedroches, that many years later I heard reports of this in various places in the district.

Lieutenant San Antón, 2nd Lieutenant Barcieiro, and Physician Lieutenant Segovia were some of the officers under General Bañuls. One section, billeted in **Santa Eufemia**, was infamous for the barbarity of its actions such as the martyrdom of Norberto Castillejo's father, that so horrified the people in the district that it is still referred to today.

During the autumn of 1940, legionnaires acted particularly viciously in **Belalc**ázar under Lieutenant Ortega and Sergeants Escobar and Rodriguez.[13] The presence of a unit of Legion troops in this town was surely due to the considerable fears the Francoists had of the great many fugitives who had fled to the mountains (prison escapes in Hinojosa 1940 and in Belalcázar 1939). There were so many groups of these fugitives that there were frequent skirmishes in the surrounding farms (Pellejeros, Ochavo, La Encinilla, etc.). Some 40 fugitives participated in one such skirmish, September 1940. Legion Lieutenant Juan Tamayo Vián arrived in Belalcázar December 1940. One of the most terrifying legionnaire officers, he was so crazy, so mad, that even the Francoist Mayor Justo Rivallo, was afraid of him, as he wrote to the Provincial Governor in Cordoba:

> "When this Legion Lieutenant came to this town on the 13th instant, to take up his command, he declared that he intended to beat a lot of people and that is just what he did. Yesterday evening, at 11 pm, he went to an establishment where several parishioners were meeting in a peaceful manner, and he began beating them with rods, ordering that the establishment be immediately closed; he did the same at a dance that he also cancelled, but not before he had rained beatings on several people who were present…"[14]

From this, one can deduce that there were aspects of Francoism that went beyond a dedication to the overwhelming repression of the defeated, to spreading terror everywhere, creating a general atmosphere of terror that distressed both the disaffected and the affected as well. If these barbarities were committed by the legionnaires in 'times of peace', one can just imagine what these troops had been capable of in times of war, as they ruthlessly conquered towns and villages, in their assaults on Badajoz, in Talavera de la Reina and everywhere they went.

The legionnaires went about the towns as if they were the owners of people's lives and property, exceeding their mandate to go after fugitives (which is what they did the least), imposing a reign of terror in the manner of barracks discipline, the only obedience they knew. It was the logical supremacy of the military over the civil society that came with the New State. Lieutenant Tamayo ridiculed the Mayor with an "I order, therefore you obey" attitude, beginning by ordering that the streets had to be swept clean as if they were patios in a barracks patios, then setting closing times for the shops and curfews for other activities, as if everyone came under martial law once *Taps* was played.

The power of the military as the essence of Spanish fascism, liberally sprinkled with the Holy Water of National Catholicism, explains all kinds of controls, excesses and abuses that occurred. Nevertheless, after all that, there are uninformed individuals who still insist that Francoism in 1941 had already become a sort of paradise. This, despite the fact that executions diminished in number, not in 1941, but in 1942, partly because there was practically nobody left to shoot. Besides, why did they want or need to execute more as society lived in terror, cowed by the many other types of repression: exclusion, hunger, blacklists, beatings, continuous raids for prisoners, shaven heads, castor oil treatments, humiliations of all kinds, rationing, daily signing-ins at the barracks under a fragile parole, not just by those who had been freed from camps or prison, but also many left-wing sympathizers, including adolescents,[x] police abuses in the capital cities, in addition to slave labour all over Spain, prisons bursting with inmates and so much more, *ad infinitum.* In other words, one cannot speak of a softening of the Regime either in 1941, or in 1942, or in 1947, or in 1948 or even later (the Law of Fugitives was applied with full force in Nerja, Málaga, in 1950). To speak of a softening of the regime is to belittle historical rigor.

Returning to the terror in the North of Cordoba province, the persecution was so great that those who had escaped to the maquis in the region, some 50 individuals, organized the so-called Great March to Caceres. There were fugitives from Hinojosa (El Francés), Belalcázar (Loro, Sincolor), Santa Eufemia and some villages of Badajoz. They entered Las Villuercas, Caceres, December 6 1940. Caceres Guardia Civil Commander, Lieutenant Colonel Manuel Gómez Cantos, got wind of this but, unable to find the fugitives, used the civil population to teach the escapees a horrendous lesson. He organized a raid of peaceful villagers, chosen totally at random, and applied

---

[x]   Ernesto Caballero, *Vivir con Memoria* (Living with Memories). Barcelona, Planeta, 1979.

a *paseo* to 12 residents of neighbouring Cañamero and 16 townspeople of Logrosán. Gómez Cantos got tired of murdering people in Badajoz, where he had been appointed Head of Public Order by Queipo, in Marbella (after Malaga fell) and in the hills around Huelva, where he chased fugitives in 1937. Responsible for the bloodbath in Badajoz bullring, Gómez Cantos proved to be so out of control that the Guardia Civil finally arrested him in 1945, stripping him of his duties. He is not totally forgotten as to this day a popular insult in the region is to accuse an individual of being 'more evil than Gómez Cantos'.

Once the Legion abandoned Los Pedroches, the Cordovan fugitives who had taken refuge in Caceres at the end of 1940, returned to the North of Cordoba at the beginning of Summer 1941. (*El Francés*, from Hinojosa, remained in Cáceres where he led a group of guerrillas.)

Let us now centre our attention on the Legion's activities in **Villanueva de Cordoba**. Beatings that were given to each and any townsperson were the norm, as in other places, part of the strategy of spreading terror throughout the rural world. Several eye-witness reports collected by Moreno Gómez at the beginning of the transition period (later, this was no longer possible as the government restricted access to archives), revealed an unsustainable hardship. Bartolomé Caballero Coleto (his brother Juan *El Hebrero* Caballero had escaped to the hills) told Moreno Gómez:

> "In April 1940, I was making charcoal in the Los Marines farm in Barranco de los Pobos (between Villanueva and Adamuz), and because I had a brother who had fled to the mountains, the Legi**onnaires went there to get me and they took me to Pedro Luís' mill. They gave me a terrible beating and then set me free. I finally made it back to the farm, with great difficulty, because of my wounds."

As it was, was something more to the above story. In the same farm, a young man who belonged to the Las Marines family, apparently was friendly with El Hebrero, the guerrilla. He left food for him at night, in a hiding place where the guerrilla would collect it later. Whether the repressor forces knew of this or not, the fact is that they beat Miguel Gutiérrez so badly that this young man could not stop crying and he lost his mind for good. Moreno Gómez was unable to determine whether it was the Guardia Civil or the Legion who beat him, nor whether the beating was given on the farm or at the landowner's mill, or in the town barracks. The fact is, they beat him so badly, they drove him mad.[xi]

Still in Villanueva, July 1940 the Legion implemented a series of intimidating actions against the country folk, most certainly with a view to sowing preventive terror against anyone thinking of helping the maquis. The legionnaires organized a warped field trip, taking with them the men and women they found on the farms. It was an exhausting expedition lasting four days and three nights, in which they gathered up some fifty country folk, including some women such as Manuela Illescas[15], who had to leave new-born children behind. "We will not stop until we find the fugitives" said the legionnaires. They travelled as far as the olive grove and the oil press belonging to Don Cionisio, close to the village of Obejo. The ill-treatment of their captives was constant. Finally, they took everyone with them to Villanueva, ending the odyssey in the Guardia Civil barracks on the Plaza del Carmen. The prize given to each for four days of deportation was a beating, especially a poor old man named Claudio (whose son Pedro Coleto Díaz was shot under the Law of Fugitives June 17 1948).

The Legion's terror in Los Pedroches grew in strength under the orders of General Bañuls as Summer 1940 advanced. In Villanueva de Cordoba, 54-year-old Juan Fernández Moreno (father of Sebastián El del Banco), an apolitical and simple man, was arrested as he worked on Navalazarza farm, August 24. They took him to headquarters and, in the presence of General Bañuls, they hung him from the rafters and beat him brutally. As he lay dying, he was taken to Romo's house on Calle Herradores that served as an improvised prison and torture chamber. According to oral testimonials from his family, the omnipresent Pepe Higuera (son of the builder Miguel Higuera) and several other notorious local torturers who helped the Legion during those terrible months, were present. The Civil Registry records his cause of death as 'died at 8 p.m. in a deserted area from gunshot wounds'. This agrees with his family's version that as Juan Fernández was clearly dying, they took him out to the fields at nightfall and gave him the coup de grâce, to simulate an attempt at escaping. They took his body away and his family was never able to find out where they buried him. Yet another 'disappeared'.

Two days later, another crime at the hands of the legionnaires: a 43-year-old apolitical man, Juan *Horozco* Cantador Cachinero, was arrested as he worked at José Cámara's farm, also in Navalazarza. His family recalls that ome days earlier several Rojos had been seen in a neighbouring farm,

---

97

the Dehesilla farm, in Torrico. For no known reason, the legionnaires went to Cámara's farm and took him off to the deadly location: General Bañuls' headquarters. The session of torture was so brutal that when Juan Cantador was removed to Romo's House, he was in such a sorry state that he died soon afterwards. The Civil Registry states 'died at p.m. from a heart attack'. If it had not been for Moreno Gómez' research and interviews with witnesses, we would have never known that this so-called 'cardiac syncope' was covering up the death of a man who had been beaten to death, a crime of *lèse humanité*.

These are the death records that never appear in the statistics. Like those, how many more hidden crimes and 'disappearances' that history will never unveil? Only oral eye-witness accounts and oral testimonials, so despised by so-called academics, can offer access to the hidden nooks and crannies of Francoist criminality.

The Legion continued its wave of crime in Los Pedroches. In Villanueva, under the watchful eye of the Mayor, the Falangist Gregorio Pedraza Cámara. October 16 1940, Bañuls' men organized another of their atypical field trips into the countryside, arresting all the country folk they found along the way, both men and women under the excuse that they were hunting down Rojos from the hills. Amongst the arrested was elderly José Huertas Valverde, aged 68, and his son-in-law Francisco Valle.[xii] They took them from Antonio Herrero's La Sierra farm down to the town, beating them along the way. There, they tortured the elderly man, making him swallow buckets of water and pushing a tube down his throat. His throat ruptured and he died that night in the Hospital; from 'cardiac arrest', according to the Civil Registry.

Some people may be confused in thinking that during the war and the post-war genocide, the dirty killing work was somehow organized by the Falangists, but that was definitely not the case: Falangists could not kill or execute anyone on their own accord. Francoist genocide was always committed under the orders of and directed by the military police (including the Guardia Civil). When victory broke out, it was a Military Police Unit that sowed the terror in Pozoblanco (100 victims of the Law of Fugitives). The 2nd Company of the Military Police, under the orders of notorious Lt. Leopoldo Mena, was the one who sowed the terror in Villanueva de Cordoba and was

---

[xii] Moreno Gómez frequently interviewed the victim's daughter, Antonia Huertas, in her house Calle Pelayo, Villanueva de Cordoba, in 1979. An extremely kindly woman, she talked to him and gave him many details of those terrible days. In addition to the tragedy of her father, she told me how one day, when she was working in the fields, her children came to tell her that there were some men in the hills. Taking care, she got a loaf of bread and went to see them: it was the group led by Julián Caballera, past Communist Mayor of Villanueva de Cordoba. "The Guardia Civil found out about this contact, arrested the whole family and took us all to the Cordoba prison. I was pregnant at the time and gave birth there. One year later, in 1941, when they felt like it, they set us free".

responsible for the first deaths under torture. The arrival of the Legion, much worse and bloodier, substituted and 'improved' on what the Military Police had started.

The Legion also acted at will in **Cardeña**, a neighbourhood of Villanueva. Moreno Gómez was able to discover at least one crime, the case of a humble stonemason, Pedro *Perico el de la Aurora* Gutiérrez Díaz, aged 46 years, married to Juana Cano and father of 6, whom they beat to death. According to the Civil Registry, he died from 'septicaemia, from infected wounds'. He did not die in any hospital, but in the Municipal Depot, at the end of the day, August 11 1940. Another crime that would have remained uncovered had it not been for the family's oral testimony.

The 3rd Battalion of the 1st Tercio of the Legion set up its first command post in Villanueva de Cordoba in Summer 1940 and that Fall, moved its headquarters to Pozoblanco. These mercenary troops were garrisoned throughout the District, because in addition to the Pozoblanco headquarters, the Legion established command posts in Villanueva (November), Belalcázar (December), etc. There is a record of the death "from a gunshot wound" of a legionnaire in the Villanueva de Cordoba barracks New Year's Eve 1940-41. The reason for his death is unrecorded but it is could have either been suicide or the result of a disciplinary procedure gone wrong. There are eye-witness accounts that legionnaires were punished by being made to sweep the Fuente Vieja square, in Villanueva, with a bare torso and sacks of sand tied to their backs with wires. Military madness.

When the Legion left Los Pedroches in Spring 1941, it was replaced by the 3rd Mobile Guardia Civil Company from Seville, under Captain Sebastián Carmona y Pérez de Vera, who had begun his bloody apprenticeship in Aguilar de la Frontera in 1936. The purpose was to chase and capture fugitives but most especially, to keep up the terror and beatings of the population, both urban and rural. The areas of action of these Mobile Units were called 'Fugitives and Bandits Districts' and they answered to the Guardia Civil Headquarters in Cordoba capital.

We know the date on which the Legion left **Pozoblanco**, May 12 1941, when they were given a 'warm farewell' after having been there for 7 months.[16] A most curious is that bloody Commander Salvador Bañuls left Pozoblanco either engaged or already married. The fortunate bride was a member of the Vizcáino family. As a 'love' present for his adopted marital homeland, when he was promoted to General and appointed General Captain of Catalonia, he donated his red sash of office to the Virgin of Luna, patron saint of

Pozoblanco. On procession days, the statue of the Virgin is still taken through the streets, adorned with this war criminal's blood red sash.[xiii]

Faced with this and other examples of the still apparent alliance of the cross and the sword, as embodied by the Causa General, it is a wonder that today's deniers of the Francoist repression have not promoted the General Canonization of all the Francoist war criminals. There are many precedents for this: if the movie Ágora, the Church blesses the canonization of Saint Cyril of Alexandria, why not also the Francos, the Queipos, the don Brunos, the Díaz Criado, Gómez Cantos and so on and so on, without forgetting the Bañuls of those times. A magnificent flowering of war criminals, smelling of sainthood Would Moses ever have thought of writing the 5th Commandment on the tablets if he could have known that the above unholy alliance was to honour it even less than it did the 6th Commandment?

Upsurge of the Law of Fugitives in 1941

> *"[Saturated with memories] … we should qualify what kind of saturation we are talking about. Who is so saturated? Is it really absurd to continue speaking of forgetfulness and silence? … In all cases, there appears to be no doubt that the intended saturation, in case it existed, is there but basically only in one direction. If there is a saturation of a memory, it is the memory of the victors, not that of the defeated. The saturated memory (of the former) and the satiation with the silence (of the latter)."*

Alberto Reig Tapa, Memoria de la Guerra Civil, p. 25.

Nobody could imagine the upsurge in the application of the Law of Fugitives in 1941. None of those who minimize the humanitarian catastrophe of Francoism, those who believe that all was 'legal' during the post-war period, who has written about the Law of Fugitives was applied during the Black Spring (April-May 1939) in the entire Centre-South region of Spain, and even less regarding how and why the Law of Fugitives was brought back in 1941. Nor has any one of those so-called historians written about how hundreds were taken for paseos during the period that Moreno Gómez calls the Triennium of Terror (1947-1949 in all of Spain, from Asturias to Malaga, the golden years of the Law of Fugitives. In the many writings about post-war Francoist government repression that have been published, despite so much talk about political violence and exemplary repression, there is little

---

xiii Although Moreno Gómez has written several times in the social media against this practice, photos of the 2017 procession show the red sash still tied around the waist of the Virgin's statue. *Vide* http://miralospedroches.es/la-virgen-de-luna/.

or no mention of the paralyzing terror, genocide, widespread extra-judicial extermination… the multiple crimes against humanity.

Something strange occurred in 1941 in quite a few towns and villages in Cordoba province when there was a series of executions that could not have been 'legal' because all the 'legally' condemned prisoners had been transferred to Cordoba Provincial Prison at the end of September 1940. These 1941 executions were summary executions devoid of all due process of law, an extra-legal, calculated surge of the repression in 1941, as the Law of Fugitives was brought back to the Cordoba towns and villages.

The so-called legal basis for this 'pull-back' as some ignoramus has called it, was the <u>Law for the Safety of the State of March 20 1941</u>, as published in the Official Bulletin of the Province on the orders of the Captain General of the 2nd Military Region, General Miguel Ponte y Manso de Zuñiga. This law contained a new list of crimes punishable by death, including armed robbery (with the activities of the maquis in mind). August 26 of the same year, an Order signed by General Emilio Álvarez Areces called, in no uncertain terms, for the 'elimination' of everybody who had escaped to the hills and their accomplices in the plains. Accordingly, all the deaths that occurred in the Cordoba countryside in 1941 were a consequence of these new means of extermination.

In **Adamuz**, there was a usual execution in the cemetery of a young farmer, Ricardo Molina Pastor, August 8, a village when there were no longer any 'lawful' prisoners left as they had all been sent to Cordoba. Without a doubt, this was a summary execution. In **Aguilar**, the Guardia Civil killed José Vega Castellón at the railway station, November 25.

In **Bujalance**, three young men were summarily executed in the cemetery, without a trial, November 22: Alfonso Alharilla, José Gallardo and Francisco Nieva. They were not fugitives but, motivated by hunger and the post-war shortages, they would go out at night to scavenge for food whilst going about their normal lives in the town during the day. They were surprised during one of these raids by the manager of an outlying farm, who shot and wounded one of them, which is how they came to be caught. They were taken to the cemetery and shot on the spot.

In **Dos Torres**, 6 young men were summarily executed during the Summer. More Gómez was unable to determine the exact reason, but presumably it was related either to the fugitives or to some kind of robbery. Eye-witnesses with whom he spoke in the village told him of a 2nd Lt. who was posted to the village and who, helped by some low-life accusers, invented false Communist plot and some supposed contacts with the fugitives in the hills, as a pretext to summarily execute 6 disaffected individuals. The Law of Fugitives was applied at dawn July 27, to Antonio Jurado and Genaro

Cazorla; July 30, to Pedro Romero, José Talero and Sebastián Lunar; and August 1 to José Romero Iglesias. These executions were recorded as the elimination of 'subversive' elements in Special Military Court for Fugitives Number 8 – a foretaste of that which would happen in 1947-49 during the Triennium of Terror.

The nadir of the criminality of this period occurred in **Espiel**, at the hands of the Carlist Militia 2nd Lieutenant José Moreno Sevillano, the notorious genocide 'Tenente Pepinillo'. Also nicknamed 'the red beret', he sowed terror when he was stationed in Villanueva de Cordoba and continued to do so after he was transferred to Espiel in 1941. Obsessed with the idea that there were Rojos all over the neighbouring fields and countryside, he dedicated himself to arresting farmworkers like crazy. He was assisted by perverted accusers such as Teodoro Valero, from Pozoblanco, and a so-called Francisco, from Espiel (brother-in-law to the olive oil producer Emilio González). Pepinillo and his henchmen were responsible for one of the most criminal post-war episodes in Cordoba province. They practiced arbitrary arrests, tortures and beatings, right left and centre to everyone they lay their hands on, without distinction.

The apotheosis of a crime of *lèse humanité* marked the July 18 1941 celebrations in Espiel, as recently described by an eye witness, the relative of two of the victims: his father – Antonio Arévalo, aged 53, and his brother Adrián, aged 19.[17] During Spring and Summer, the local jail and the Espiel Municipal Depot were packed with working men Pepinillo had arrested. He would strip the inmates' chests, handcuff their hands and tie them to their legs, and then beat the unfortunate men on their backs. He would send their clothes for washing back to their families soaking in blood and with strips of skin sticking to them. One inmate, Adrián Arévalo, our witness' brother, wrote the following to his fiancée: "*I don't know whether we will ever see each other again. We are being made to pay for something we did not do.*"

One day, some of the inmates asked to confess to the village priest. Some of the inmates took this opportunity to tell the priest of the unfair treatment they were being subjected to, especially as they had not committed any crime and were only hard-working farmhands, with no involvement in anything political or with the guerrillas in the mountains. The priest, believing the truth of their declarations, went to Pepinillo telling him that he was mistaken regarding those individuals. Pepinillo was absolutely furious: he slapped the priest hard across his face and accused him of being a Rojo. The next day, the priest went to Seville, to complain at military headquarters that he had been slapped by Pepinillo and he did not return to Espiel. The military authorities acted swiftly and an order arrived from Cordoba Military Headquarters ordering Pepinillo to present himself immediately in Cordoba, within a maximum of four hours, unarmed. This was late on the eve of July 18.

Pepinillo's revenge was swift and terrible. The very next night, July 18, he ordered a truck to collect all the inmates in the town jail and to take them to the cemetery, whilst he would go with another truck to the Municipal Depot where there were another 15 prisoners. Arriving at the cemetery, Pepinillo unloaded his truck and had all 15 prisoners executed. Meanwhile, the driver of the first truck, upon arriving at the cemetery and terrified with what he saw and was about to happen to the men in his truck, said "I am going to risk my life", floored the gas pedal and drove the truck and the prisoners post-haste to Cordoba.

No sooner were the executions over, Pepinillo went to a town dance where the townspeople were celebrating the date and asked a young lady out to dance. Soon afterwards, in the middle of the dance, he took out his revolver and shot himself in the head, thus ending his life. The young woman was so shaken by his act that she suffered mental problems for the rest of her life.

Among those executed on that date: 7 were from Pozoblanco, 4 from Villaralto, 3 from Espiel, and one from Pueblonuevo. Blaz Muñoz Márquez, brother to Baudilio Muñoz Márquez, one of the victims from Pozoblanco, provided a background account of the events that led to his brother's death. At the end of the war, he said, there were many deplorable and painful events. There was a man in Pozoblanco, Teodoro Valero, who owned an olive grove in Peñon de Lazarillo, Espiel, and who saw a potential communist in every man in the village. This man spent his time accusing men of proven honesty of this and they were arrested and taken to Pepinillo's headquarters in Espiel. It is useless to describe that scenes of what they did to some men there for whom there was no specific accusation and whose fabricated confessions were obtained by the most tremendous beatings. Teodoro and a so-called Francisco dedicated themselves to going to the farms in the mountains and, on Pepinillo's orders, capturing men they accused of being Rojos or communists. One notable case was that of a Falangist, a so-called Teodoro, who owned some money to the Pozoblanco judge, Antonio García Ruíz. The latter forgave Teodoro his debt on the condition that they stop beating his shepherd. Even the Espiel parish priest began to complain of Pepinillo and his gang's behaviour.[18]

Pepinillo's activities included the economic destruction of his victims and their families, which was usual Francoist behaviour in those days. Farmhands who were arrested in the fields near Espiel also suffered the loss of their belongings and, occasionally, their homesteads. A case in point was that of the Arévalo Bajo family: Pepinillo seized their herd of goads, a mare and other belongings which ended up in a military barracks in Cerro Muriano. After death had decimated the family, his widow and her surviving sons went to Cerro Muriano to retrieve their cattle. The soldier in charge understood her outrage and, taking pity on the family, told her: "Most of the goats have been killed, but the mare is over there. Take them." Thus, a family that had been plundered of most of its belongings returned to Espiel with the few animals they had left.

This was not a case of an occasional excess nor an individual's fit of madness by a Francoist officer, but yet another example of the fact that Francoism consisted precisely of excesses, arbitrary actions and unlimited cruelty. With the onset of the military coup, bloodthirsty individuals popped up like mushrooms all over the country, like the policeman called Naranjo, one of Pepinillo's more diligent assistants. Under his orders, women's heads were shaved, they were stripped naked and forced to drink castor oil and everyone was terrorized. One day, the travelling puppeteer arrived in the town with his goat but he did not know how to play *Cara al Sol*. Pepinillo had him arrested and beaten until he learnt how to play the tune and then made him spend an entire day playing the fascist hymn throughout the town.

In **Fuenteobejuna**, Jesús Franje Carlos, a young working man of whom nothing else is known, was summarily executed by firing squad February 9.

In **Hinojosa del Duque**, two men were executed in Summer, perhaps in relation to robberies on farms, supposedly by suicide, possibly due to torture. A man whose name is unknown is recorded as having died supposedly by hanging in the Guardia Civil barracks, June 22. Likewise, July 2, the cause of another unknown prisoner's death is recorded as having 'wounded himself'.

In **Hornachuelos**, 4 victims were summarily executed in 1941: Julio Ramos, February 13; Antonio Sevilla and Francisco Moyano, February 17; and José Castaño, August 6. There is no record of any trial.

In **Villaviciosa**, Francisco Martínez Aguilera is officially presumed as having committed 'suicide by hanging' in the municipal jail, August 10. Even if this were a true case of suicide, the disproportionately high number of suicides in the prisons is, on its own, an indication of Francoist methods and criminality.

In **Santa Eufemia** prison, July 13, another peculiar cause of death in the jail, officially due to 'alcoholic coma' (were alcoholic drinks available in jail?) Moreno Gómez' informants in the town, however, assured him that he died from a beating.

Lastly, a complicated case in **Torrecampo** where another 2nd Lieutenant posted to this town was busy doing his own thing. The evening of July 31, two men who had been arrested were being viciously beaten. When the tormentors broke one of Florencio Rísquez Andújar's arms he exploded like a caged wild animal, attacked the Lieutenant and ran out of the jail. As one might expect, he was caught in the Torrecampo main square where he was shot and killed. The Lieutenant also ordered the execution of another prisoner, Sebastián Pastor Romero, who had also attempted to escape from the jail but was hit on the head with a stone and brought back, where he was sitting quietly in his cell. Sebastián's wife was also beaten on the Lieutenant's orders. All this occurred in the evening of 31 July.

It appears that in all the above cases, this was related to presumed contacts between these men had with those who had fled to the hills. Men working in the fields were continuously subject to raid after raid and tempestuous beatings, always because of malicious allegations. As the post-war period progressed, the climate of terror spread from the urban centre to the rural world as official interest in repressive activities acquired a new impetus. By 1941, the New State was no longer centring its attention on the wartime causes of anti-Francoist activities but on all sources of post-war clandestine and reorganizational political activities, including support of the populace to fugitives. The punishments the authorities meted were terrible indeed.

Causa General raids

The *Causa General de la Guerra Civil Española, la dominación roja en España* (Causa General of the Spanish Civil War, the Red rule over Spain), was a procedure instituted by <u>Supreme Court Decree April 26 1940</u>, retroactive to April 1 1939, endowing Franco's Miinistry of 'Justice' with the means to investigate and punish the nature and extent of the "criminal activities of the subversive elements who openly opposed the existence of the essential values of the Fatherland that were saved, at the last moment, by the Liberating Movement".

The Causa General was essentially an archive containing evidence with which Francoism could prosecute any remaining Republicans and all it considered disaffected, for crimes against Spain. Public prosecutors were sent into the provinces to collect documents and compile witness statements, although legal standards of proof were not always observed. The more than 1500 files that were complied, were used to complement the military and political repression and as a justification for swooping down on towns and villages to collect prisoners and later, as evidence, for the trials that were organized in the provinces before 1943-5.[19] This triggered thousands of raids and arrests throughout the country and thousands of summary proceedings that ended up in thousands of executions. *Vide* APPENDIX IV

One particularly scandalous trial, or *processo*, the *Processo de La Parrala* or *de la Centena* – the Parrala or de la Centena Trial - Causa General Case 1,546/41, was the outcome of the great November 21 raid in several towns and villages in Cordoba province, especially in Villanueva de Cordoba, with ramifications in Jaén and Seville, after which over a hundred were arrested.

The cause of the November raid was the activities of an extensive network that had been created by wives and relatives to help the prisoners who had been taken to Cordoba Provincial Prison and who were dying by the dozens from hunger and starvation, prison extermination practices typical of the Nazi regimes. Despite the support to the organization to provide assistance for the imprisoned and which, under Victoria Fernández, undoubtedly saved many lives, more than 500 inmates died in 1941 alone (a total 756 died during the entire decade). During the post-war period, more men died in the Capital from hunger and other causes than by firing squads. *Vide* APPENDIX V.

Moreno Gómez obtained a great many witness accounts of this raid in the early 1980s. In the Vallecas neighbourhood of Madrid, he interviewed one of the accused, Isabel *La Chata* Gutiérrez Romero, from Villanueva. He interviewed María *La Loba* in Villanueva de Cordoba and then went to Puertollano, the home town of another of the Villanueva accused, Juan Reyes Gómes (brother-in-law to La Moejea of the maquis), who gave him many more details.

Isabel – La Chata, Maria Muñoz – La Loba, and other women who were prominent members of the local PCE, were already targeted because they fled to the mountains in the first days of the Nationalist victory. They had gone to the La Garganta area but they only stayed away for fifteen days before returning home because they found that kind of life unbearable. Upon their arrival, they were picked up by the authorities, soundly beaten and subjected to the castor oil and shaven head treatment, and labelled 'the Mayor's whores'. As Rojas, their names were on a list. This brings us to 1941 and the scandalous high mortality from starvation of the prisoners in Cordoba. Many of the aforementioned Rojas, as well as Victoria Fernández (Adriano Romero's wife) and his sisters Dolores and Isabel, began to gather food to try and save their lives.

Victoria Fernández was the first one arrested 21 November and with this, the link to Seville and Villanueva de Cordoba was established. The Jaén connection was established through José Lupiáñez from Jaén, who was already imprisoned with Adriado Romero in Cordoba.

The raid began in Villanueva de Cordoba November 21 with the arrest of Maria – *La Loba*, Isabel – *La Chata*, and several other women, as well as quite a few men: Juan Reyes Gómez, Miguel *El de la Fragua* Cabrera, José Vioque García, Juan Capitán Gutiérrez, Román – *El Carbonero*, Diego García *El Mosico* García Cachinero, Manuel *Mazo* Torralbo Cantador, the schoolmaster, and several others.

Under Francoism, arrests were not simple conventional judiciary procedures but the first step for terrible beatings. First came the beatings and the rest would follow. In this case, under the orders of a rabid Guardia Civil Captain, all the arrested were subjected to torture, beatings and humiliations in the Fuente Vieja Schools improvised jail. Juan Reyes testified that he was cruelly beaten on the grounds that he was a 'communist accomplice of those who had fled to the mountains'. Manuel Mazo, the schoolmaster, was accused of being a 'Communist leader'. The women were not beaten.

All these charges were idiotic as the only thing that brought them together was a simple organization to help the Cordoba prisoners. Victoria Fernández and Dolores Romero (Adriano Romero's wife and sister, respectively) were imprisoned in Cordoba; Rosa Alcaraz was imprisoned in Jaén and several Sevillians, José Muñoz, Faustino Garcia Marin, Salvador Galiana Serra, Antonia and Carmen Navarro, Rosarito Navarro and others in addition to José Merino Campos from Seville, were captured in Cordoba.

A few days later, the hundred prisoners who had been caught in the raid were tied two by two and taken to the railway station and from there to Cordoba capital prison, and then on to Seville where they spent a year in prison awaiting trial. Cause 1,546/41 was tried in Seville by a Council of War presided by Judge Carlos Ollero y Sierra. Considering that the charges were inconsistent: assistance to rebellion, plotting, clandestine reorganization of the Communist Party, etc. he avoided handing out any death sentences. By October 1942, many of the accused were out on parole, with all that this implied: daily checking in at the local barracks and regular doses of 'syrup of the rod'. Some, such as schoolmaster Manuel Mazo Cantador and Juan Reyes, although allowed out on parole, were not formally tried until October 20 1945, when they received a light sentence already served with their first year in prison. Mazo, the schoolmaster, was re-arrested in June 1948 and killed under the Law of Fugitives.

These raids, based on Causa General information and carried out without any pretext, served from the onset to keep the disaffected with Francoism on their toes and make their daily lives unbearable. After many raids, the military authorities didn't even bother with arrests or any legal procedures, they just held the persons they caught as prisoners of the local government. Even when there was a semblance of due process, the result was the e: several months in jail, the children abandoned, jobs lost or work remained undone and fields untended. The purpose: do not let the disaffected rest and make it clear who were the bosses in Spain and who held the upper hand. This was so characteristic of Spain during the 1940s, that the jails became a kind of unholy social meeting place for supporters of the Left, as when some left, others arrived. All were tortured and beaten to one extent or another.

These comings and goings went on for an entire decade, with another aggravating factor: all those who were released, were released on parole, that is, under vigilance. What did this mean? That every afternoon they had to present themselves at the doors of the barracks and have their names checked off a list, a humiliating ceremony. Every day, some were lectured and others were taken into the barracks to be 'warmed up'. As a result, quite a few fled to the hills. The famous guerrilla Juanin, from Cantabria, fled to the mountains because of the daily beating he received in his home town. All this extreme behaviour is ignored by Julius Ruiz and the deniers who are still determined to believe that the repression consisted only of shooting a handful of disaffected criminals. They have no idea or still choose to ignore what was going on in the depths of the country, where exclusion, hunger, beatings, humiliations, constant persecution, slave labour, blacklists, castor oil, shavings, and all sorts of abuse were the order of the day.

Generally speaking, most people today have very little idea of just how chancy life was for the defeated during the first years of the 1940s, of the relentless persecution of fugitives in most of the Spanish provinces as a pretext for stoking the fire of terror, not only in the mountains but also in the countryside, in the rural world. Just reading the list of individuals executed does not tell us anything of this or of the multitude of raids that were launched for the most banal reasons. The following witness account of one of those who was caught in such a raid, Juan Gutiérrez Romero, a native of Villanueva de Cordoba but resident in Villafranca, is witness to this:

"In November of the same year [1939], I was arrested for the first time, after the maquis' attack on Pozoblanco. We were accused by Blas *El Sillonero* Carbonero and held in Villanueva jail until September 1940 we were taken to prison in Cordoba, together with all the other prisoners in the province. One year later, the accusation was cancelled and we were allowed to return to Villanueva. January 1942, I was free but on parole. I could not go far out of town because every evening I had to present myself at the barracks to mark my presence.

At the beginning of 1943, several men from Villanueva maquis (Diego – El Chato and others) went to the mountains to join Julián's maquis in Las Umbrias... A few days later, all the farmworkers from the region were ordered to Torrico farm in la Loma del Caballero and they kept us all under arrest for three months, first in Montoro and later in Cordoba capital. I was lucky and they did not discover my contacts with Julián.

December 1944, I was arrested for the third time. They caught Isidoro – El Lobo and because of that they caught me also. I was taken to the Villanueva Mobile Headquarters in the Fuente Vieja Schools jail where I was beaten then released.

At the beginning of 1945 I was again taken and made to take part in a raid looking for Rojos. By then, other friends had also been released from prison by then, such as Pablo Agenjo and Diego El Mosico. The latter was made to go along several raids with me. A sergeant told us: "In war, when you catch a confident, you liquidate him, and we are at war."[20]

Another example from the 1941 year of terror occurred in the Fall of that year, when November 25 a mixed patrol of Guardias Civiles and Falangists, under the orders of 2nd Lt. Eduardo Solar, was carrying out a routine inspection in the countryside. The patrol was searching to the left the Villanueva-Adamuz road, when the Lieutenant walked off towards some shrubs where a group of Julián Caballero's guerrillas were hiding. The guerrillas had no choice but to shoot the Lieutenant on the spot and to run for their lives. The next day, the Falangist Diego El Chunga and his usual group of Falangist civilians and soldiers rounded up all the farmworkers in the region and took them under arrest. They beat a family they nicknamed 'Los Quemados' to death. The system was always the same and repeated itself constantly: incident in the mountains > general raid and roundup of farmworkers > beatings all round.

The 21 Roses of Cordoba during the post-war period

Francoists exterminated 21 women in Cordoba province during the post-war period. Many more fell during the war, especially in 1936, both in the capital and the province. Table 1 gives the names of these *21 Roses*, divided into three groups: those who were summarily executed during the first two post-war years, those who were killed in the fight against the guerrillas, and those who were shot under the Law of Fugitives in the countryside.

The designation '21 Roses' is applied here as an honour and as being similar to the case of the *13 Roses of Madrid*, is the name given to a group of thirteen young women who were summarily executed in Madrid just after the conclusion of the civil war. Their execution was part of a massive execution campaign known as the *"saca de agosto"*, which included 43 young men, among them a fourteen-year-old.

Table 1. The 21 *Roses of Cordoba.*
Women executed in the province after the end of the war

Location	Name	Date
Shot by firing squad during 1939 and 1940		
Belalcázer	Carmen Rubio Cáceres, age 32	06-08-1939
	Matilde Medina Pizarro, age 50	20-08-1939
Belmez	Leonor Expósito Palomo, age 38	09-05-1940
Hinojosa	Carmen Aranda Caballero, age 47	14-08- 1939
Montoro	Patrocinio Juárez Pareja, age 39	20-09-1940
Pedro Abad	Josefa Ortega Egea, age 37	03.10.1940
Peñarroya	Martina Alcántara, age 53	11-12-1939
	Dionisia Alcántara Calvo, age 60*	16-12-1939
Pozoblanco	Tomasa Díaz Moreno, age 21	28-10-1939
Killed while fighting with the guerrillas		
Fuenteobejuna	Isidora Merino Merino,,	27-02-1947
Belalcázar	from Esparragosa	
	Soledad Moreno García,	02-06-1947
Villaviciosa	from Guadalmez	"
	Luisa Lira Montero,	11-06-1947
El Viso	from La Granja	
	Maria Josefa López Garrido, from	05-03-1948
	Villanueva de Cordoba	
	Sergia Flores Sanz, in Ciudad Real	
Assasinated under the Law of Fugitives in the countryside		
Fuente Tójar	Josefa Briones Molina, age 58	27-12-1946
Villanueva de	Catalina Coleto Muñoz, age 52	08-06-1948
Cordoba	Amelia Rodríguez López, age 49	10-09-1948
Pozoblanco	Amelia García Rodríguez, age 18	"
	Isabel Tejada López, age 60	"
Cardeña	Brígida Muñoz Días, age 60, from	14-09-1948
Belmez	Obejo	27-02-1949
	Teresa Molina Sánchez, age 26, from Espiel	
TOTAL: 21 women murdered after the end of the war		

*Not shot. Recorded as having collapsed and died, probably after being tortured.

TABLE 2. ESTIMATED BALANCE OF VICTIMS OF FRANCOIST REPRESSION IN CÓRDOBA PROVINCE AND CAPITAL

LOCATION	EXECUTED BY FIRING SQUAD TOWNSHIPS		EXECUTED BY FIRING SQUAD CAPITAL		NAZI CAMPS	CÓRDOBA PRISON 1939-1946	LAW OF FUGITIVES 1939-1950	MAQUIS KILLED	TOTALS	TOTAL CÓRDOBA CAPITAL	WARTIME RIGHT-WING VICTIMS
	WARTIME	POST-WAR	WARTIME	POST-WAR							
	1	2	3	4	5	6	7	8	9	10	11
ADAMUZ		3	(5)	(29)	0	22	6	10	41	(+34)	61 (+48)
AGUILAR	140	1	(16)	(3)	2	2			145	(+19)	0
ALCARACEJOS		1	(2)	(11)	4	4	1		10	(+13)	36
ALMEDINILLA	20		(0)	(0)	0	1			21	(+0)	1
ALMODOVAR DEL RÍO	30	6	(9)	(8)	2	5		1	44	(+17)	14
AÑORA			(1)	(1)	3	3	3	2		(+2)	30
BAENA	700	32	(6)	(8)	14	13	1		760	(+14)	110
BELALCAZAR	1	30	(1)	(18)	2	9	6	23	71	(+19)	170
BELMEZ	40	36	(25)	(6)	8	16	2	3	105	(+31)	41
BENAMEJÍ	45		(10)	(1)	1	0			46	(+11)	0
LOS BLAZQUEZ	16		(0)	(0)	0	2			18	(+0)	0
BUJALANCE	3	55	(15)	(13)	3	13	3	22	99	(+28)	112
CABRA	100		(7)	(1)	1	7	1		109	(+8)	0
CAÑETE DE LAS TORRES		3	(6)	(4)	1	4			8	(+10)	25
CARCABUEY	20		(2)	(0)	1	2			23	(+2)	0
CARDEÑA	3	5	(0)	(0)	0	6	1	4	19	(+0)	4
LA CARLOTA	110		(17)	(2)	2	4		1	117	(+19)	0
EL CARPIO	3		(8)	(6)	3	2			8	(+14)	25
CASTRO DEL RÍO	40	167	(16)	(18)	6	7			220	(+34)	79
CONQUISTA		1	(0)	(0)	0	1	1		3	(+0)	0
CÓRDOBA CAPITAL			4,000	584	15	26	2	2	4,629		1
DOÑA MENCÍA	20		(15)	(1)	1	4			25	(+16)	0
LOCATION	EXECUTED BY FIRING SQUAD										

111

	TOWNSHIPS		CAPITAL		NAZI CAMPS	CÓRDOBA PRISON	LAW OF FUGITIVES	MAQUIS	TOTALS	TOTAL CÓRDOBA CAPITAL	WARTIME RIGHT-WING VICTIMS
	WARTIME	POST-WAR	WARTIME	POST-WAR		1939-1946	1939-1950	KILLED			
	1	2	3	4	5	6	7	8	9	10	11
DOS TORRES		6	(3)	(8)	1	13	7	3	30	(+11)	78
ENCINAS REALES	10		(0)	(0)	0	0			10	(+0)	0
ESPEJO	80	6	(9)	(7)	6	2			94	(+16)	64
ESPIEL	?	16	(3)	(11)	2	9	5	1	33	(+14)	23
FERNÁN NÚÑEZ	150	4	(13)	(0)	1	5			160	(+13)	11
FUENTE LA LANCHA			(0)	(3)	0	3		2	5	(+3)	0
FUENTEOBEJUNA	400	40	(5)	(5)	14	19	8	10	491	(+10)	57
FUENTE PALMERA	15		(2)	(4)	7	6			28	(+6)	0
FUENTE TOJAR	10		(1)	(0)	0	2	4	4	20	(+1)	2
LA GRANJUELA	10		(8)	(0)	2	5		1	18	(+8)	14
GUADALCÁZAR	?		(4)	(1)	0	0			0	(+5)	0
EL GUIJO			(0)	(0)	0	2	2		4	(+0)	0
HINOJOSA DEL DUQUE	16	67	(3)	(20)	8	23	9	31	154	(+23)	124 (+34)
HORNACHUELOS	40	8	(11)	(19)	7	2	4	1	62	(+30)	18
IZNÁJAR	80		(3)	(3)	1	3			84	(+6)	0
LUCENA	127		(12)	(1)	2	5			134	(+13)	0
LUQUE	31		(12)	(4)	3	5			39	(+16)	13
MANTALBÁN	17	1	(2)	(0)	1	0			19	(+2)	0
MONTEMAYOR	25		(6)	(0)	2	0			27	(+6)	0
MONTILLA	200	22	(8)	(2)	7	7	1		237	(+10)	10 (+1)
MONTORO	40	21	(16)	(40)	7	25	2	5	100	(+56)	118
MONTURQUE	15		(1)	(0)	0	1			16	(+1)	0
MORILES	10		(1)	(0)	0	1			11	(+1)	0
NUEVA CARTEYA	70		(10)	(0)	1	1			72	(+10)	0
OBEJO	?		(2)	(7)	1	2	6	2	11	(+9)	0

LOCATION	EXECUTED BY FIRING SQUAD				NAZI CAMPS	CORDOBA PRISON 1939-1946	LAW OF FUGITIVES 1939-1950	MAQUIS KILLED	TOTALS	TOTAL CORDOBA CAPITAL	WARTIME RIGHT-WING VICTIMS
	TOWNSHIPS		CAPITAL								
	WARTIME	POST-WAR	WARTIME	POST-WAR							
	1	2	3	4	5	6	7	8	9	10	11
PALENCIANA	20		(4)	(0)	0	2			22	(+4)	11
PALMA DEL RÍO	300	40	(10)	(22)	14	7			361	(+32)	0
PEDRO ABAD	20	40	(11)	(11)	3	6	1		70	(+22)	42
PEDROCHE			(3)	(11)	0	11	1	1	13	(+14)	26
PEÑARROYA-PUEBLONUEVO	40	88	(11)	(4)	10	24	1	5	168	(+15)	69 (+3 0)
POSADAS	20	19	(16)	(24)	17	12			68	(+40)	20
POZOBLANCO	1	209	(10)	(10)	11	8	25	7	261	(+20)	77
PRIEGO	80	2	(4)	(1)	0	8			90	(+5)	55 (+1 26)
PUENTE GENIL	900	29	(32)	(17)	5	10			944	(+49)	0
LA RAMBLA	60		(2)	(6)	8	0			68	(+8)	115
RUTE	55		(2)	(11)	2	3	4	2	66	(+13)	8
S. SEBASTIÁN DE LOS B.	23		(2)	(0)	0	0			23	(+2)	0
SANTAELLA	36		(1)	(0)	1	0			37	(+1)	0
SANTA EUFENIA		21	(1)	(6)	0	6		5	32	(+7)	0
TORRECAMPO		3	(0)	(4)	3	8	2		16	(+4)	37
VALENZUELA	25		(1)	(11)	1	9			35	(+12)	33
VALSEQUILLO			(0)	(0)	0	3	1		4	(+0)	19
LA VICTORIA	?		(6)	(0)	1	2			3	(+6)	0
VILLA DEL RÍO	75		(3)	(28)	3	8			86	(+31)	30
VILLAFRANCA	51	8	(9)	(11)	1	2	5	2	69	(+20)	13
VILLAHARTA	60		(4)	(1)	9	2	1	1	73	(+5)	32

LOCATION	EXECUTED BY FIRING SQUAD — TOWNSHIPS WARTIME (1)	TOWNSHIPS POST-WAR (2)	CAPITAL WARTIME (3)	CAPITAL POST-WAR (4)	NAZI CAMPS (5)	CÓRDOBA PRISON 1939-1946 (6)	LAW OF FUGITIVES 1939-1950 (7)	MAQUIS KILLED (8)	TOTALS (9)	TOTAL CÓRDOBA CAPITAL (10)	WARTIME RIGHT-WING VICTIMS (11)
VILLAFRANCA	51	8	(9)	(11)	1	2	5	2	69	(+20)	11
VILLAHARTA	60		(4)	(1)	9	2	1	1	73	(+5)	13
VILLANUEVA DE CÓRDOBA		102	(2)	(35)	4	23	22	20	171	(+37)	32
VILLANUEVA DEL DUQUE	?		(1)	(4)	2	7	2	3	14	(+5)	98
VILLANUEVA DEL REY	15		(2)	(5)	1	14	7	3	40	(+7)	4
VILLARALTO	4	1	(0)	(20)	1	7	4	2	19	(+20)	12
VILLAVICIOSA	40	3	(13)	(13)	6	22	4	24	99	(+26)	32
EL VISO		6	(1)	(3)	0	10	4	7	23	(+4)	33
ZUHEROS	10		(2)	(0)	1	0			11	(+2)	33
Elsewhere in Spain 1947-1950						150	6	51	207		0
POST-WAR						98			98		78
VILLAFRANCA	51	8	(9)	(11)	1	2	5	2	69	(+20)	13
VILLAHARTA	60		(4)	(1)	9	2	1	1	73	(+5)	32
TOTALS	4,472	1,102	4,000	584	246	756	160	262	11,582	4,629	2,107 (+239)

Column 1: Victims of the Francoist repression in the towns and villages of Cordoba province during the war (4,472 executed by firing squad).

Column 2: Victims of the Francoist repression in the towns and villages of Cordoba province during the post-war (1,102 executed by firing squad). Some towns are left blank or with few victims; this may be due to the fact that the executions were carried in larger neighbouring towns, in party headquarters elsewhere or there is no available data.

114

Columns 3 and 4: These figures are in brackets because they are not computed in the totals as they are included in the data for Cordoba capital. They serve solely to indicate the number of residents of towns and villages executed in Cordoba capital. These total 4,000 shot during the war and 584 during the post-war.

Column 5: Cordovans who died in Nazi concentration camps (246).

Column 6: Inmates who were starved to death or who died from the sub-human conditions in the Provincial Prison in Cordoba capital. The victims are listed by towns until 1946. From 1947-1950 accounted for jointly (98 victims). Total number exterminated in this fashion for the decade 756.

Column 7: Victims of the Law of Fugitives from 1941-1950, as a result of summary executions, on suspicion of collaborating with the guerrillas, because related to someone who had fled to the hills, os simply to extend the terror (160 assasinated in this manner).

Column 8: Estimated number of maquis shot by the Guardia Civil in the Cordoba mountains (262 victims).

Columns 9 and 10: Estimated number of republicans killed by the Francoist genocide in Cordoba province: total: 11,582 victims. By locality: in Cordoba capital: 4,629 victims; in towns and villages, 6,953 victims.

Columna 11: Right-wing victims, by location: General total 2,107 victims (2,029 during the war and 78 in the post-war) 239 victims are given in brackets as they were not killed in Cordoba province but elsewhere in Spain, especially in Valencia through the actions of the People's Court.

Note: Until the Spanish government offers free access to all sorts of registers and archives to confirm the exact number of arrested, dead, etc, historians will only be able to present incomplete figures.

Firing squad executions in Cordoba capital

"Everything that is told here is true, because I believe that it will be
useful for History, and I like it when History tells the truth."
Rosario La Dinamitera, in *Tomasa Cuevas*, Barcelona, 2004.

"The day that one truly knows the history of the repression in these
villages of Toledo, Extremadura, in all of Spain, there will be
those who believe that it is not possible that so much happened,
and that human beings, because we have to call them something, were
capable of taking their sadism and their hatred to such tremendous extremes."
Carmen Machado, in *Tomasa Cuevas*, Barcelona, 2004

The genocide in Cordoba capital was shocking. During the war, Francoism ended the life of 4,000 persons in the capital, not all of them from that city but also from many towns and villages in the province, who were taken to Cordoba to be shot, together prisoners whom they captured on the Los Pedroches front lines and members of the international brigade they captured on the Lopera-Porcuna front.

The terror was supervised by Commander Zurdo and the bloodbath was at the hands of Lt. Colonel Bruno Ibáñez, both of the Guardia Civil, and other bloodthirsty repressors who emptied Cordoba of Republicans.[21] Rafael Castejón y Martínez de Arizala, past-President of the Real Academia of Cordoba, assured Moreno Gómez during an interview July 13 1983, that, according to Spanish Red Cross archives, the number of victims in Cordoba capital during the war totalled 7,770. In Moreno Gómez' opinion, this number is excessive but there are no means by which we can confirm or correct it.

To make matters more difficult, the current Director of the Spanish Red Cross in Madrid, Carmen Flórez Pérez, refuses to allow historians access to the archives. As Moreno Gómez already had reliable confirmation that up to the middle of 1938, 3,495 prisoners had already been executed in Cordoba capital, he wished to further his research at the Red Cross. Ms. Flórez Pérez denied him access on the grounds that: "We are subject to Law 15/1999, Data Protection Law, and consequently, personal data will only and exclusively be made available to the interested parties themselves and/or their relatives".[22] It was quite clear: the freedom to do historical research in Spanish archives still shines by its absence. The right to privacy after death, over the rights of historical science.

1939

The list of victims executed in San Rafael and the La Salud cemetery in Cordoba capital during the post-war period, was again outrageous. Executions by firing squad began anew in Cordoba capital with the onset of the courts martial. At first, there were few sacas, mostly involving people from outside the province – from Jaén, Málaga, and Badajoz. Basically, the Regime was liquidating the last groups of prisoners taken during the war.

November 8

The largest saca that year, with 11 victims, among whom Ricardo Rubio Calero, aged 27, son of El Calor, a well-known elderly socialist from Pozoblanco. The young man was a prisoner of war who had been captured in Vinaroz , Castellón, in 1938. There were two major strikes against him: on the one hand, he was the son of a time-honoured Socialist leader; whilst on the other hand, he had served as a political commissar in the Army. Although some attributes and occupations were immediately fatal in the great Francoist cleansing operation, the executioners usually looked for additional, albeit false, specific accusations with which to advance ulterior motives. more specific accusations, whether these could be legally proven or not. Accordingly, Ricardo Rubio was also accused of having belonged to the local War Committee, a totally false charge, but the reality was that the Regime had decided that all of El Calor's family had to be exterminated. Several other prisoners executed in the same saca were from Puente Genil, the Cordoba town that, after the capital, sacrificed the greatest number of individuals.

December 6

Six more men were led to their death, a few more from Puente Genil, among them one of the heavy-weights of Cordovan Socialism, Justo Deza Montero. Actually, he belonged to the Young Socialists and as a member of the War Committee, was one of the angry townspeople who rose against the military coup in Puente Genil and managed to thrash the equally furious local Fascists. Indeed, the Republicans enjoyed a brief victory when August 1 they repealed an attack by General Castejón's Legionnaires who in this town, later perpetrated one of the largest acts of genocide in Spain. During the war Justo lived in Pozoblanco where presided over one of the Community Councils. It is no surprise that there was a price on his head. He is reported to have faced death valiantly, shouting: "Compañeros, you have to revenge so much bloodshed!"

1940

At the beginning of 1940, the Regime began executing a certain number of professional soldiers, members of the Republican Army. In Cordoba, the professional soldiers were executed in a killing field of their own, the Polígono de Casillas. Considered by Franco as war criminals, in their dossiers they are only described with the rank they held before July 18, not the rank they rose to in the Republican army during the war. First, however, the officers were stripped of their highest rank in the Republican army and reduced to the rank they held before 18 July.[xiv]

January 17

Two high-ranking Republican soldiers, prisoners of a defeated army and therefore subject to the Geneva Convention which Franco always ignored, were executed on this date, thus marking the beginning of a new series of war crimes at the hands of the Regime. Executed were: Lieutenant Colonel [*Artillery Commander*] Narciso Sánchez Aparicio, 50 years old, in reality a Lt. Colonel and member of the Central Army Chiefs of Staff, and at the end of the war, Head of the Chiefs of Staff of the XVII Army Group and then of the XXIII Army Group. Executed with him: Artillery Commander [*Lieutenant*] Esteban Rodríguez Domingo, from Valencia, Captain in 1936 and Comandante in 1938.

January 27

Two more Republican soldiers executed in the Polígono de Casillas. [*Captain*] José Bueno Quejo, a valiant Basque, who defended the Republic in the North of Spain. He commanded the 2nd Division of the Santander Army Group, where he rose to the rank of Comandante. When the North fell, he went to France and from there returned to the Centre of Spain to defend the legal government. At the end of the war, José Bueno was Head of the Chiefs of Staff of the 22nd Division of the Army of Andalucia. Defeated and taken prisoner, he was denied his rights under the Geneva Convention and was executed. Furthermore, also charged under the Law of Political Responsibilities, he was fined 5,000 pesetas that his family had to pay. Executed next to him, [*Lieutenant*] Luis Soler Espianba, from Cartagena, who although he had retired from the army in 1936, when war broke out, re-enlisted to defend the Republic. He rose to the rank of Captain, then to

---

[xiv] In the following descriptions, the officers are honoured with the ranks they lawfully rose to during the war; the ranks they were reduced to by the Francoists is given in italics and in brackets.

Comandante (1938) and he fought in the Granada sector. He ended the war in the 54th Battalion of the 23rd Division of the XXII Army of Andalucia.

February

That February, they executed a great loyal soldier, Lieutenant Roberto Garcia Domenech, who had come to Cordoba in 1936 with the Alcoy Unit, commanded by Colonel Giralf. When this unit was divided into two sections (one to Cerro Muriano and another to Espejo), Lieutenant Garcia was sent to Espejo where September 23-25 1936 he fought with great valour under Colonel Jesús Perez Salas.

March 18

The wholesale killing of civilians in 1940 Cordoba capital began March 18, in this case with a saca of 19 victims from several towns in Cordoba province - Hornachuelos, Villa del Rio, Obejo, Almodóvar and more. Among the executed: Gonzalo Obrero Duque, a notable local trade union leader, was from Villafranca. Francisco Haro Manzano, belonged to a family from Bujalance that was all but exterminated – 4 brothers were executed and another one spent many years in prison in Puerto Santa Maria. Only one sister survived[xv]. The workers' movement in Bujalance was wiped from the map as the last activists, the Jubiles brothers, died as guerrillas in the mountains.

Spring

April 5

April 5, 6 Republican military prisoners of war, were executed: [*Lieutenant*] Lorenzo Almaraz de Pedro, had fled from Badajoz to Portugal in 1936 and was one of the passengers on the ship *Nyassa* to Tarragona where he re-joined the Army. Promoted to Captain, he fought in Catalonia, then in the XXII Army Corps, in the Army Group of Levante, in 1938, when he was taken prisoner; [*Lieutenant*] Damián Contreras began in the Jaén Volunteer Battalion. October 1936, promoted to Captain, he commanded the 148 MB of the 37th Division of the VII Army of Extremadura. He was promoted to

---

[xv] Moreno Gómez recently discovered that a nephew of the Haro Manzanos lived near him, in Getafe (Madrid). "I would have liked to hear what he had to say about these events, but I never did because every time I brought the subject up, he burst into tears. This is why I repeat that Francoism represented a river of blood for the dead and a river of tears for the living. Still, these features are ignored by all those who neither investigate or show any interest in the victims and their families."

Comandante June 1938; [*2nd Lieutenant*] Felipe Gallardo Linares, retired as 2nd Lieutenant early in 1936, re-enlisted and rose to the rank of Lieutenant, then Captain and in 1938, Comandante, always with the Army of Andalusia. [*Lieutenant*] Eugenio Muñoz Hoyuela, a *Guarda de Assalto*[xvi] who was posted to Linares in 1936. He has been described as very active during the entire agitated Summer 1936, especially in the creation of the Jaén Militia where he became famous as the soul of the resistance to the coup in the entire Upper Guadalquivir River region. He was promoted Captain in October 1936 and Comandante in 1938 when he was posted to the Army of the Centre. [*Artillery 2nd Lieutenant*] Antonio Fernández Sánchez was always posted in Cartagena. He was promoted to Lieutenant in October 1936 and Captain in March 1938; last, [*Captain*] Enrique Medina Vega, who retired in 1936 but re-enlisted to defend the Republic, rose to the rank of Comandante and served with a Machine Gun Unit in Almería until the end of the war.

April 8

Another huge saca April 8 of 24 victims. We know little or nothing about these men other than their names. There were quite a few from Villa del Río, Hornachuelos, Adamuz, Villafranca and some other provincial towns. Although there is no information regarding their professions, the men themselves, nor their lives, at least their names have been recorded for History.

April 20

Civilian executions in Cordoba were usually held in the City Prison but April 20, some unknown reason, 5 men were executed in the Provincial Prison: 3 from Posadas, one from Villa del Río and another from Adamuz.

June 4

16 executed, several from Palma del Río, Hornachuelos, Posadas, Espiel and other towns. This month there was a saca practically every day.

June 6

17 executed. The sacas were getting larger and larger and the panic in the jails was terrible. The men shuffled off to their deaths like robots, resigned to their fate, at the same time that Francoists were shooting their countrymen extra-legally in all the towns and capitals of Spain, namely in Villa del Río, Montoro, Espiel, Villafranca. This was the great cleansing of Spain, to the rhythm of rural and Catholic Fascism.

[xvi] An elite army corps, similar to a Praetorian Guard.

14 men from Palma del Río, Montoro, Villa del Río and other Cordoba towns executed. Included in this saca, Rafael Polonio Delgado, a native of Montilla, resident in Palma del Río. He belonged to the JSU where he was very active, as were his brothers. His brother Francisco, also imprisoned in Cordoba, had come from a French concentration camp. He was permitted to accompany Rafael in the chapel to say farewell. A third brother, Antonio, had already given his life for the Republic on the Peñarroya front.

22 June

18 executed. The most notable individual in that saca was Paco Dios, Francisco Dios Muñoz. "El Capitán Paco" as he was known, was a young bricklayer from Villafranca, the heart and soul of the Villafranca Battalion and later of the 74 MB and another great fighter of that irreplaceable generation of the 1930s. At the beginning of 1980, Moreno Gómez interviewed his brother Juan, in Cordoba, who wold him of the valiant end of his brother, as referred to earlier. Capitán Paco encouraged his companions at all times and when facing the firing squad, behaved like a hero: he asked permission to say a few words and that was granted. Paco spoke with such inspiration and high ideals that all present were amazed, including the executioners and the chaplain. Pedro Garfias dedicated a poem to this great man from Villafranca in his book *Héroes del Sur*[23] and he truly was such a hero. Joe Monks, a member of the international brigade, also mentions him in his book *Con los rojos en Andalucía*[24] Today in Villafranca, despite the fact that since the war all the Mayors have been socialists or communists, there is nothing to celebrate the memory of this exemplary leader, not a street, or any kind of commemorative plaque named after him, or after Comandante Castillo, nor the great poet Pedro Garfias who sang of Villafranca and died in exile in Mexico. It would appear that all these politicians are latter-day accomplices of those who preach the historic amnesia.

Summer-Fall 1940

July 20

6 executed, almost all from Montoro.

September 2

11 executed, many from Villaviciosa, among them a local trade union leader, Tomás de la Torre Barbero.

September 20

7 executed.

September 30

6 executed

November 12

Execution of Juan *El Gato Negro* Rojas Arenas, an anarchist from Pedro Abad. He had belonged to the War Committee and was a great fighter. Imprisoned in San Miguel de los Reyes, Valencia, for his participation in the revolutionary strike in Bujalance in December 1933, he was released after the Frente Popular elections.[25] He was co-founder of the *Nueva Aurora* workers' association. The Prosecutor asked for 10 executions by garrotte. His brother Antonio had been executed in Pedro Abad the previous year.

December 18

4 executed.

December 20

3 from Santiago de Calatrava, Jaén, executed.

December 27

Francoism celebrated the end of the year with bloody fireworks of 34 executions, the largest saca so far in post-war Cordoba capital. Many were from Montoro, Belalcázar, El Carpio, Puente Genil, Alcaracejos, Castro del Rio and other towns. In other words, a sampling of the entire province.

1941

January 31

1941 began with a great saca of 25 victims, 31 January, mostly men from Los Pedroches district: 6 from Belalcázar, 7 from Hinojosa, 4 from Villaralto, 2 from Fuenteobejuna and other towns. The most notable prisoner in the saca was Félix Chaves Caballero, past Socialist Mayor of Fuente La Lancha. From Belalcázar they took the elderly socialist Antonio *El Sabio* Vigara Regidor, a peaceful, venerable man, a typical nineteenth century individual and past

President of the *Casa del Pueblo*. He had lived in hiding for a year until he was discovered by Fernando Ballester, a municipal policeman, who denounced him to the Legion when it arrived in Belalcázar October 16, 1940. His son Agustín was executed 3 months later, in May. One of the victims from El Viso, Manuel Ruiz Fernández, was accused by the Causa General of belonging to the War Committee.

This particular saca had a huge impact both inside and outside the prison, which is exactly what the Francoists wanted. Never before had so many been killed in this manner, either in Cordoba or in all of Spain. Still, it appears that society had become inured to the lists of so many executed, but to see so men killed at one go, one after the other, is much more criminal than anything else that the cold mentality of today can grasp. "The bourgeois aloofness", as Reyes Mate calls it.[26]

Winter 1940 – Spring 1941

In Cordoba , the rest of the winter and much of Spring was undisturbed by the terror of the sacas because the sentenced to death from Cordoba and other Andalusia provinces had been sent to Burgos where they would be tortured by the bitterly cold winter weather until Francoism decided to kill them once and for all. To give you an idea of how harsh the 1940-41 Winter was, the thermometer on Christmas Day registered -4ºC (24.8ºF).

Cordoba capital, however, was not free of the effects of the extermination during this Winter and Spring. For the moment, there may not have been many sacas, but the prisoners were dying like flies in the Provincial Prison. Retain this fact: 1941, in the prison of Cordoba, more than 500 inmates died of starvation in the new Cordoba Prison, almost as many as were executed by firing squads in all of post-war Cordoba – 584 in all. This number continued to rise during the entire 1940s, during which 756 inmates in the new Cordoba Prison, the Spanish Auschwitz, died of hunger.

April & May

Once Winter was over, in April and May 1941, the prisoners who had been sent to Burgos for the winter were returned to Cordoba for the sole purpose of carrying out their sentences, in several trains known as "trains of death". From the onset, the condemned men knew their fate and there were a few desperate attempts to escape the cattle wagons in which they were travelling.

It seemed that there were no limits to Francoist cruelty as in all of Spain it became customary to celebrate executions on festive dates and public holidays such as February 16, April 14, May 1, November 7, and so forth. There could be no more cruel way of teaching the townspeople a lesson than scheduling a saca to coincide with local festivities. The traditional May 1 working men's holiday in 1941 Cordoba was such an example.

May 1

The train of death with the condemned had arrived from Burgos a few days before, and the 34 men on board knew why. They came from many towns and villages in the province: 4 from Villanueva de Cordoba, 3 from Villaralto, 3 from Hinojosa, 3 from Bujalance; others from La Rambla, Cañete, Montoro, etc. Manuel *El Perla* Sánchez Ruiz, aged 33, past Socialist Mayor of Montilla, was the most famous member of this saca. He was an outstanding person who had held leading positions in the JSU and the local Workers' Society, was secretary of the provincial FNTT and promoted national vice-president in 1938, in Valencia. He was captured in Alicante and sent to Albatera concentration camp. His wife and two sons were fortunately able to take a ship to Oran, Algeria. Manuel was taken from the Montilla jail to Cordoba.

Blas Gómez Medica, a native of Villanueva de Cordoba, had been a leading member of the PCE for many years, was alderman for the Frente Popular, presided over a Community Council and served as an early volunteer with the Garcés Battalion. He was about to flee on a ship at the end of the war when he was denounced by a countryman, a so-called Aplicos, who handed him over to the Nationalists with the words: "Take him. You have caught yourselves a great Communist leader". After being sent from one prison to another, he ended up in Villanueva where he was exhibited to the Señoritos at the Casino. Later, it was the *via crucis* of all the prisoners, including the train of death from Burgos. According to Pedro Molinero, a cellmate, when Blás Gómez' name was called out for the saca " he became totally downcast, shuffling to his death like a sleepwalker".

Another native of Villanueva executed on this day, José Maria Sánchez Jurado, a solicitor and clerk, local director of the Unión Republicana, alderman and member of the Frente Popular. An inoffensive person, he never imagined that he would be killed. Harking to his experience with the law, he attempted to console his companions saying: "Don't worry, the only thing they can take from us is the right to vote." Sadly, he appeared to ignore that Fascism has no laws. A cellmate, Manuel Pascual Soler, told Moreno Gómez that when they called his name, he shared his personal objects among his

124

cellmates, in such a way that they were all very moved. That was one of the most terrible nights in Cordoba prison: you heard nothing but nobody slept."

Pedro Padilla Moreno, another native of Villanueva, was executed for no "revolutionary" reason, just because he had committed "an act of war". When Padilla was fighting on the Belalcázar front, at the end of 1938, he was sent out on patrol for the nightly relief of the sentinels. They left one at his post, but as they left this guy attacked them behind their backs as he intended to go over to the enemy. As the patrol threw itself to the ground, Padilla shot and killed the traitorous sentinel. When the family of the dead man found out what had happened, they filed a suit in Villanueva against Padilla, Afonseo Militos Torralbo, a soldier from Villanueva, and another soldier from El Horcajo. All three men were arrested and Padilla assumed full responsibility, justifying his actions as legitimate self-defence in an obvious act of war. The authorities refused to accept his defence.

Lastly, of the four natives of Villanueva who were executed, José Telesforo Torralbo Espósito was denounced by the family of José Fernández Martos, who had died in battle in 1936. He left a widow, Maria *La Lavandera,* who later became stepmother to the well-known Rev. Pedro León Moreno, a high-ranking Dominican monk, currently posting in Seville.

Other victims of that May 1 saca included Bartolomé Parrado Serrano, of the Bujalance War Committee; Francisco Casado Pedrajas, from Pozoblanco who had been photographed smoking a cigarette whilst sitting on the body of a dead Nationalist; Agustín Viagara, from Belalcázar, son of Antonio El Sabio Vigara, who had been executed three months earlier; Antonio Guerra, from Pedro Abad, member of the UGT, accused of belonging to the War Committee, but with no specific charges. He was imprisoned in the Granada bullring at the end of the war, then in Padul concentration camp (so-called Camp of Glorification, according to Francoists) and finally transferred to Cordoba capital.

May 3

Another great saca, again 34 victims, executed in San Rafael cemetery. It was a matter of expediting all the passengers on the first train of death that had arrived from Burgos some days earlier and had not been executed in the May 1 saca: 5 victims from Pedro Abad, 5 from Santa Eufemia, 3 each from Hinojosa, Belmez and Castro del Río; several more from Montoro, Villaralto and other towns.

Vicente Blanco García, a communist leader from Belmez, ex- Captain in the Militia, was accused of having organized a People's Court from the City Hall balcony in 1936, to try a group of right-wingers who ended up being shot. Vicente Blanco was the scapegoat for all these events and he was cruelly tortured, including by Falangist women. In Cordoba prison he attempted suicide by cutting his wrists, but his wounds healed and he was executed. In the same saca: Alfonso Gómez Gutiérrez, from Castro del Rio, whose brother Juan had been a member of the War Committee; Tomás Pizarro Rodríguez, from Belalcázar, whose brother Juan had been a member of the War Committee; Francisco Muñoz Gutiérrez, from Montoro, accused of the death of some right-wingers in Ventorrillo de la Lola, Montoro, in July 1936. A similar accusation was made against Manuel Ocón Fleitas, from Adamuz, and Antonio José Calero Tirado, from Pedroche. The latter was accused by the family of José Manosalvas, a Falangist who was killed inside the church in 1936. All of these Causa General accusations were accompanied without a shred of proof of any kind, therefore unreliable.

June 3

Another great saca in Cordoba prison following the arrival of another train of death Burgos, this time with 28 victims. These trains full of Andalusians sentenced to death, were sent not only to Cordoba but also to Jaén and other locations. It was the terrible Winter during which the Francoists 'amused themselves' at the expense of the Andalusians in Burgos.

Claro González Sánchez, a native of Fuenteobejuna, who managed to escape from one of the trains of death, describes their despair:

> "We arrived in a convoy of prisoners from Burgos, destination Cordoba, straight to the cemetery. The doctor bade us farewell in Burgos with these words: "You know where you are going." Before we arrived at Arévalo Station in Avila, a group of 18 of us escaped, with the idea of going to Portugal where there was a British ship and for which a teacher from Villa del Río had some documents.
>
> Unfortunately, we were all immediately recaptured. A Lieutenant Colonel took me and four other men and pretended that he was putting us before a firing squad. If it had not been the intervention of a sergeant, I truly believe that he would have killed us there and then. We were imprisoned in Avila for three months and between one thing and another, by the time we were sent to Cordoba it was May 1942 and we were able to save ourselves."[27]

Another time, Santiago Cepas Romero, a native of Villanueva de Cordoba, told Moreno Gómez that on another occasion, when the train slowed down to go through Despeñaperros station, a group of prisoners tore strips off the side of the cattle wagon and escaped. Some of them were immediately recaptured but others managed to disappear. Antonio Ramos, from Almodóvar del Río, told him of Juan Pato Velázquez, also from Almodóvar, who like others, made a hole in the side of the goods wagon that was taking them to Cordoba to be executed, and escaped, but his footprints in the snow led the guards directly to him and he was recaptured. Then there was the convoy of prisoners from Madrid to Cordoba, at the beginning of Summer 1941, when a prisoner from Badalatosa, Seville, escaped when the train stopped in the Linares-Baeza station. He was immediate surrounded on the platform by Guardias Civiles who shot him on the spot.[28]

Of the 28 who were executed June 3, 11 were natives of Villanueva de Cordoba and some of them were well-known in the community. The most famous of the lot was Pedro *Cuadrado* Torralbo Gómez, Communist alderman in 1931 and 1936, provincial Member of Parliament in 1936 and Militia Captain in the Garcés Battalion. His adventures when he returned to his home town in 1939, on foot from Jaén, and his capture, were described earlier. Pedro Torralbo was tried as Causa General Case 27.404/39 and suffered considerable torture before he was sent to spend the winter in Burgos. He was tried in Villanueva May 1 1940 in the Torres hall, with Francoist Pedro Luengo Benítez as the Presiding Judge of the Military Court. , sentenced him to death. He immediately appealed his sentence, to no avail. He had never been involved in any violence nor did he belong to the War Committee, as he was accused. The only thing that they could hold against him was that he had had differences of opinion with landowners in City Hall in 1931 regarding the social problems of the people. It was his political significance alone that led to his death. The Captain General of the II Military Region approved the sentence April 23 1941. A copy of the last letter he wrote in the chapel is reproduced in APPENDIX I.

Also from Villanueva de Cordoba, the Castro family alleged that Bartolomé Viveros Torralbo had been present when t Miguel - *El Fresco*'s house was examined by the police in July 1939 and where Falangist Juan A. Castro Díaz died. Manuel Orellana Gómez and Avelino Nevado Asencio were denounced by the widow of Victoriano Muñoz, whom they went to arrest in the countryside in August 1936, when a man called Rojas shot and killed her husband. Avelino Nevado and his brother Alfonso were members of the PCE and they served as volunteers in the defence of Madrid; they belonged to a family that was well aware of its social standing and that was greatly persecuted by Francoists. Alfonso Bujalance Gallego, also from Villanueva and executed in this saca, had been a Militia Commander and was related to the above Falangist. Victoriano Muñoz. Francisco Illescas Palomo, from Villanueva, the especially tragic case of the man whose wife and three children died when the Las Navas powder magazine explored February 28, 1939, was also executed in this saca.

29 executed were from several other towns in the province, including Ángel Trujillo Medina, from Villanueva del Duque, accused of belonging to

the War Committee and Manuel Madueño Navarro, from Montoro, accused by the Cause General and the FAL Militia, of being responsible for several deaths during the evacuation of the village, Christmas 1936.

One of the most notable victims of these deaths was Eduardo Bujalance López, a socialist from Hornachuelos, whose brother Antonio, Member of Parliament for the Frente Popular, was murdered in Cordoba by the Nationalists soon after the coup, July 30 1936. Eduardo was executed solely because of who his brother was. It was a purely political elimination, like so many thousands in Spain, as there was nothing of any importance of which he could be accused. The landowners in his town accused him of totally false crimes, with the sole purpose of erasing the Bujalance family from the map. When Moreno Gómez visited Hornachuelos, he was given a copy of Eduardo's last letter, written in the chapel, that clearly illustrates the political nature of his execution.[29] This letter is also recorded in APPENDIX I.

June 9

9 executed: Blas Gajete López, from Villafranca, 26-year-old public school teacher about whom Moreno Gómez wrote; more men from Pedro Abad, a small village that was terribly punished during the post-war they imprisoned 150 men and executed more than 50; Francisco Olanda Garrido, Socialist who served with the 108 MB on the Madrid front. He was accused of participating in the negotiations for the surrender of the Guardia Civil barracks. In the town and of several unproven other acts. From Palenciana, a neighbouring village to Pedro Abad: Joaquín Antequera Gámez, who according to the Causa "took up arms against the Glorious National Movement" and engaged in guarding and arming patrols (the so-called Self-Defence Groups); Rafael Rojas Navarro, member of the UGT and the same Self-Defence Groups. Apparently, he was on guard in the jail August 10 1936 when the Militia from Alcoy arrived in the town and took a saca of seven right-wingers whom they killed in exactly in the same place that Francoists had shot and burnt a group of townspeople 22 July 22 1936.

June 28

9 executed in Cordoba, including Francisco Moya Gómez, from Pedroche, accused by the family of landowner José T. Gutiérrez Rane, executed in July 1936 (Causa General data).

A few individual executions on different days

July 15

Next large saca with 14 victims from different townships, including Francisco Pedragosa Velasco, a native of Valenzuela, accused of belonging to a War Committee. Moreno Gómez regrets that he was unable to obtain more information regarding the history of the multiple and tragic personal activities for so many of these victims, in order to honour their memories.

August 20

8 executed, including Rafael Deza Montero, a native of Puente Genil, brother of Justo, a great trade union leader, member of the JSU, who was executed 9 November 1939. A third brother, Marcos, was also executed. Another family total eradicated by the Regime.

September 12

11 executed, 5 from Villanueva de Cordoba, including Juan Cantador Zamora, whose story Moreno Gómez told earlier as a typical example of Francoist 'justice', when referring to the riot and the violent treatment of the prisoner that followed a case of mistaken identity at his trial under the notorious Juan Calero Rubio. Executed on the same day, Juan Lorenzo *Cucharas* Cantador, ex-Militia Captain. It was alleged, as all the others were, that he had participated on the attack on the Villanueva barracks, belonged to the War Committee and other such activities, all without any proof whatsoever. All these prisoners arrived from Burgos to Cordoba in another train of death September 8; Miguel Campos Toledo, accused of persecuting right-wingers in Villanueva July 24 1936; Faustino *El Peno* García Calero, well-known native of Pozoblanco, ex-Militia Lieutenant, accused, probably without cause as usual, by the families of two right-wingers executed in 1936 (José Alcaide Dueñas and Antonio Cañuelo).

September 29

One of the 3 executed on this day, Juan Flores López, past Mayor of Espiel, and José Palomo Huertas, a native of Villanueva de Cordoba and another one of the many who fell because he had taken part in a carnival prank involving a ditty ridiculing a well-known landowner who was running for office in 1936.[30] José Palomo Huertas and his wife Francisca Gómez Cuevas belonged to a large, Communist, working class family. His wife, together with other brave women in the town, stood in front of the Guardia Civil horses to prevent them from charging against their husbands

José Palomo was sent to a concentration camp in Valladolid until June 1939, when he was released to return to Villanueva. No sooner had he arrived home that he was arrested on totally false charges June 22 1939, beaten and tortured until daybreak the next day when they took him to the Fuente Vieja Schools prison. They had placed slivers of wood under his toenails and beaten his arms to bits and had beaten his body so badly that he was left him lying on the floor. His cellmates took care of him and he recovered. The charges against him were totally false. He was sentenced to death by court martial at the end of 1939. 26 September 1940, he was transferred to Cordoba New Prison with all the other local prisoners and then to Burgos where he spent 11 months from where he returned to Cordoba shortly before he was executed. As to his wife, Francisca Gómez Cuevas, she was arrested with all the other Roya women in the town and imprisoned in Juan Herrero's house on Calle Conquista, where she gave birth to a son. The child fell ill and died without ever knowing his father (his father was imprisoned in Fuente Vieja Schools jail at the time).

In Cordoba, the men were sent to the new prison and the women to the old one. Francisca suffered many years in jail, like Juana *La Flora* and other front-line Rojas. The tragedy of the Palomo family did not end there. Another brother, José Antonio, was killed in 1948 under the Law of Fugitives after he was caught listening to the *La Pirenaica* radio station[xvii]

October 11

7 executed in San Rafael cemetery, including a well-known individual from Villaviciosa, Nicomedes de la Fuente, an anarchist, who had become known for his role in the October 1934 revolutionary uprisings, which is why he fled the town and took refuge in Bujalance. He was now being executed on the anniversary of those events. Tomás Cuadrado Ruiz was another activist involved in the Adamuz uprisings.

November 6

8 executed, including several from Villanueva de Cordoba. Juan Escoriza Segura, a native of Almeria, one the famous *materos* whose job was to keep the bushes and shrubs in hillsides under control. He was accused of "participating in the attack on the village and in a shooting in Fuente Vieja", which he denied. As his family told Moreno Gómez, Judge Juan Calero propositioned Juan's daughter, with the promise of promising to save her father in exchange for her 'services'. As she snubbed him, he refused to process Juan's appeal

---

[xvii] *Radio España Independente* was a clandestine radio station broadcasting from Bucharest from 21 July 1941 to 14 July 1977, nicknamed *La Pirenaica* because it was believed to be broadcasting from somewhere in the Pyrenee mountains. Run from Moscow by the Spanish Communist Party as the voice of the victims of Franco's regime. *Vide* article by Armand Balsebrea and Rosario Fontova at http://www.davidpublisher.org/Public/uploads/Contribute/55079243ce777.pdf.

and had him placed in solitary confinement, where he suffered all the usual mistreatments until he was shipped to Burgos.

Juan F. Chuán Soso, from the same town, was condemned under the usual accusations of "attack on the town and shooting in Fuente Vieja" that the authorities indiscriminately levied against all Almeria townspeople they captured. It is said that Chuán refused to confess with such force, that he began to shout and they had to muzzle him. José Domenech Martínez, a native of Montoro, was a member of another of the exterminated families whose sons Valeriano, Lucio and José were executed. In Montoro, the charges were the same: everyone was accused of attacking the Falangists inmates of the local jail July 22 1936.

November 17 1941

This saca of 3 is remembered as when one of the three victims, Antonio Baena Moreno, schoolmaster from Pozoblanco, who had presided over the War Committee was executed. An influential socialist, somewhat of a visionary and very kind, who truly never participated in any kind of blood event, quite the contrary, he avoided all conflicts he could. To make matters worse for him, he had been the political commissar of the 8th Army Group, and later General Political Commissar for the Army of Andalusia. Throughout his imprisonment, he attempted continuously to demonstrate his innocence, with detailed appeals, to no avail. The fact of the matter was that the great 'crime' in Franco's eyes, was the 'political significance' of an individual, not whether he had been involved in bloodshed or not.

Antonio Baena wrote a lengthy diary in prison, that his family kindly allowed Moreno Gómez to consult and copy, that is a perfect description of the disgrace, constant humiliations, shortages, hunger and terror that everyone inside a Francoist prison suffered.

Baena was tried by court martial in Pozoblanco April 22 1940. He was accused by several local Falangists: the Bosch Caballero family, relatives of Lázaro Delgado Cabrera, Juan García Tirado, Bartolomé Caballero, Domingo Márquez, José Delgado Dueñas, and others. In other words, the majority of the Pozoblanco bourgeoisie, most of whom wanted to revenge relatives of theirs who had fallen victim to the People's Court in Valencia. With all these accusations, there was no way out for Antonio Baena. September 20 1940, he was sent to Cordoba with the local prisoners, then onto Burgos for the winter. November 2 1941, after a year and a half with a death sentence hanging over his head, he was returned to Cordoba on the train of death for execution. That same day, he concluded his diary with the following words: "I leave Burgos for Cordoba, having lost all hope. How I think of you, my children!"

Two weeks later, he was listed for the saca. A cellmate of his from Dos Torres, Carlos Menéndez, told Moreno Gómez that he bade farewell to Antonio Baena, when they took him. He went with another prisoner from Pozoblanco, tied to each other with wires. Baena was depressed and was crying. He didn't say anything. Carlos Menéndez was assigned to work in the prison office and that night he was made to stand guard and to accompany the Head of Services to confirm the departure of the sentenced.

Jerónimo Jurado Carrillo, Baena's companion, had been accused by Falangist Francisco Peralbo's family. Jerónimo had served as a guard over several Falangists imprisoned in the Teatro jail and they accused him of having been present at the November 20 1936 executions.

November 25

Only 1 execution that day, Miguel Lindo Serrano, from Adamuz, a member of the famous Lindo family, two of whom, the Luque Lindo brothers, had escaped to the mountains because they were tired of being so badly and frequently beaten in their town. They joined Claudio Romera's Socialist fighters and survived as guerrillas until around 1949.

December 10

10 sentenced executed from several towns, namely: Villa del Río, Posadas, Castro del Río, Pedroche and Pedro Abad. Francisco Carrillo Cobos, from Pedroche, was accused by two families whose relatives had died while serving in Franco's army. Julián Claudio Carrillo, also from Pedroche, was accused by the family of José Tirado Vaquero, who had been killed by a fugitive but, so they said, because he had been called Falangist by Julián. He was also accused by relatives of being responsible for the death of Antonio Rodriguez, a right-wing student, who died in 1936. The accusation against Juan Castilla Rivera, from Pedro Abad, was a novel one: that he was responsible for organizing the "Children of the Night" who put petards on the railway line at night, as well as of belonging to the typical local Self-Defence Groups, of course.

December 20

The last execution of the year in Cordoba capital, with 6 victims.

January-February 1942

Fewer sacas during the year, but with more victims each time.

January 10

9 victims.

March 10

2 executed. Moreno Gómez considered that this execution was especially significant because of the extremely moving letter that Joaquim Morno Muñoz, a native from Baena, wrote his family from prison, a copy of which he obtained from Arcángel Bedmar. Dated February 4 1942, it reflects the enormity of the suffering of the prisoners under Francoism.[31]

> "Mother, regarding what you say you sent me, I received everything and you have no idea how much good it did me as I have improved from the debility I suffered, so you can continue bringing or sending me clothes and what food you can, as it will all help me feel better. If you cannot, without it I will find it impossible to continue... A couple of handkerchiefs to wipe my nose, some size 38 cord sandals, and tobacco.
>
> Dear brother, you have no idea how happy I was to read your letter and... don't forget me. You have no idea the satisfaction that it is for a prisoner to know that he is remembered, especially under the circumstances in which I find myself, because nobody knows it better than he who has the misfortune to go through such situations; this eats me up. Tomás of my heart: Do what you can, both for my health and for taking this weight off me, as it is unbearable..."

Everything ended for this unfortunate man March 10 but at least Moreno Gómez was able to record the suffering he endured, for History. Regarding so many others, it has been impossible to get any information but at least we have most of their names, which is not a little.

March 25

5 Executed., Juan Sánchez Pozuelo, second son of María La Loma's, from Villanueva de Cordoba, whose brother Alfonso was executed September 12 1940. Juan had been hallmarked, as were another 2,000 militiamen, for having participated in the great anti-coup uprising July 1936 with the assistance of 20 miners from Puertollano, a technically perfect operation in which the Republicans fought the Nationalist by breaking through the walls of adjoining houses as they moved through the town, instead of fighting openly along the streets, a most unusual military operation. The Republicans were ultimately defeated and thereafter, all the townspeople were considered guilty of 'the attack on the town'.

For some unknown reason, the Francoists waited until March 1943 before executing a third of Maria's, Juan El de la Loma, who was denounced by *El Cuco* who lived on Calle Pozoblanco. Juan's family later told Moreno Gómez that he caught tuberculosis in Cordoba prison and that he attempted suicide by throwing himself onto the prison patio from the third-floor gallery, but did not die. As customary, his guards probably waited until he recovered before they executed him.

June 25
    11 victims

August 8
    7 victims

November 7
    8 victims. This date, the anniversary of the Russian revolution and the first offensive against Madrid, was always celebrated with one or more sacas.

1943

Executions by firing squads occurred less frequently during this year and most often, only one prisoner at a time. Frankly, there were not many left to kill, at least for the time being, because it was not yet time for the 1945-1947 Triennium of Terror. Meanwhile, other assorted features of the "multi-repression" program that began to be applied. (Reyes Serroche, executed February 6, is not included in the list because unlike the others, he was a common criminal.)

Table 3. Civil Registry Data: Post-war firing squad executions in Cordoba Province towns and villages only

Location	Number executed	Location	Number executed
Adamuz	3	Hornachuelos	8
Aguilar de la	1	Montalbán	1
Frontera	1	Montilla	22
Alcaracejos	6	Montoro	21
Almodóvar del Rio	32	Palma del Río	40
Baena	30	Pedro Abad	40
Belalcázar	36	Peñarroya-	88
Belmez	55	Pueblonuevo	19
Bujalance	3	Posadas	209
Cañete de las Torres	5	Pozoblanco	2
Cardeña	167	Priego	29
Castro del Rio	1	Puente Genil	21
Conquista	6	Santa Eufemia	3
Dos Torres	6	Torrecampo	8
Espejo	16	Villafranca	102
Espiel	4	Villanueva de Cordoba	(8) 1
Fernán Núñenz	40	Villaralto	3
Fuenteobejuna	67	Villaviciosa	(8) 6
Hinojosa del Duque		El Viso	

TOTAL post-war executions by firing squad in Cordoba Province: 1,102

The first stage of the Francoist repression, in terms of executions by firing squad for reasons related to the civil war itself, can for all intents and purposes be considered closed in 1943. If on the one hand there were fewer prison inmates sentenced to death for this kind of crimes left to kill, there were other means by which the repression could be enforced and resort to these was rising to new heights: forced labour, beatings in the barracks, blacklists, the humiliation of being freed on parole with the attending restrictions, the continuing drama of those serving long prison terms, not to mention Law of Fugitives, in itself a budding catastrophe. Typical causes of post-war crimes were those connected with the clandestine reorganization of political parties, partisan support to the Maquis and guerrillas, and so forth. These would be typically resolved with large sacas in the Fall of 1944.

Table 3, gives an indication of the forces of death that enraged and asphyxiated the provincial towns and villages during this first stage of Francoist repression. Cordoba capital was no exception to the overall severity of the Regime, as we saw summarized in Table 2. This, because martyrized Cordoba capital had already been enduring an unbearable genocide since July 1936. How many shootings, how many bloody dawns, how much bloodshed in the cemeteries. In Cordoba, there were many nights in which so many were executed by firing squads that the bloodbath often lasted three hours, as groups of 8 or 10 men fell together, one after the other, falling onto the bodies of those who preceded them.

In Cordoba capital, as in all other towns and villages, the people continued to live the same nightmare of terror that they had endured since the terrible days of 1936, even though in the post-war period the executions were more directed at those who had already been sentenced to death and were incarcerated. Few were left to execute in the capital, but the harassing and the insistent climate of terror persisted in the neighbourhoods mostly populated by the working classes. The Guardia Civil, the municipal Police and the Falange took it upon them to ensure that the population would continue to be subdued by the threats, the beatings, the castor oil treatments, the registrations, detentions, denouncements, accusations, the apprehension of children by the Social Welfare program, exclusion, pursuit of the black market and hunger in the most literal sense of the words.

Guardia Civil, Police and Falange multiplied their efforts to sacar Rojos whom they said were hiding under stones everywhere. Many persons who had been in the Republican zone in both capital and townships, tried to live incognito in the city, without success. The Cordoba capital *vox populi* had not forgotten the group of Fascist policemen who were forerunners of the of the New State's agents of repression and who would kindle tragic memories in the 1939 immediate post-war period: Commissar José González de Lara and policemen Aparicio Romero, Ricardo de la Fuente, Heredia Espinosa, Ruiz Molina, López Linares, Rafael del Olmo Garcia, and others. In 1942, Commissar Aurelio Cortegero de la Cuerda and an extensive list of especially active political policemen.

Amongst the Francoist Guardia Civil, another body devoted to the political repression, we note the tragic notoriety of Corporal Payán (José Payán Porcel?), Corporal Arenas and Corporal Manolo El Colorao. The latter, from the La Magdalena barracks, took pleasure in torture and in applying enormous beatings for the most trivial reasons such as the theft of a cabbage or a head of lettuce. If he caught someone hunting birds in the countryside, he made them eat them raw; if he caught someone picking olives, he made them eat the green [unripe, bitter] ones, to all of which he added the well-known beatings. Another Guardia Civil nicknamed *El Bizco* was feared for the savagery of his tortures, even before the October 1934 uprisings. Another one was known as *El Dino*, who specialized in torturing and applying the castor oil purge to women who were caught with goods they had purchased on the black market. Others, such as Corporal de Asalto Ballesteros, municipal policeman Moreno, Guardias Civiles Baltasar El Maño, Rafael El de los Bigotes, and a so-called Urbano Cantizano who had served as a Legionnaire during the war and immediately re-enlisted in the Guardia Civil.

Likewise, engaged at their side, there was an entire cohort of Falangist admirers, social-climbers and servants to the army of evil, in uncountable numbers. The names of some of the more notorious are still remembered in Cordoba: Juan El Gitano, a Falangist sergeant, and his local contacts Isidoro El Comandante and Antonio El Loco, suppliers of the barracks and rabid hunters of women black-marketers whom they beat viciously when caught.

Powerful Falangist women were no less evil than the men. One, Conchita Costa, Director of the Prison for Women, was particularly notorious for her ruthless and inhumane discipline. Another, Maria Campos y Carmelita *Caraquemá*, a leader of the Falange would send her centurions down the streets of Cordoba to arrest women in the working-class neighbourhoods and then take them to the Falange barracks where they shaved their heads and purged them with castor oil, a treatment invented and widely applied by Italian Fascists. Other groups of puritanical Falangists organized raids of women and took them to the Roman baths behind the Alcázar and there, on the pretext of hygiene, they shaved and mistreated them.

The Falange paramilitary barracks were located: in the Rinconcito, in front of the Isabel la Católica movie theatre, another in the Calle Jesús María, near the Góngora theatre, another in Calle Carbonell y Morand, near Capuchinos square. All of this and much more, formed the climate of harassment, abasement and humiliation of those who were disaffected with the Regime. Together with the firing squads, they formed the essence of the Francoist repression.

Some clandestine reorganization (1944-1945).
Causa General Case 94/44.

> *"Our party has never thought that the solution to this war might be the establishment of a Communist regime. If the mass of the working classes, the farmworkers and the urban bourgeoisie follow us and support us, it is because they know that we are the most resolute defenders of national independence, liberty and the Republican Constitution."*

José Díaz, letter to *Mundo Obrero* newspaper, 19 March 1938.

Despite the defeat of the Republic, the workers' political parties, especially the PCE, never ceased attempting to reorganize themselves even in the face of the relentless Francoist repression, with its torture, imprisonments and executions, both in Cordoba and throughout Spain. In Madrid, the provincial reconstruction of the PCE involved the well-known playwright Antonio Buero Vallejo, who produced false documents and was almost shot. Curiously, the most reliable witnesses state that the principle leaders of the political reorganization were interned together in the same prisons. Considering that the best-known leaders were under arrest, as were the most combative members of the workers' movements, it is not surprising that the important base at the origin of the clandestine fight against Francoism could be found in the prisons.

During Moreno Gómez's research into the clandestine reorganization in Cordoba, he recorded observations regarding the spontaneous home-grown nature of the reorganization attempts, regardless of any directions from outside the country (almost impossible to apply, at any rate), as well as the lack of homogeneity in the dynamism of any kind of political opposition. At the same time, while there is information regarding the Communists who were clearly active and the Anarchists who were less consistently so, there is practically no available data regarding the clandestine activities of Cordovan Socialists who virtually drop out of sight in the province in 1939.

On the other hand, the harshness of the Francoist repression against any attempt at reorganization was a powerful deterrent: frightful: to be found with clandestine propaganda or being listed in the flowchart of a local or provincial party committee, was punished by death. Already in 1941, political activists such as Heriberto Quiñones and Enrique Sánchez in Madrid, began to fall like flies before the firing squads, not because they had committed a crime of war but because they had engaged in crimes of clandestine activities. Matilde Landa and Buero Vallejo escaped by miracle. Still, regardless of the underlying reason for their arrest, when tried, all offenders were charged with a 'crime of military rebellion', the only charge allowed under Military Law.

Moreno Gómez therefore extended his research into mass executions after 1942 beyond the repression of defeated Republicans and those considered guilty of crimes of war, to include aspects of the government's recent multi-repression policy directed at a new civilian target – everyone involved in some form of 'clandestine' activity – meaning almost everyone who opposed Francoism in Spain. Beginning with an intent to behead the nascent clandestine organizations and to maintain the climate of terror by which Francoism controlled the civil population, the government refined and updated its tried and true methods of repression. As the Causa General became increasingly active in its investigations, the number of raids of suspect organizations rose exponentially, as did the number of individuals arrested and tried by the courts and condemned to death.

Causa General Case 94/44 that was instructed and tried in Cordoba capital July 27 1944[32], provided details of the clandestine organization of the Communists since 1943, beginning with the creation of a local committee in Cordoba capital, then a Provincial Committee, followed by several branch committees in several towns. (The Communist party was doing the same in Galicia and in Madrid, at about the same time.) All this organization came crashing down at the end of 1943 following a massive raid in which 145 individuals were arrested (primarily in Cordoba, La Rambla, Castro del Río, Belmez and Peñarroya-Pueblonuevo), of which 68 were formally tried; of these, 8 were executed by firing squad October 19 1944.

The events that led to this disaster began August 1943, primarily due to the initiatives of three Communist leaders: Antonio Guerrero Lebrón, recently released from Málaga prison, and two other activists: Adriano Romero from Villanueva de Cordoba, past member of Parliament for the Frente Popular and José Lupiáñez, from Jaén, both of whom were imprisoned in Cordoba capital. This was a matter of divulging the politics of the Unión Nacional, a new populist creation of the PCE, already being disseminated throughout Spain by Jesús Monzón from France.

Summer 1943, one of the first local PCE committees was created in Cordoba capital, with the following officers:=

José Molero Berlanga, Local Secretary
Alfonso Cerezo Regalón, Financial Secretary
Antonio Fernández Cuenca, Uprisings Secretary
Juan Vélez López, Organization Secretary
Celestino Lara Ruiz, Propaganda Secretary.

This local committee's immediate objective was to provide assistance to the prisoners (the same thing that was the basis for Causa General Case 1.546/41), contact with like-minded organizations and to attract members. Contact with the Communist organization in Madrid was managed quickly thanks to José Molera Berlanga's efforts. October 5 1943, Madrid sent a delegate to Cordoba, Manuel Santuagi Alvarez Aguado, who had to confirm his identity before the Cordoba Committee with the password *on behalf of Maruja*. Manuel Álvarez had been exiled in France but he returned to Spain via Catalonia with false documents. He had served as a political commissar with the military during the war. Under his direction and assistance, the local officers intended to expand the Communist organization in the region. Cordoba province was divided into four sectors (La Rambla, Belmez, Villafranca and Castro del Río). Sub-committees were created in some of these towns and several cells in the capital (Campo de la Verdad, Calle San Fernando; Higuerón Station, Santa Marina, Olivos Borrachos and Barrio el Naranjo).

The Provincial Committee was created and the following were appointed as officers:

Manuel Álvarez Aguado, Political Advisor, nicknamed *Santiago*
José Molero Berlanga, General Secretary
Francisco Medina Rodriguez, Organization Secretary
Juan Vélez López, Military Secretary
Alfonso Cerezo Regalón, Financial Secretary
Antonio Fernández Cuenca, Uprisings Secretary
Celestino Lara Ruiz, Propaganda.Secretary

Contact with the Party Regional Committee in Seville was soon established. One of its members, Manuel *Bartolo y Luisa* Castro Campos proposed two Secretaries for Cordoba: Manuel Álvarez and José Molero. The latter did not accept and was substituted by Emilio Jiménez Rascón. Manuel Álvarez made another change to the first Provincial Committee: Juan Vélez was replaced by José Fernández Braga as Military Secretary, whilst Juan Vélez, Celestino Lara and Francisco Medina Rodriguez were put in charge of the Cordoba Capital committee's activities involving creating cells in several neighbourhoods in the capital.

It is important to keep in mind that these clandestine activities in Cordoba city and province abided by the guidelines of the new National Union policy disseminated by the PCE and Jesús Monzón from France, that had already begun being infiltrated throughout Spain. In Cordoba, clandestine National Union pamphlets and handouts were distributed, with the enormous risks that this entailed. The handouts were written on Rogelio Díaz García's typewriter. The police discovered other in Julio Priego Ordónez's home.[33] All the above were indicted under Causa General Case 94.

Local committees were created in three provincial towns: La Rambla, Belmez and Peñarroya-Pueblonuevo. Shoemaker Bartolomé Mendoza Caballero tried to do so in Castro del Rio, but without success.

The Belmez Committee comprised José Békar Luque, Daniel Gallardo Gallego, Andrés Diaz Bonilla and José Fernández Braga (the latter was a representative on the Provincial Committee and senior officer in Belmez).

The La Rambla Committee was directed by Andrés Ruiz Urbano, followed by Martin Peinado Alcaide, both of whom had been attracted by Juan Vélez's activism and in whose boarding house in the capital, Manuel Álvarez the link with Madrid, was staying.

The Peñarroya-Pueblonuevo Committee was directed by Pablo González Calvo, Secretary General, whom Moreno Gómez interviewed many years later in his house in Madrid. The remaining Secretaries were Cipriano Tapia Quintana (Organization), Antonio Igualador Gómez (Information), Mariano Fernández Romero (Finances) and Juan Manuel Muño Mansilla (Raising funds for prisoners).

All the above committee members were arrested in the great raid at the end of 1943, as were many supporters or subscribers from each town. 32 were arrested in the capital, including Benito del Puerto Baltanas (head of a radio station and several cells in the capital) and Blas Herencia Burgos (who was in contact with Castro del Río) and many more.

In Belmez, in addition to the Committee, another 7 activists who, according to the Causa General, acted in three-by-three cells, were arrested. In La Rambla, the Committee and another 9 members fell into the clutches of the Regime's political police The Peñarroya raid arrested 8 activists, in addition to the local Committee. One, Juan Gallardo Sánchez, was arrested on the grounds that he had donated 15 pesetas to a fund for prisoners. The raid was carried out by police from Madrid and from Cordoba.

All the oral witnesses stated that at a first stage, 145 were arrested in 1943 and 1944. Many remained in prison as 'guests' of the government, without trial; 68 were tried under Causa General Case 94/44.

The great raid was disastrous for the organization that had worked so hard to get it going from prison as early as 1941. When Adriano Romero was transferred to prison in Granada July 1942, he had to stop being the soul of the clandestine organization in Cordoba. Adriano has recorded their actions in his memoires:[34]

"When I arrived in Cordoba, I ran into Alfredo Caballero and many other Party leaders. José Lupiáñez arrived later and with Guerrero Lebrón, also of the Cordoba Provincial Committee, the three of us did out utmost to help the Party leaders in the prison and on the street, without ever taking over their jobs. The main work involved: information, preparing leaders and legal and economic assistance, as much as possible. Alfredo Caballero was in Sevilla, where there were also many but less important members, and Lupiáñez in Madrid."

Captain Manuel Álvares Núñez was the Presiding Judge for Cause General Case 94/44; Captain Fructuoso Delgado Hernández prosecuted the July 27 1944 court martial. He had been instructed to be very harsh and so he was: he asked for 45 death sentences. 18 indicted were sentenced to death, 5 to life imprisonment, 1 to twenty years in jail, 8 to 12 years in jail, 28 to six years in jail and 7 were absolved. The court martial was held in the same building as the Provincial Prison.

August 5 1944, the Seville Judge Advocate approved the 18 death sentences and they were confirmed August 10 by decree from Captain General Miguel Ponte y Manso de Zúñiga, General Headquarters for the 2nd Region. Nevertheless, the Government's *enterado* of October 3 1944 only sent the following 8 to the firing squad, to be shot at dawn October 19:

- Manuel Álvarez Aguado, 29, single, bank worker, from Madrid
- Juan Vélez López, 32, married, plumber, from Posadas, resident in Cordoba
- Celestino Lara Ruiz, 29, married, manual worker, from Cazorla, resident in Cordoba
- Francisco Medina Rodríguez, 34, married, metalworker, from Cordoba
- Antonio Fernández Cuenca, 29, single, salesman, from Brazil, resident in Cordoba
- Alfonso Cerezo Regalón, 40, married, bricklayer, from Adamuz, resident in Cordoba
- Emilio Jiménez Rascón, 29, married, employed, from Cordoba
- José Molero Berlanga, 33, single, telegraph operator, from Espiel, resident in Cordoba.

Another five activists who were also caught in that raid were sentenced to death in a different Cause General trial,, details of which Moreno Gómez was unable to find. One, Corporal Antonio Cobos León, from El Carpio, had been found with propaganda for the Union Nacional. He only knows the name of one of the four other victims: Sebastián *El Niño del Dinero* Caravaca Martínez , one of the Los Jubiles guerrillas who had dared to come down from the mountains in Bujalance, to see his family, and there he was either captured or he turned himself in. They beat him, made him talk, then executed him.

Julio Priego Ordóñez who was caught in the great trial and sentenced to 30 years in prison, told Moreno Gómez the following in an interview, some years later:

"I remember the words of those unforgettable companions, when 19 October 1944, they were taken in a saca from the Cordoba Provincial Prison to face the firing squad. They shouted Viva la Republica! and they asked us to ensure that the blood they were about to shed was not forgotten. 11 December 1943, at 3 a.m., we were arrested by Falangist police who shut us up in the Puerta del Rincón Falange barracks in Cordoba. The repression was so severe that it continued through January and February 1944, with 145 arrests. The raid began in Cordoba capital and later spread to the towns of Peñarroya-Pueblonuevo, Belmez, Villafranca, Pedro Abad, El Carpio, La Rambla and Castro del Río. They leaned on us so harshly that for the supposed crime of military rebellion they asked for 45 death sentences, 9 were shot outright without any accusation. This was the most criminal trial in History."[35]

The repression was undoubtedly out of control, considering that the only proof the authorities found and the only 'subversive' material they were able to present to the Court was twenty flimsy eight-line leaflets from the Unión Nacional. The Regime did not appear to be at all magnanimous, as some swear it was.

There is some information regarding the clandestine activities of the PCE during 1945, based primarily on an undated letter from Bartolomé Fernández Sánchez, Socialist from Pozoblanco, who served as a Major in the Militia, was captured and at the time of writing, was imprisoned in Cordoba. In his letter, Bartolomé refers to a December 30 1945 report from imprisoned Communists, in which they reflect on the evolution of their Party's political aspirations during that year. The Communist information consisted of six items proposed for discussion by the Party's bases:[36] According to Bartolomé, the report consisted of six items that the Party proposed for discussion by the base:

1. Difficulties and hardships that the prison committee identified, following the Cause 94 prosecution [assistance provided to prisoners];
2. The authority that today the leaders of the prison committee today share with the Provincial Committee of the PCE, thanks to the strength of its base;
3. It is said that the union of Republicans, Socialists and themselves is a certainty as there exists a committee of relationships between them, although many are highly critical of their confederates;

4. Preparation of union leaders for the future: directing them along the Communist lines. Knowing how, for this purpose, to take advantage of the masses at the right time, as the people are aware of the PSOE's reformist position and its revolutionary passivity throughout the world.

5. The work of reorganizing the UGT involves accepting as a transitory fact, all that connects it with obtaining the desired relationships, and that the work of the PCE within the UGT tends towards creating a single Central Committee of the Proletariat and ceasing with factory, company, workshop and general field committees, by uniting workers and farmers the implantation of the Supreme Soviet;

6. Give strength of purpose and action to all Communists who, as members of the PCE, can express their opinion and elect, in a democratic manner, those comrades who are best prepared to give political guidance within the Party. If this is not being done today they say it is because of the repression by the current Regime's repression;

7. This Agenda shall be discussed by all the Communists in the prison and later sent, with the opinion of all the members, to the Party leaders.

From this document, one deduces that the clandestine political activity in the prison was active and hegemonically Communist. The usual Communist pretension of its being the supreme authority is quite clear, despite its unspoken recognition that the Socialists and especially, the Anarchists, were reticent when faced with such unitary policies. Nevertheless, some Socialist prisoners such as Bartolomé Fernández, imprisoned in Cordoba, became involved in the PCE's deliberations and activities.

Communist base in Cordoba replied to the above report as follows:

"All the Communist cells, having discussed the six points of the report via the committees of radios, sectors and subsectors, approve the report as it describes the work of the Communist Party during one year and because it complies with true Communist guidelines and doctrine. Although it reveals defects and great omissions that today are irreparable because we are engulfed by a dark cloud, if we are to ensure the success of our efforts, we must strive to bring about a unity with the other political sectors, especially the CNT/UGT and generally-speaking, avoid an in-depth attack on confederates not censure the few young imprisoned Socialists, as this would seriously harm unity.

We also wish that this leadership were more democratic when appointing the comrades that will have to fill the different positions, that it disseminate all the propaganda material it receives, that it allow every Communist to associate with anyone whom he believes good for the Party and that it cease all censorship of this kind.

We ask that you inform the Party base, as soon as possible and in general terms, which political line is to be followed at these times of repression of the Spanish people, whether the U.N.A. or the Democratic Alliance. Communists are not much concerned with the colour of the politics as long as all the anti-Francoist forces are united."

Bartolomé Fernández attached an interesting commentary on the report, that he appears to have sent to his organization:

> "As you can see, this is a summary of the comments, but they are sincere and revolutionary and do not admit any partisan criticism, simply a desire to break the yolk that oppresses us today; tomorrow will be something else, and shall stir the attention of the mass of working men. The political movement inside the prison is, as you can see, an agreement of criteria within the Marxist parties and an alliance of combative political forces…"

Outside the prison, capturing clandestine communists was the Regime's order of the day. There was another great raid in Cordoba capital, tried as Causa General Case 443/1945. This court martial of 24 accused, two of whom were women, was celebrated inside the Provincial Prison July 24 1946. The Socio-Political Brigade of the Cordoba government police arrested them on charges of attempting to reorganize the Communist Party.

Accused under Causa General Case 443/1945	
Cordoba residents	
Domingo Escola Verde	Antonio Carrasco Expósito
Antonio Sánchez Alcaide	Juan Conde Navarrete
Sebastián Fernández Martínez	Antonio Rivas Garcia
Rafael Obrero López	Juan Sánchaez Cabrera
José Dás Bueno	Francisco Catalán Higuera
Joaquin Cabello Labrador	Manual Jiménez Escribano
Pedro Moreno Pino	Jaime Cuello González
Benito Núñez Vélez	Antonio Rabadán Carmona
Fausto Contreras Hervás	Francisco Páez Ortega
Rafael Camargo Montes	Manuel Jiménez Sánchez

Seville residents:	
Ildefonso Becerra Galindo	Ana Ponce Barneto
Josefa Arévalo Pozuelo	Ángeles Vargas[xvii]

The crime for which they were indicted was summarized by Francoist military jurisprudence in a single expression: military rebellion. As evidence, the police presented some brochures entitled the "Booklover's Guide" which consisted of a whole a bunch of news clippings from *Mundo Obrero* regarding the policies of the Union Nacional, dated 1944.

They were accused of creating the provincial organization of the PCE, as successors of those who had fallen in Causa General Case 94/43. Domingo *Antonio el Misterioso* Escola Verde, considered one of the most important accused, had returned covertly to Spain from France where he was living in exile, April 1944. He arrived in Cordoba in May and in January 1945 he contacted the Regional Committee in Seville, to where he went. Upon his return to Cordoba, he dedicated himself to organizing the When he returned, he centred his activity on organizing the so-called Young Communist Fighters of Cordoba, along Jesús Monzón's guidelines. At as assembly in March they agreed to merge with the Communist Party. Domingo Escola Verde suffered terribly after he was arrested. To prevent saying anything that could damage the organization, under torture, he attempted suicide by throwing himself off the top floor of the Police Headquarters to the patio below. He was seriously injured but they treated his wounds and court-martialled him with the other accused.

Another eminent accused, Antonio Carrasco Expósito, was an officer of the Cordoba Regional Committee. A representative of the last Regional Committee of Seville where he held the position of Assistant Secretary for Organization and Finance, he also was a regional instructor for the Party with the mission of reorganizing the Cordoba City Committee. At this time there was a so-called First Committee that functioned until March 1945 when the Young Communist Fighters and another group that had been created independently, merged with the Cordoba Committee, hereinafter known as the Second Committee.

Identification of the members of the First Committee is difficult, because some of its members were sentenced and executed under Causa General Case 98/44, regarding whom there is no data. Also tried as belonging to the First Committee under Causa General Case 443/45: Arturo Sánchez Alcaide,

---

[xvii] Ildefonso Becerra Galindo's wife, the 24th accused in this trial·

Secretary General; Juan Conde Navarrete, Organization and Finance; and Juan Sáchez Cabrera, Agitation and Propaganda), were not executed.

After the 1945 merger, the following are known to have been officers of the Second Committee: both Antonio Rivas García, Agitation and Propaganda, and Rafael Obrero López, Organization and Finance, had earlier belonged to the independent activist group; Fausto Contreras Hervás had been a member of the Young Fighters.

In 1945, Cordoba province was divided into three sectorial or provincial subcommittees: the First Sector (North), the Second Sector (South) and the Third Sector (possibly Cordoba capital).

The Committee for the First Sector was comprised of, among others: Manuel Jiménez Escribano, Secretary General); Joaquin Cabello Labrador, Agitation and Propaganda; and Sebastián Fernández Martínez, Organization and Finance, in the name of whose wife, Barnarda Gárate, the Regional Committee sent its correspondence to Cordoba.

Three of members of the Committee for the Second Sector, are known: Francisco Catalán Higuera, Secretary General; José Díaz Bueno, Organization and Finance; and Juan Conde Navarrete. Only one member of the Committee for the Third Sector could be identified under Causa General Case 443/45: Juan Sánchez Cabrera.

Of those indicted under Causa General Case 443/45, those who were resident in Seville were tried in that city because they received communist correspondence in their homes: Josefa Arévalo, Ana Ponce Barneto and Ángeles Vargas, Ildefonso Becerra's wife

Only one of the accused, Domingo Escola Verde, was sentenced to death by this court martial July 24 1946, even though the Prosecutor had asked for seven death sentences. Six accused were sentenced to 39 years in jail, one to 20 years in jail, three to 12 years in jail, one to 6 years in jail and three to 3 years in jail. The death sentence was confirmed by the Seville Judge Advocate September 6 1946 and by the General Capitania on the 17th of that same month. The Government commuted Domingo Escola Verde0s sentence January 20 1947.

It has been extremely difficult to reconstruct the labyrinth of raids and arrests during the 1940s. Much information comes from the reports of oral witnesses who have spoken of many of these caidas, or nettings, such as the *Caida del Horno* because it left from a brick factory in the Campo de la Verdad, in Cordoba capital. A great many number of communists were netted on this occasion, such as Melchor Ranchal Risquez, a native of Añora. When at the end of 1945, five months later, the police were again looking for him in another raid, he chose to flee to the hills where he joined the guerrillas with the nickname of *Curro de Añora.*[xix]

The members of clandestine organizations who were netted and arrested in the caídas, were subject to the traditional beatings and tortures of all prisoners under Franco. We cannot forget that an outstanding feature of Francoism was that nobody who was arrested escaped a beating. For many of the political prisoners, the arrest alone would have been punishment enough. Torture obeyed various ends and where the clandestine were concerned, it was as a means of obtaining the names of Party members and details of their links. In the case of Melchor Ranchal for example, told how after suffering a non-stop 24 hour torture session, his wife went to see him in prison and she didn't recognize him. That is why he fled to the hills, not because of a whim or because of any desire to become a guerrilla fighter.

The repressive terror reached such heights during 1945-1946, that more and more fled to the hills, which undoubtedly explains the rapid increase in the number of guerrilla groups at that time. Many of those who discovered that they were thought to be or identified as clandestine, had no other choice than to flee to the hills. José *Felipe* Merino Campos is an example of a young man who, believing that he may have been discovered for having set off some firecrackers in Cordoba to celebrate July 18, fled to the hills and joined Julián Caballero's guerrillas.

During the entire decade of the 1940s, every time that was a raid and netting of country folk, both men and women, in the neighbourhood of a town on the grounds that they were giving support to the guerrillas, there followed an outbreak of extra-legal shootings, deaths and imprisonments. Whenever a guerrilla turned himself in to the authorities, it was the same. There was a constant in and out of imprisoned individuals, justified by the authorities as anti-guerrilla repression. Of the many thousands imprisoned during this decade, according to an official source, at least 60,000 individuals were imprisoned for this reason. No less than 5,349 were arrested in Toledo province between 1941-1948 and there were other 'hot' regions such as Galicia, Asturias, León, Levante, Málaga, Granada, Cordoba and so on. To those numbers we must add the thousands who suffered the great repression of clandestine activities in major cities such as Madrid, Barcelona and Seville. The great penitentiary world of Francoist prisons was so hyperbolic that one could be forgiven for thinking that any understanding of it is almost beyond one's reach.

[xix] He died in the Umbría de la Huesa, Villaviciosa, tragedy in 1947, when all the leaders of Julián Caballero's 3rd Guerilla Group were executed.

Endnotes for Chapter II

1   Constanza de la Mora Maura, *Doble splendor* (Double splendor). Gadir, Madrid, 2004, p. 550.
2   Bartolomé Cabrera Peralbo, eye-witness reports, interviewed by Moreno Gómez in Pozoblanco, November 21 1985 and October 17 1986.
3   Antonio Baena Romero, *Prison Diary*. Lent to Moreno Gómez by his family.
4   Francisco Moreno Gómez, *Villanueva* newspaper, Villanueva de Cordoba, number 12, April 1981.
5   *En solidaridad con la Comisión y Proyecto de Monumento* (In support of the Monument Committee and Project), *Villanueva* newspaper, Villanueva de Cordoba, nº 19, Nov 1981.
6   Manuel Bedmar, eye witness accounts during several interviews with the author in Puente Genil.
7   Juan Gutiérrez Romero, a companion of his in prison. Eye witness report.
8   Antonio Bahamonde. *Un año com Queipo de Llano. (Memorias de un Nacionalista)* [A year with Queipo de Llano. (Memoires of a Nationalist). Espuela de Plata, Sevilla, 2005, p. 113.
9   Letter from the *Todos Los Nombres de Porcuna* [All the names from Porcuna] project, sent to the author and dated 30 January 2013. Blog entitled *Religión en Libertad*: http://www.religionenlibertad.com/blog/tomas-de-la-torre-lendinez--297.html.
10 Francisco Moreno Gómez." Hombres que dejan huella. Nemesio Pozuelo" (Men who have made their mark. Nemesio Pozuelo), biography of this leader in the *Villanueva* newspaper, Villanueva de Cordoba, issue 5, September 1980.
11 For a more complete biography of Miguel Ranchal, see Francisco Moreno Gómez, *Villanueva* newspaper, Villanueva de Cordoba, issue 23, March 1982.
12 Alfonso Vaquero Zamorano, interviewed by Moreno Gómez, 16 October 2013.
13 *Azul* newspaper, Cordoba, 16 October 1940.
14 Letter from the Mayor of Belalcázar to the Civil Governor in Cordoba 16 December 1940. Belalcázar Municipal Archives.
15 Eye-witness account to Moreno Gómez from Manuela Illescas, one of the woman who had to leave her newborn child behind.
16 Book of Minutes of the Sessions, Box Number 246, Pozoblanco Municipal Archives.
17 Sr. Arévalo Bajo, personal testimony and eye witness account to Moreno Gómez at the entrance to the Pozoblanco Old People's Home, December 12, 2013.
18 Information received from Blas Muñoz Márquez, Pozoblanco, 21 November 1985.
19 Mary Vincent *The Sprintering of Spain: Cultural History and the Spanish Civil War,* Edited by Chris Ealham and Michael Richards. Cambridge University Press, 2005, p. 75.
20 Juan Gutiérrez Romero, from Villanueva but resident in Villafranca. Interviewed several times by the author during the 1980s.
21 Francisco Moreno Gómez. *1936: El genocidio franquista in Cordoba* (1936: The

Francoist Genocide in Cordoba), Crítica, Barcelona, 2008.

[22] Carmen Flórez Pérez, letter to Moreno Gómez, denying him access to the Red Cross archives, 13 November 2013.

[23] Pedro Gafias. *Héroes del sur* (Heroes of the South). Madrid-Barcelona, 1938.

[24] Joe Monks, With the Reds in Andalusia. London, 1985. (pp. 110 et al. In the Spanish translation).

[25] Data provided by the Gaitán brothers – Adán, Félix and Juan Manuel. *Mártires de una esperanza* (Martyrs to Hope), about Pedro Abad. Lopera (Jaén), 2009, p. 495.

[26] Reyes Mate, *Memoria de Auschwitz* (Memory of Auschwitz). Trotta, Madrid, 2003.

[27] Claro González Sánchez, interviewed by Moreno Gómez in Fuenteobejuna, August 1979.

[28] Miguel Navarro González, oral testimony given to Moreno Gómez in Obejo, 24 August 1985.

[29] Copy of the letter given to Moreno Gómez by his sister, Salud Bujalance, Hornachuelos, April 1981.

[30] One of the stanzas of the ditty, which the author's mother taught him, was based on the idea that the right-wing won the 1933 elections because women were allowed to vote for the first time.: *Si la mujer no tu-viera / voto ni tampoco voz, / no nos hubieran ganado / las derechas a traición* [If women had not been given the vote nor a say, the perfidious Right would never have beaten us.].

[31] Arcángel Bedmar gave Moreno Gómez a copy of this letter, which was mentioned earlier in this book.

[32] True copy of the dossier for Cause 94/44, provided to Moreno Gómez by one of the indicted, Pablo González Calvo, from Peñarroya.

[33] Moreno Gómez interviewed Julio Priego several times and he still has his address in Cordoba.

[34] Adriano Romero Cachinero, *Eurocarrillismo y oportunismo* (Eurocarrilism and opportunism). Bilbao, 1984, p. 102.

[35] Julio Priego Ordóñez, interviwed by Moreno Gómez , 2 January 1983.

[36] This document is kept with Bartolomé Fernández's family archives, in Pozoblanco.

APPENDIX I

FAREWELL LETTERS FROM PRISONERS TO THEIR FAMILIES, WRITTEN IN THE PRISON "CHAPEL" AS THEY AWAITED EXECUTION

Joaquim Moreno Muñoz. BAENA. Letter to his family written from jail February 1942. A returnee from Baena, aged 43, he was imprisoned in Cordoba. One month later, 10 March, he was executed in San Rafael cemetery, Cordoba.

- "My dear parents and brothers... Mother, I received everything that you say you sent me, as you do not know how much good it did to make me better from the weakness I was suffering. If you can continue to come or send me clothes and what food you can, I will be better off; if you cannot, it will be impossible for me to go on... You have no idea how grateful a prisoner is to know that he is remembered, more so in the circumstances in which I find myself; nobody knows that better than one who has to endure these situations and how they devour you. Tomás of my heart: do whatever you can, both for the sake of my health and to relieve me of this unbearable burden..."

Francisco Copado Sánchez. VILLANUEVA DE CÓRDOBA. Executed in Paterna, Valencia, 1 November 1939. First cousin to Fr. Bernabé Copado, S.J., the famous Jesuit chaplain to the Nationalist Redondo Unit conscripts. Arrested on a trumped up false allegation. His wife wrote letters and tried to visit his cousin in Málaga to enlist his help in obtaining his release but he ignored her. A few days before his execution, Francisco wrote Maria, praising her attempts in his favour but clearly expressed his resignation to his fate which he decided was predetermined.

- "Yesterday you wrote of your determination and plans to go and see cousin Bernabé in Malaga and have him come to our home town. Dear girl, I do not want you to undertake another difficult trip, but when I consider what is and has been done, go ahead. Because, even if you can get Bernabé to go to Villanueva and despite that, he is not successful in getting the reversal of that denunciation whilst he is there, it is because their 'secret committee' met and they did not agree to do so. I imagine, Maria, that you will arrive in Málaga and you will be nicely and well received by Bernabé, but even though you are going there with good intentions and firmly

151

decided to prove what you can, and try to convince him to accompany you to Burgos, you won't manage it, because these men have their agenda for every moment, and in Villanueva, the slanderers will continue with their own plans. It was a great triumph on your part that you were able to get a pre-trial hearing, the results of which are already in my case file, and if I were not already a 'caged cat', this would be enough for my sentence to be commuted… I am thinking, although I have not yet decided to do so, of writing to that stupid guy, influenced as he is by his wife and other relatives, the slanderer Rodríguez."

- "Valencia, Modelo Prison, 31 October 1939.
  My dear parents and brothers,
  Today is the last day of my life and I am facing it as calmly as any other day because I am innocent, as you know, of that which I am accused. I wish you good fortune and that you get some pleasure in this world. Receive my heartfelt gratitude for all that you did, to the very end, to save me, but those men did not want that.
  Farewell my parents and brothers. Many hugs and kisses.
  Francisco Copado."

Francisco "Curro Beatas" Sánchez Muñoz. VILLANUEVA DE CÓRDOBA. Member of the Izquierda Republicana and alterman for the Frente Popular. Executed 17 My 1940 in Villalnueva. Wrote several letters in chapel, two of which, both undated, are reproduced here.

"Please deliver to:
  Agustina Cerezo Garcia
  Plaza del Carmen 11
  Villanueva de Cordoba

- To my dear wife and children,
      When you receive these four letters, if they arrive, I will be no more, but as I have no other way to bid you farewell, I do so in this way, also because I believe it is more suitable as if it were any other way, none of us would have the courage to bear it.
      Agustina, I trust that you will be strong enough to bear this new trial that you must face, even though for no other reason than for the sake of our children who, given their ages, more than ever need your care and love. I am very aware, dear Agustina, of the extremely difficult situation in which you are left, but trust in the future; this situation will not last forever and as they grow older, our children will soon be able to help you. So, be strong, accept matters and try to give them a good education. Make them respect you as you deserve and as is due to all honourable and hardworking people. Keep them from suffering from the lack of a father.

To you, my dear children, I charge you to be respectful and obedient to your mother, who deserves it all, for no matter how much you do for her, you will never be able to repay her for all that she deserves and has done for all of us. You, dear Rosalía, as the eldest, must care for and rebuke your younger brothers whenever necessary and help Mother in every way you can; avoid giving her any trouble and do not allow anyone to do so.

I also tell you all, no matter how much you hear others say about me, that you have nothing to be ashamed of, as your father died without ever having killed or robbed anybody. On the contrary, I always did my utmost to help those who needed it, never failing in my duty, even though on this occasion some say not, some because they are afraid, others because of ill will, as to the best of my knowledge nobody has done anything to help my situation.

Dear Agustina: I would also like you to show these letters to my brothers, so that they may become aware of the situation in you find yourselves and as I would expect, help in any way they can, as I always did when they needed it. The only person I do not want you to even bother to contact is that shameless nephew of mine, whose veins I very much doubt run with my brother's blood since he has behaved so badly towards you and me after I did so many favours for him. I die convinced that sooner or later he will reap his just reward.

I will not tire you any longer, my dear wife. Please give my regards to your parents and your brothers, to my parents and the rest of my family and friends. To you, my dear children and wife, receive this last heartfelt embrace from your father and husband who will keep you in his thoughts until his very last breath.
Francisco Sánchez

A second letter which he most certainly had delivered by a different means, although also addressed to his family and also written in chapel is not personal, as the above one, as in it he denounces those who tortured him in Villanueva, adding the wish that some day they shall as they deserve.

- "My dear wife and children: If I am trying to make sure that you receive these lines, I do so because I want you to know what happened to me during all the time that I was in prison and who are the principle persons guilty of the monstrous accusations with which I was charged, as I believe that, in the not too distant future, you can denounce them to the powers that be, not with lies, as they did with me, but with the truth.

When I went to the barracks where I was beaten with rods until I signed a confession. I was forced to sign everything they put before me, and whenever they wished to add something, they would beat me again. My principle tormentors were "Berenguer", Matias Pedraza, "El Tiraor",

Miguel Higuera's son and Manolito el Panadero's son, all who beat me viciously, as you would not do even to the wildest animals.

Gregorio Pedraza, Miguel Higuera, Pedro Cano, Pablito and two or three more whose names I don't remember, made an endless number of false accusations, something that none of them had a reason to do so in the way that they did. They had warned me, when I defended Don Dionisio's sons, that if ever I continued to do so they would repay me in this way.

As to the witnesses for the accusations, they may have said nothing more than what was read to me: Pedro "Cascanueces" said that I had taken statements from those who were arrested and Alfonso [Fernández] that I, as a member of the War Committee, had prevented his execution, contrary to the other twenty-one, implying that it was I who was responsible for ordering the executions; this, so you know what it is that you have to thank them for.

For now, I do not ask you for anything more, but if you can avenge me, do so. I also beg my sons not to be ashamed of me because I never stole from, nor killed anybody. I am guilty of nothing else than supporting a legally constituted Government; also, I never exceeded my powers when I duly carried out my duties as a member of that Government.

I have nothing more to say, except to you, my dear children: I charge you to be always respectful to your mother and that you love her as she deserves, for no matter how much you do for her, you will never be able to repay her for all that she deserves and has done for you.

To you, my dear companion, be strong and care for our beloved children as if I were with you, and wait for the better times that shall soon come, for the good of Spain. With a heartfelt embrace from your father and husband who will keep you in his thoughts until his very last breath."

Luís Prat Blanco. BELALCÁZAR, age 32. Local Secretary of the PCE lost a leg from gangrene on the Madrid front. Executed at the end of 1939 in Hinojosa del Duque. Two farewell letters exhibited to Moreno Gómez by his niece Guadalupe.

- "To my dear sisters, nephews and brothers-in-law,
    It is with the greatest pain and with tears in my eyes, that I dedicate these words to you so that you may remember me.

    Sisters, at the last moments, as I am about to be executed, my heart beats with the memory of such dear sisters of mine alone, as you have had no other brother; you who have always been my greatest joy and hopes, you who have been the mirror of my soul, you who were everything to me, my dreams and my joy, who on this tragic day, fate will take me from me.

    I ask you to be always good, that you look after the girl of my dreams, that you forgive everyone as I forgive them, that you educate my little niece well, to be truthful and when she grows up, you tell her that she had and she still has, albeit underground, an uncle who loves her with all his heart and soul, that she was my only joy.

Sisters, live in peace knowing that your brother was never bad; you know that I always was, as far as I could be, an honest worker. Goodbye dear sisters and brothers-in-law, forever. Goodbye with all my soul, goodbye until eternity, your brother,
Luis Prat Blanco

- To my dear parents, from prison
    With pain in my heart and sadness for myself, in the last moments of my life, I dedicate this letter to you, so that you always remember with fondness, the advice from your son Luis.

    Dear parents, bad luck now that my life is ending, despite the misfortune of my leg, the best time of my life. Father, keep in mind what you must do in the years left to you, resign yourselves to the calamity and do all the good that you can for everyone, most especially for my sisters and nephews, be truthful and good, forgive everyone as I forgive them in my last hours.

    I hope that you will live for many years, considering that I in my last and best years of my life, am being separated forever from you. Although it pains me, I ask that you do not go into a corner of pity for me, that you try to dry up as much of the pain as you can, in the hope that you may live life as well as possible, because I am going to rest forever, and my sole and only concern is for you, for how much you will suffer for me.

    Be certain that your son always believed that he was good to you as you always were to me. I beg you to forgive me for anything I might have done to offend you, as I myself I leave without ever having been offended.

    Goodbye dear parents, goodbye forever and for eternity. Goodbye with all my heart and soul. Your son,
Luis Prat Blanco."

Eugenio "Palmera Jurado Pozuelo. VILLANUEVA DE CÓRDOBA. Executed 26 May 1940 in Villanueva.

- "My dear wife:
    Convinced as I am that, despite all the efforts of our family to save me, it will all be to no avail because those who hold my fate in their hands, although insignificant in number, today are the people's arbitrators. I am writing you these lines so that you know who are the principle authors of our misfortune and the cruel manner by which they persecuted me during the year and half of my Calvary.

    I am convinced that the future of the world is in play today and that it lies in the fight to death between tyranny and the freedom of the people, which has only just begun, and I die knowing that those who are responsible for my death will not wait long before they are made to pay for the blood lust that led them to commit so many crimes. When the time for justice comes, I beg you do your utmost to avenge my death.

I assure you, as if you ever had any doubts, that I have never taken part directly or indirectly in any of the deaths that occurred in our town and that I did as much as I could to avoid problems for many who today may have turned their backs on me. Of these, I can truthfully mention, among others, Diego Higuera, Paco Ochoa, Pepe "El Florista", Andrés Cabrera and Cristóbal Arellano. As regards my political behaviour, I did no more than do my duty, not as a member of a certain political party, but as a simple citizen, in support of a Government whose legality even its enemies recognize. Circumstances obliged me to accuse (not with lies as they have done with me) before a Court, those who to their shame are the material authors of my death and of the suffering that I have been subjected to.

You need to know that the first to arrest me was Andrés Pontes (a carpenter) from Daimiel, who undoubtedly wishing to curry favour, presented me to the authorities of that town as a terrible criminal, which led them to shut me up in an attic with other unfortunates. Later they brought me here the day that we met in the jail, put there is no point in listing the suffering and aggravation that I have endured since then.

My tormentors have not missed a chance nor a pretext, no matter how base, to mistreat me with word and deed, resorting to shocking and shameful things.

Those who most persecuted and were angry with me were primarily: Matías Pedraza and Pepe Delgado, who beat me two or three times, and Manuel Delgado (Pepe's father), and Blas el Sillonero, who were guilty of many beatings that I received in the barracks, as well as the brothers Valero and Vicente "Salado" Muñoz. Others who did their best to make sure that I would not be saved, by making declarations in my dossier against me: Diego López, Gregorio Pedraza Cámara and Ángel Díaz, son of Manolo el Panadero, many of whom I never bothered at all, and some of them, such as don Gregorio, who at least in part owes me his life. These are those who ostensibly prepared my death, but I have no doubt that as regards those who collaborated with them, you shall one day reward them in the way they deserve.

As regards my brother Zacarías, I want you to remind him to whom he owes his existence, as nobody ignores that he is my brother, if for no other reason because when he was arrested and tried [sic. in Jaén by the Republican People's Court, at the beginning of the war], I went and spoke to the prosecutor and to Nemesio on his behalf, to try and influence the jury, which is why he was not sentenced to death. Behave with him with as much consideration as he has behaved with us, as I do not know with any certainty how he will react to my situation.

Try to do for my father, if he survives so much disgrace, all that you possibly can and comfort each other.

I know that your affection is sufficiently sincere and deep to understand the causes of our misfortune and I am sorry that because of me you will also suffer what you shouldn't. Be strong in your adversity and trust that the time shall soon come when my death shall be avenged.

My affection to all, as I hold you all in my heart. First you and our daughter, with whom you shall soon share your misfortune and who will help you with her love and company; my poor father, who has struggled so much; my brother José, who has always been so kind to me; my sister and all my nephews and nieces; your parents who have done so much for us; my friends who interested themselves in my fate. To all, a warm embrace from your husband who loves you with all his heart.

Eugenio."

Pedro "Cuadrado" Torralbo Rico. VILLANUEVA DE CÓRDOBA. Executed 3 June 1941 in Cordoba. Copy of letter given to Moreno Gómez by Pedro Torralbo's son, José, from Sallent, Barcelona.

- "Dear wife and children: I dedicate this to you at the last moments of my life. Dear wife: You know how I have acted and that I have nothing to be ashamed of. Continue to be good with our children, don't impress anything bad on them so that they do not absorb any of the hatreds that poison Humanity. A very deeply felt remembrance to all my brothers and to your parents. Embrace our children, as I would, and you, my dearest wife, receive my last embrace with love.

Darling daughters Petra and Paquita: It is at a very sad time that I write these lines, a remembrance for you. As I think of you, my emotions prevent me from telling you everything I wanted, but I will try to recommend two things: be honest and good with your mother and brothers. Think of your father every so often, but you need be ashamed of nothing, as I always was an honourable man. When you are grown up, you will understand why your father died.

Dearest sisters and brothers-in-law: At these last moments of my life, I write these words of farewell. My spirit is calm and my conscience even more so, because I never did any harm to anyone as I always followed my conscience and am ashamed of nothing. At these last hours of my life, I tell you with all sincerity, that I never participated in any crime of blood, either directly or indirectly, therefore, neither you nor my children have to bow your heads before anyone. I only ask you to look after my children, as I die for my ideals. I don't mind dying; I only feel for them. Regarding the rest, I am content. Please do not shed any useless tears for me and help my children understand why their father died. I ask you to look after them, as you will do my wife, and care for her as you would a sister. Many hugs and kisses to the nephews and nieces whom I never met. Hugs to Santiago. Say farewell from me to all the family. And to you both, forgive me if I ever offended you in any way.

With a warm embrace from your brother, Pedro Torralbo."

Juan José "El Conejero" Mohedano Sánchez. VILLANUEVA DE CÓRDOBA. Executed 26 May 1940 in Villanueva de Cordoba.

- At this very tragic moment in my life, when seventeen of my companions have just been taken out to be shot, I pick up my pencil, dearest companion and dear children, to ask you to forgive me if I have ever, at any time, offended you and, at the same time and if you receive this letter, to let you know my last Will and what you shall have to do if there ever is some justice…

  I only wish that you are never ashamed of your father, who committed no other crime than to guard the prisoners at Los Grupos, from 23 July to 23 September 1936, when I thwarted outside attempts to free the prisoners from the prison. But as they could find no crime to accuse me of, they introduced four false accusations that I was prevented from defending with true facts, with which they ensured that I was given the maximum sentence."

Juan Luna Enríquez. VILLANUEVA DE CÓRDOBA. Communist member of the Villanueva Committee. Fragment of a letter he wrote his wife while in the chapel.

- "…and to my María Josefa, tell her to be good and, as the eldest, that she helps you with your hardships, and that she nailed a thorn in my heart the day she came to see me and said: "Father, do not worry." Also, my Magdalena, mi Teodora and my boy, tell them to never forget their father, not to be ashamed of him: their father was neither a criminal nor a thief; nobody could prove that. Also, help your mother. With no further ado, I, your dear father, bid you farewell, and you, my Luna, as this is the last time I shall speak your name…"

Letters from residents of Cordoba Province who were executed elsewhere in Spain

Miguel Ranchal Plazuelo. VILLANUEVA DEL DUQUE. Socialist leader and Mayor of Villanueva del Duque during the Republic. Executed 13 June 1940 in Modelo Prison, Barcelona.

- "Miguel Ranchal, Modelo Prison

  To: Maria Josefa Luna

158

5th Gallery, cell 448, Barcelona
Barriada de la Estacion
Villanueva del Duque, Cordoba
13 June 1940
My dear wife and children,
As I have always told you, I saw the coming of the last hour of my life and it arrived this morning, 13 June. I go in peace and in the knowledge that you shall never be ashamed of my actions, as I neither robbed nor killed anybody. All the people know that. I shall only tell you one more thing: teach our children as much as you can so that tomorrow they will be men of good will. For my sister, for Bartolomé, for your father and all the family many hugs, in the knowledge that I always remembered them. Last, for you and our dear children, thousands of hugs and kisses, until eternity. Your Miguel."

José Cantador Huertos. VILLANUEVA DE CÓRDOBA. Banesto bank employee resident in Játiva where he was an alderman for the Frente Popular. Executed 29 August 1940 in Valencia.

■ "To: Isabel Sánchez de Cantador   Calle Reina 12, Játiva

My dear wife,
When you receive this by such an extraordinary channel, I who was your husband, will have ceased to exist. There is nothing we can do about that. I suggest that you clothe yourself with calm and patience and that you try to organize your life for the future in the best possible way for yourself and for our children. As last favours, I ask that you do your utmost to give our children a good education so that they can learn a profession that will bring them a good living and that you don't spend any money on my remains.

Try to move back to our hometown as soon as the means you have at your disposal make it possible. There, surrounded by family, you may possibly feel better. Please thank all those who, in my absence, did something for me and for you, and tell them that I am only sorry that I cannot repay them.

I believe that you are keeping the receipts from the Montepío de Banca. Do not ever let them go and if the situation shall ever change, and I wish it does, if you are advised by somebody, you may perhaps be able to recover some of our savings. This is the only capital that I, this man who worked his entire life, can leave you. Regarding our household goods, if there is anything left, they are all yours during your lifetime and afterwards, our children's.

Bid farewell to the children for me and tell them that it is their father's wish that they do their best to be good, honest and hardworking and that they give you all the love that you deserve; that they learn a lot from their father's example and, most especially, that they only make friends with honourable people. Tell them that their father dies because of those who owed him the most favours, as they could not accuse him of having done them any harm.

The war, in my opinion, was a waste of energy, albeit dedicated to good and to the defence of my class – bank employees – yet it is this family that abandoned me at the worst moment and even let me die. They have documents? I don't know. I saved their lives and for them I went to as many places as I had to. Except for one you know; the remainder deserve being reviled. Especially Ricardo Diego Ruiz who is a prototype of perversity.

It does not pain me to die in such circumstances, not more than not being able to repay you for the many sleepless nights you suffered on my account; but if it brings you some solace, I swear that if it is true that there is a life beyond this one, I will watch over you all… Never think of revenge. Revenge dishonours the person who exercises it! Think of justice and use it to defend me and defend yourself.

Many hugs for the children and for our family; for you, receive the heart shot through with pain and bullets of he who was your husband, José Cantador.

Valencia, 29 August 1940.

(Post script)

Dear wife,

At this moment (5 p.m.), I am being taken to fulfil the sentence dictated by the court martial. I repeat, go to Villanueva and care for our children and do your utmost to educate them in the best way possible. Many hugs and kisses for everyone, and for you, the love of he who shall forever watch over you. José Cantador. Regards to my brother."

Rafael Porras Caballero. POZOBLANCO. Son of Antonio Porras the Republican poet and politician. Executed 19 May 1943 in Madrid. Wrote two letters in chapel, one to his sister Carmen and one to his parents and brothers which is reproduced below.

■ "My dearest and never forgotten parents and brothers.

In a few minutes, I will deliver my soul to God. I have said confession and I die as a Christian in that I forgive my enemies, with all my heart. Therefore, my last request is that you do the same as your son is doing in the last moments of his life.

Carmen shall arrange my funeral and she will always offer you the solace of being able to pray at my grave and every so often, to bring me some beautiful flowers. I die as a Christian, with resignation and a clean and tranquil conscience, as you and I know that I never hurt anybody. If I have a great regret, it is that I cannot embrace all of you for a last time and tell you that I always, always have held you in my heart and in my thoughts.

Carmen will explain how I invested the money for the house; if I spent too much for some reason, please forgive me. I do not want to remain quiet regarding Carmen and her husband's behaviour towards me: they never abandoned me for a single moment. They did more for me than they could imagine, which is why I trust that you will know how to acknowledge this as they deserve.

I may be rambling a bit, but I cannot concentrate on writing it as I should. I just want to tell you all, dear parents and brothers, that I die thinking of God and you. Farewell. I do not want to go on any longer as you will suffer more. Be resigned, be good and live in peace, you certainly deserve it. My last embrace holds all of you together, to make it stronger and more heartfelt.

Rafael.

José María San Ildefonso dies with me. He leaves a widow and children. Please do as much as possible for them. They live at Carretera de Aragón number 15, Ventas."

Eduardo Bujalance López. HORNACHUELOS. Member of Parliament for the Frente Popular. Executed by the Nationalists 30 July 1936 in Cordoba. Letter lent to Moreno Gómez by his sister, Salud Bujalance, Hornachuelos, April 1981.

- "Dear father, wife, brothers, nephews and other relatives, Today, the last day of my existence, I am writing you these last lines, that you will remember for a long time, never forgetting, above all, that when I was tried for the first time, everything that I said to my sister and wife.

As you know, because of what I have told you before, I never took direct nor indirect part in blood crimes. There are charges against me, but you know who is accusing me, so that my conscience has nothing to regret and your pride as father and honourable family, as always, remains unblemished.

There is only one certainty that I have had from the very first day (I noticed this when I became aware of the way they were focusing on my declarations): They do not want me to live so that tomorrow I cannot press charges against those who were responsible for shooting my brother. It is not by chance that the military judge told me that the worst that could be said of me was that I was the brother of Antonio Bujalance, the Member of Parliament; that is why they are interested in that I no longer continue to exist.

It does not hurt me to die because of death, no; the only thing that pains me is that they are eliminating me without just cause, that is, for false reasons.

161

The irony of Destiny planned dubious things for us; for you, my father, it allowed the loss of your three sons, in the flower of their lives. Sister of mine – I beg you to not to abase yourselves for anything in this life; fight for the future of your children.

Carmen, my dear wife, what can I say to you? When I try to speak to you I get a knot in my throat, not because of the pain in my heart, but because I feel responsible for destroying a young life such as yours, although you will never have to bear the burden of having loved a man who loved you and in which you deposited all your trust... Today, destiny separates us. You are alive, you are young; do not waste the chance of living your life well, because I want you to be as happy on this earth as when you were at my side. That is my wish.

Lastly, to all of you, do not waste time nor energy with useless matters and shedding tears. Be as strong as I am in these last moments. Get along well with each other, as true sisters who help each other. Look after Father, who is already very old, and remember your brother, son, husband and uncle, who sends you his last kiss. Eduardo Bujalance.

(Written in the chapel, hours before my execution.)"

APPENDIX II

WRITINGS AND LETTERS FROM MEMBERS OF THE CLERGY OR CHURCH INSTITUTIONS. EXCERPTS FROM REV. GUMERSINDO DE ESTELA'S DIARY

Father José M. Gallegos Rocafull, Professor at the San Pelagio Seminary and of the Universid Central de Madrid.

Extracted from a manifest entitled *Palabras cristianas* (Christian teachings) by Fr. José M. Gallegos Rocafull and Fr. *Leocadio Lugo*. In: *La pequeña grey. Testimonios religiosos sobre la guerra civil española.* (The small congregation. Religious Testimony on the Spanish civil war). Barcelona, Península, 2007, pp. 211 et al.

> "The Church will never stop teaching the respect and obedience due to the established power..." Collective declaration by Spanish bishops 20 December 1931.

> "...failure to obey and to encourage sedition is a crime of lèse majesté..." Pope Leon XIII, Inmoratale Dei.

> "...the Church has always condemned the doctrines and the men who rebel against the legitimate authorities." Pope Leon XIII, Au milieu.

> "Fight, Catholic men, in defence of the rights of the Church, with perseverance and energy, but without ever using sedition and violence." Pope Pius XI, Gravissimo.

> "The truth is that a few men have burdened the shoulders of the innumerable multitude of proletarians, a yolk that is very little different to the one of the slaves." Pope Leon XIII, Rerum Novarum.

> "The economic organization violates the true order when capital enslaves the workers." Pope Pius XI, Quadragesimo Anno.

Pronouncement of Fr. Rocafull's, recorded in the above book:

- "In the Catholic world (albeit more in Europe than in America), at the first there was a spontaneous movement of surprise, of protests, of fear of the intervention of the clergy in the war, even more so because this was a civil war between some insurgents and a legally constituted government."

Ernesto Caballero Castillo. *Vivir con memoria.* (Living with memory). Cordoba, El Páramo, 2001, pp 66 et al. Son of Julián Caballero, ex-Communist Mayor of Villanueva de Cordoba, who at the time of these events was a guerrilla commander in the North of Cordoba province. He was taken from home by the Welfare authorities and placed in a convent school in Villanueva de Cordoba.

"Those days of profound beliefs were horrendous times for me. I was permanently terrified of the punishments that God might hurl against me. Everything was a sin and God saw everything.

In summary, my bad memories of the Cristo Rey Convent are of old and musty chick peas, lentils and dried beans, ridden with bugs, served with only a bit of fat, inedible... I hated lentils for years afterwards; broad beans forever. I had nightmares of the scary stories Mother Maria Josefa told us; of the loud bells; of Mother Rucio's wicker cane and the way she beat us on our heads with the pot in which the food was served, to shut the children up... of the terrifying religious lessons and, quite obviously, the day of my confirmation...

When I was 7 years old, the nuns sent me to work as an apprentice blacksmith at Domingo Torres' forge on Calle Cañada Baja. Domingo Torres was, unwittingly, the person who most influenced me to stop believing in God, as much as the nuns tried to make me believe in Him. I had to go to daily mass before I began work in the forge, early in the morning.

Domingo swore constantly, blaspheming as the nuns would call it, slanging Christ, every saint, virgin, blessing and consecration of the communion host in the Book. The first times that I heard such things, I looked at him in fear and amazement. I expected God to strike him dead as the nuns had taught me that this is what happened to all who blasphemed."

"The missionaries appeared in 1943 or 1944. These were young Jesuit priests intent on Christianizing every left-wing individual who was still alive and not yet imprisoned, as well as his relatives and the relatives of those who had already been executed. The imprisoned were Christianized in the jails.

For quite some time, the missionaries taught a whole series of classes, giving those who attended some economic compensation in exchange, a few bags of food, clothes. As the authorities were again compelling the rich to accept that the workers had to be believers before they could hire them, anyone who did not convert found it difficult to find any kind of work.

It saddens me greatly when I remember those poor people, crowding around those priests like so many sheep, hoping for some clemency, a bag of food, some clothes to cover their bodies and a reference that they were good Christians."

EXCERPTS FROM
REVEREND GUMERSINDO DE ESTELA'S DIARY

22 June 1937. Terse dialogue in the chapel wiith Don Tregídio, Socialist, Secretary of the Escatrón Municipality near Casp. He was a friend of Father Gumersindo's. Condemned to 30 years in prison by the court martial, his sentence was overruled in Burgos and he was condemned to death.

- "He was a tall gentleman, about 50 years old… He was nervous as he entered… When he saw the altar, he stood straight, raised his arms and exclaimed:
  - Why have I been brought here? Let them kill me quickly, with four shots; do not keep me here suffering.
  He sat down and again asked:
  - Am I permitted to know why I have been brought here?
  I felt that this was a good time to speak to him, so I said:
  - You can imagine my deepest sympathy at seeing you suffer. I would like to help with lessening something of the pain you must be suffering. This is why I have come to offer you some religious comfort.
  He looked me straight in the eye and replied:
  - What are you saying? What religion are you talking about? If you are referring to the religion that I learnt in my mother's arms, that one is very good for consoling someone… But the religion that now has set your lot to killing a million Spaniards, that one comforts no one; don't even mention that one; that one is a fascist religion…"

TORRERO, ZARAGOZA, CEMETERY. **Execution of Don Tregídio and another prisoner.**

"…We had arrived at the cemetery. We drove along the wall to get to that part of the wall at the front, facing the city and neighbourhood of Torrero, from where we had just come. And … we found a detachment of some one hundred soldiers. They were formed in rows facing the wall, but about fifty metres distant. Sixteen of them were closest to the wall…

As we arrived, our truck stopped. We got off and began to walk towards the soldiers. They looked at us with curiosity. I walked next to Don Tregidio. The other prisoner was accompanied by Fr. Victor, who could not contain his roughness. We walked past a Red Cross van, almost touching it… Next to the van, two gurneys that had been prepared to receive the bodies of both men. And they could see it all! What a terribly sad walk! Sixty or seventy bitterly difficult steps for the condemned men and for anyone who had been born with a bit of heart...

Nobody asked the prisoners whether they wanted a blindfold. I still did not abandon my friend. I stood at his side, stroking his right arm and neck with my hand, and I repeated the prayer: 'Merciful Jesus, save my soul'. He repeated it and he kissed the crucifix. I offered it to the other prisoner for him to kiss, but he shook his head. The silence was deafening. I realized that the officer who had to give the sign to fire was waiting for me to leave. I walked away and stood behind the advance squad of soldiers.

The officer shouted: 'Aim!' Don Tregidio shouted: 'Long live God and Socialism!'. The officer shouted again: 'Fire!'. The fatal shots rang out. Each body was riddled by eight bullets. They fell backwards, onto the ground... Some Guardias Civiles approached to remove the metal handcuffs that bound their hands.

I approached to administer extreme unction to one and absolution and a prayer. Both bodies were lying in a large pool of blood that had run down their legs and was mixing with the dew... A lieutenant shot them each twice in the head. The doctor approached to confirm their death. The members of the Brotherhood of the Blood of Christ picked them up and placed them on the gurneys...."

21 September. After consoling six Nationalist soldiers who had been condemned to death: three from the quartermaster's, three health workers and one from the artillery.

> "The six confessed, attended Holy Mass and took Communion with great devotion. Some cried. They were so very wretched! One of them sobbed: "What is my poor mother going to think that I did, when she hears that I have been shot? How horrible! All for nothing...!"

22 September. Report of three women who entered the chapel because they had attempted to go over to the Republican zone. Two of them were carrying young children. The execution the followed was horrific and so upset the Capuchin monk tha he left alone, walking like a robot.

> "I had entered the chapel, in which everything was prepared for Mass, when I heard the heartrending cries of women outside... Sobbing appeals...
> – My daughter! Don't take her from me! Have pity, don't steal her from me. Kill her with me! I want to take her to the next world with me!
> – I don't want to leave my daughter with these executioners...! Daughter of my heart, what will become of you?
> ...Meanwhile, a fierce fight broke out between the guards who were trying, with all their strength, to tear the children from their mothers' breasts and

arms and the poor mothers who held onto their treasures as tightly as they could...

When I heard those poor little creatures cry, as they did not want to be taken from their mothers, terrified at the sight of the guards, as I heard the heartrending cries of those unfortunate women, I felt my heart breaking... I never thought that I would ever have to see such a sight in a civilized country. I never believed that there could be a king, or leader, or caudillo on this earth who could decree such a thing. To anyone who intended to do such a thing I would say: Either you pardon those poor mothers, or you admit that you are the shell of a human being without charitable feelings..."

At the place of execution, there was an entire company and a squad of 24 soldiers who formed the firing squad – six for each of the four prisoners (three women and one man)

"...We began the slow walk towards the place of execution. It was the most horrible walk of my life. The three women wobbled as they walked, their hands had been tied, their clothes were in disarray, their hair was a mess (the babies of two of the women had been torn from their breasts as they entered the chapel) ... One of the women shouted: 'So many men just to kill three women...!'"

11 October. Execution of a miner from Asturias. As the prisoner entered the chapel and saw the Dictator's picture on the altar, he protested and refused the comforts of the Church:

"Can't you remove Franco's photo from the alter?", he asked.

3 February 1938. Execution of two prisoners-of-war, the first who was taken prisoner in Celadas, on the Teruel front, and the second, taken in Santoña when Vizcaya was lost to Franco:

1. "When I spoke to him of confession and other religious practices, he flatly refused them. Relatively calmly, he said that religion had been falsified by those who called themselves supporters of the right, priests included, those, he added, who were responsible for everything that we are suffering..."

2. "When Mass was over, he became notably more dejected and he began to panic at the thought of the execution. He asked that he be given some chloroform to deaden his awareness. But they refused, as was expected. When he saw the soldiers, he faltered a moment and refused to walk. Finally, with wobbly steps, he arrived at the site of the execution. He had

nothing to say. You only heard him crying: *Ay, Dios mío! Ay, madre mía…!* As I had suggested, he turned his back to the rifles."

17 March. Following the execution of two high-ranking Republican prisoners and prisoners' state of mind as they arrived in the chapel:

> "I did not ask these condemned men to make a full confession, because their state of mind was comparable to a person who was seriously ill. Some prisoners were truly moribund; in some cases, their nerves were so on edge that they shook violently and their arms and legs jerked. Others vomited. Some fainted."

12 May. Description of a saca of nine inmates, possibly all prisoners-of-war from Alcañiz, one of whom was a woman. When Maria de Asis Figueras entered the chapel:

> "…She began to cry again and shouting at the other prisoners, especially the one called Tomás: 'Look at our misfortune, Tomás, Tomás. This is horrible. Why are they killing us? ' That is not all she shouted and then all the others began shouting at the same time, protesting their innocence. They accused the courts of cruelty. Their yells formed a strident and extremely tragic concert.
>
> I confessed another two during all that shouting… They all took Communion, except for the oldest, Miguel Andrell, who was 61 years old.
>
> When several Guardias Civiles entered the chapel and began to bind their wrists, Maria stood up and shouted: 'Don't take me, don't tie me up, shoot me right here! Tomás, why don't they just kill us right here…?"

At that moment, Father Gumersindo noticed that the woman appeared to be pregnant, so he approached the Judge Executioner:

> "Take a look at the young woman, María Figueras. Look for yourself, if you have any doubts as to what the female prison guard said, that she could be pregnant.
> - 'If for every woman who had to be tried we had to wait for seven months' the judge replied, 'you will understand that it is not possible…' and Maria was tied up, like all the others.
>
> In the truck in which we all went, and which was filthy with bits of earth inside, we continued to hear the mournful concert of heartrending *ayes*, of anguished cries and weeping. I attempted to console them, holding my crucifix in my hand, speaking unending words of comfort.
>
> They sat on wide benches on either side of the truck. I knelt on my knees in the middle of the truck, as there was nowhere else for me to sit.

Old man Andrell, who was the calmest of all, looked at me with anger and finally said: 'You really know how to play your role..."

When we arrived at the place of the execution, we placed ourselves between the wall and the firing squad. I suggested that they turn themselves to the wall so that they would not suffer from looking at the soldiers. Old man Andrell (61-year-old Miguel Andrel), seeing the soldiers arrive, spoke to them:

- Men! You are about to kill sons of the people...!

I stood between the wall and the condemned, unceasingly begging them, one by one, to have faith in God... Suddenly, I heard the prison director's voice shouting: 'Fr. Gumersindo! Get out of the way!' He wanted to give the order to fire and I hadn't realized that. In fact, the officer hadn't noticed that I was still talking to the prisoners. There still was very little daylight.

Young Maria was twisting and turning in place. She continued to sob and cry: *Ay! padre mío! Ay, padre!* Why are they killing me...?' This excited the soldiers and I saw their indifference and disgust mirrored in their faces.

No sooner did I get out of the way than the shots rang out. Four rifles for each prisoner. None of them died instantly. They were not mortally wounded. One of the wounded, rolling about on the ground, cried out: 'They have finished us; we only have a minute left to live!'

They all cried out with pain and some begged for the mercy shot. I went up to each one and absolved them. An officer administered the mercy shot, sometimes repeatedly shooting the dying three times in their heads."

14 July. Description of the execution of eight prisoners from Alcañiz. The firing squad forgets their ammunition.

"As we approached the soldiers, the truck stopped but we were ordered not to get off. A quarter of an hour later and we still had not been ordered to get off. I jumped down and asked a soldier what was happening and what was the reason for the delay. He told me that the soldiers had not brought their ammunition. Fifteen minutes later, some soldiers arrived in a car...

That delay was very harmful to the condemned. Some lost patience and began complaining: 'Why are they keeping us suffering here? How pleased they are to make us suffer! Then they dare say that it is the Rojos who are cruel!... Hurry up and kill us! Please, kill us and be done...!'

Finally, we got there. The soldiers made another mistake that added to the suffering. After lining the eight condemned in a single row, they decided that they would execute four first, then the other four. Right there, in full view of the last four, the officer gave the order to fire against their companions.

They saw the soldiers take aim and fire and they heard the shots. They then watched their companions lying on the ground, rolling in the pools of their blood and crying with pain. Then the same soldiers took their positions in front of the surviving prisoners, who fell next to the first.

Looking at the eight wounded lying on the ground, you got the impression that this was a battlefield."

26 July. Description of the execution against the wall of Torrero cemetery, of 7 victims, almost all prisoners of war, several from Gelsa and one from Belchite.

"The victims of the 26th suffered a great deal. The soldiers shot badly. They were apathetic. One of the executed fell to the ground shouting 'Hurry up and kill me!' All cried and screamed with pain. A deplorable and sorry spectacle…!"

18 October. Description of the execution of another 4 prisoners.

"The soldiers who on that day had the misfortune of being the executioners or part of the firing squad, shot badly. The unfortunate prisoners rolled around on the ground, with pitiful cries and screams that tore at my soul. The unfortunate Martín raised his feet and legs, whilst harsh, deep *Ayes!* from his chest, sounding like a death rattle.

The two who refused confession, exclaimed just before they were shot: ''Viva the Republic! You will soon suffer the same fate!'".

Regarding Isidoro Franquesa, a prisoner-of-war from Vich, on the Teruel front who was denied all spiritual comfort:

"No sir, don't ask me to get involved in religious practices. The right-wing is killing in the name of religion and it has declared war in the name of religion. I want nothing to do with a religion that inspires so much cruelty."

It was 11 June 1938 and he was still in the chapel when he stood up and started walking towards the door. The matter was that the Director and several military officers, as well as the Judge Executioner, had entered the chapel and were standing next to the altar. On the altar, above the crucifix, hung a portrait of Franco. In his opinion, it was a typical political and military farce.

I accompanied the unfortunate prisoner to the identification room. Two prison officers followed us. When he saw those officer, he regretted that as a prisoner of war, he was going to be killed, contrary to the rights of Man. He added that in the Republican zone they did not kill their prisoners, they respected their right to live; as he himself had done."

APPENDIX III

SELECTION OF CAUSA GENERAL FILES FOR CORDOBA PROVINCE

Causa General archives can be consulted
on the Spanish Arcives website at www.pares.mcu.org
Not all the CG file numbers are available for the following,

Bartolomé Fernández Sánchez [Causa General Case number 5,753/39. Pretrial hearing in Cordoba, 16 March 1943.] POZOBLANCO. Sentenced to death but the sentence was commuted.

■ Bartolomé Fernández Sánchez was one of the most famous defenders of the Republic in the Cordoba mountains. His case file states that he was a socialist, 'an extremely active propagandist in the February 1936 elections' and that as a result of these elections, 'the accused and other low-life of the same kind, attacked City Hall and appointed themselves town councillors.' This was totally false, in addition to being absolute nonsense.

Although there are entries to the effect that he organized the Pedroches Militia Battalion 31 August 1936 and served as its first Commander, which was correct, the authorities did not discover that he was also Commander of the 73rd Battalion of the Mixed Brigade. It is noted that he was promoted Major in the Militia 14 September 1938 but not that he commanded F Column during the Cordoba-Extremadura battle of January 1939. In addition to all these military-related charges, in themselves punishable by death, his case file includes a typical, presumably false, allegation from a private individual: 'According to a reliable witness, José Plazuelo, he commanded firing squads against noted individuals and himself administered the *coup de grâce*,' to ensure that the accused would be executed.

Moreno Gómez was unable to discover how Bartolomé Fernández managed to get the latter, totally false, accusation erased from his file. It may have been that as he was tried in 1943, when the Regime's deadly arrows were already soaked in blood, there was a certain lessening of the repressive fury. Besides, this type of accusation could be easily proven false because the firing squads and the coup de grace always were a senior officer's responsibility, never the commanding officer's, in this case, Fernández Sánchez. Bartolomé was still sentenced to death but miraculously, his sentence was commuted.

Antonio Baena Moreno. POZOBLANCO. Executed in Cordoba 17 November 1941.

▪ Antonio Baena Moreno, a 37 year-old socialist schoolteacher, was in a worse predicament than Bartolomé Fernandez. He had served as President of the local War Committee, although at heart he was a kind and reasonable individual who tried to impose law and order but did not know how to go about it. Despite his efforts, many of the right-wing prisoners in Pozoblanco in 1936 who were evacuated to Valencia after Pozoblanco surrendered 15 August 1936 to the rebel troops, were executed by Republicans in Valencia. To add to the seriousness of his situation, he also served as a high-ranking political commissar: no less than Commissar for the VIII Army Corps and, finally, for the entire Army of Extremadura. There was no escape for him. Although he had been sentenced to death by strangulation, he was shot by a firing squad in Cordoba 17 November 1941.

José Madueño Serrano [Causa General Case number 26,298/39]. POZOBLANCO. Originally sentenced to death but later comuted to 30 years' imprisonment.

▪ José Madueño Serrano, an attorney, was tried by court martial 30 September 1939. His case file states that he had once been a member of the right-wing Acción Católica, the Juventud Liberal and the Patriotic Union. However, when the Socialist party arrived on the scene, he ran unsuccessfully for office as Socialist Deputy for Seville in 1936. Served as town councillor in Pozoblanco and later as Provincial Deputy for Cordoba. His file acknowledges that he remained in his house during the insurrection, but one informer declared that "he remained in contact with the Rojos". The file also stated that although he was a mine owner and had access to dynamite, he did not give any to the Rojos. A particularly negative allegation states that at the beginning of the war Madueño Serrano travelled to Elche, Santa Pola and Madrid 'and that during his journey he did not avoid the challenges and crimes committed by the Marxists'. Lastly, the absurd charge: 'considered to be conceited'. Although the case file clearly showed that the accused was never implicated in any kind of disorder, he was sentenced to death but this was later commuted to 30 years' imprisonment.

Antonio Varo Granados [Causa General Case number 26,454/39. Pre-trial hearing in Pozoblanco, 22 April 1940.] AGUILAR/POZOBLANCO. Sentenced to death by strangulation but commuted.

- The pre-trial hearing case file for Antonio Varo Granados, from Aguilar, a public prosecutor in Pozoblanco by profession, was an anthology of false allegations and other irregularities. The notation *'educated'* on his dossier is underlined.

All the charges against Antonio Varo focussed on the supposed nefarious influence of his being an educated person. He was accused of:

- great leftist importance, being an effective propagandist of leftist ideas and using the press to disseminate them, propaganda that was extremely dissolutional, and in view of the personality of the accused and the lack of culture on the part of the worker element, of having considerable influence over the workers, the constant target of his propaganda;

- the beginning of the Glorious Uprising finding him in Madrid and having in his hands the destiny of the people, far from presenting himself to the authorities [*sic.* in his town of residence] who would prevent the commission of outrages and excesses, he continued to remain in Madrid;

- having employed Masonic tactics, as there is a strong presumption that he belonged to that sect; (*Unbelievable! He must have been a Mason because he had all the characteristics of one! FMG*)

- his house in Madrid is said to have been the regular meeting place for all the significant Marxist tycoons;

- his file includes a supposed allegation by relatives of a right-winger who had been murdered in Pozoblanco, Moisés Moreno, saying that Varo was the 'instigator' of that death and that someone heard somebody else say: 'Antonio Varo murdered your father.' (*Varo was in Madrid at the time.*)

Based on that mountain of garbage and of insidious comments, the special Court convened in Pozoblanco presided by Pedro Luengo Benítez, one of the major Fascist magistrates in Cordoba, sentenced Varo to death by strangulation, after declaring that all the information given agreed with the statements that the defendant was the leading individual responsible for all the crimes committed in that town and that he was an extremely dangerous person. Antonio Varo did not stop appealing and 10 January 1940, he appealed to Military Court No. 9 in Pozoblanco, in which he:

"requests that you receive the sworn declaration of Don José Sánchez, Captain of Infantry Regiment 3, of the Badajoz garrison", stating that the defendant sheltered him in his house in Madrid, despite his belonging to an army that was fighting the Republic. Varo adds: "Many right-wing persons from Pozoblanco came to my house to ask for advice and assistance and I received them all." He concludes: "My daily routine basically involved going to work in my office and not going out when I returned."

173

Without a doubt, the testimony of the Badajoz soldier bore some weight as Antonio Varo's terrible sentence was commuted. He was transferred back and forth from one Francoist prison to another, among them, the Burgos prison.

Cesáreo Romero. [Causa General Case number 11.113/39, pre-trial hearing, Pozoblanco, 15 June 1939.] TORRECAMPO. Executed.

- Cesáreo Romero's case file was another pack of lies. His problem was that he had served as Mayor before the coup and the right-wing in his town were baying for his head. His family told Moreno Gómez that Cesáreo was in Espiel when the military coup broke out and he remained there until October 1936, totally removed from any kind of disturbance that might have occurred in Torrecampo. He returned to his town and was not reappointed Mayor until February 1938, many months later. Although he could not be accused of anything, unless it was his political beliefs, his file contains the following allegations and charges for which he received the death penalty:
  – bad behaviour
  – being a Socialist
  – a supporter of the class war
  – instigator and leader of the masses
  – serving as Mayor of the town until four months before the Movement and later re-elected to the same position
  – gave unfavourable information against brothers Alfonso and Esteban Márquez, who were murdered, and
  – every witness considers him to be an extremely radical individual and a danger to the National Cause.

Juan Pulido Cantador. [Ministry of Agriculture proceedings against Juan Pulido Cantador and multiple interviews with Moreno Gómez who was provided with many details of those tragic times.] VILLANUEVA DE CÓRDOBA. Sentenced to death but commuted.

- Juan Pulido Cantador was sentenced to death, not for blood crimes, but on such flimsy charges as: 'the Movement found him in Cuesta del Hornillo, in the county of Montoro, where influenced by his ideals and the aims of the Red revolution, he supported the latter by walking to a farm located one kilometre from the place denominated El Niño Herruzo, where Marxists were staying. The accusers alleged that he got into contact with those Marxists and participated with them in the fight to recapture Villanueva de Cordoba, where they committed murders, then served their cause by first collecting arms from the farms and later grain. The reality of the matter is that the Falangists wanted to get rid of this individual because he had been a leader of several agricultural cooperatives, but he somehow survived, as his sentence was later commuted.

A sample of the many CG files with backdated allegations in Villanueva de Cordoba

<u>José Romero Cachinero.</u> [Causa General Case number 26,709, pre-trial hearing, Villanueva de Cordoba, 24 April 1940.] Sentenced to 30 years in prison.

- José Romero Cachinero was accused by Sebastián Cepas Díaz (brother of the notorious "Berenguer") of having participated in the attack on the town in 1936 and having destroyed bridges in Monterrubio, Castuera and Cabeza del Buey as a member of the guerrilla. He was sentenced to 30 years in prison. He died soon after leaving jail in very poor health from the mistreatment he had suffered.

<u>Luis Sánchez Torralbo.</u> Executed 17 May 1940.

- Martina Castro Díaz accused Luis Sánchez Torralbo of having arrested her husband Antonio Ruiz Justos, who was later shot in Fuente Vieja. Although he denied this, Luíz was still sentenced to death and executed 17 May 1940 in Villanueva de Cordoba.

<u>Juan José Serrano Cepas.</u> [Causa General Case number 27,324/39 pre-trial hearing, Villanueva de Cordoba, 31 January 1940.] Executed 27 December 1940 in Cordoba.

- The charges against Juan José Serrano Cepas were listed on a form signed by a group of Falangists who dedicated themselves to collecting allegations. Miguel Higuera Días, Alfonso Fernández and Matías Pedraza appeared as witnesses to the charges that Serrano Cepas 'participated in the occupation of the town', 'had been a guard in local prisons', 'was a member of the Confiscation of Property Committee', and 'had volunteered' to serve in the militia. No crime was listed, but Serrano Cepas still was sentenced to death and executed in Cordoba 27 December 1940.

Juan Miguel Amor Garcia. [Causa General Case number 1,200/39, pre-trial hearing, Cordoba, 5 February 1941.] Sentenced to 30 years in prison.

- Juan Miguel Amor García a teacher at the Centro Obrero, was accused by Pedro Serrano and Roque Díaz. Pedro Jesús Torres and Juan Ocaña were witnesses for the defence. Juan Amor García had been an active member of several political parties and was accused of being a member of the local War Committee, which he denied. He was also charged with witnessing accusations against Francoists in the Republican People's Court of Jaén. Sentenced to 30 years in prison.

Diego Fernández de Haro. [Causa General Case number 27,453/39, pre-trial hearing, Villanueva de Cordoba, 14 March 1940.] Sentenced to 30 years in prison.

- Diego Fernández de Haro (whose brother, Fernando Fernández de Haro, a private schoolmaster, was executed 25 May 1940). Diego Fernández faced the flimsiest of accusations by Matías Pedraza and Arcadio Herrara who alleged that he beat the priest Fr. Rafael García and was a member of the Supply Committee. In this case, there were two witnesses for the defence: the priest himself who said that when he was a prisoner of the Republicans, he was only hit once because he was walking too slowly in line, and Ángel Chaparro who said that he owed him his life. Despite the inconsistency in the accusations, he was condemned to 30 years in prison. By the time Diego Fernández was released, he had lost his wits as a result of the mistreatment he had received.

Pedro "Cuadradro" Torralbo Gómes. [Causa General Case number 27,404, pre-trial hearing, Villanueva de Cordoba, 1 May 1940.] Executed 3 June 1941 in Cordoba.

- One of the most upstanding Republicans in Villanueva de Cordoba was Pedro "Cuadrado" Torralbo Gómes, one of the founders of the PCE in 1921, city councillor in 1931, provincial deputy in 1936, active organizer of the rebuilding of the town after the military coup and a Captain in the Militia. He was not an extremist, but a prudent and well-organized individual. He was beaten to a pulp after his arrest in 1939. They could not charge him with blood crimes, just of being a leader. His accuser, the landowner Bartolomé Torrico, declared: "I know that Pedro Torralbo himself did not kill anybody, but he did nothing to prevent others from being killed." Pedro was executed in Cordoba 3 June 1941.

Selection of CG files for women in Villanueva de Cordoba

The case files for the numerous women who were charged in Villanueva, exhibit the same bizarre accusations and allegations.

Catalina "La Mojina" Buenestado Herrero. [Causa General Case number 26,708, pre-trial hearing, Villanueva de Cordoba 21 December 1939.] Sentenced to 20 years in prison.

- Catalina "La Mojina" Buenestado Herrero was accused by Mayor Gregorio Pedraza Cámara, of belonging to the JSU and to *Mujeres Antifascistas* [Antifascist Women], of taking part in registrations and seizures and of supporting the International Red Aid. Nothing else of any importance. Sentenced to 20 years in prison.

Ana María Gómez Ruíz. [Causa General Case number 37,131/39, pre-trial hearing, Cordoba, 4 July 1943.] Sentenced to 30 years in prison.

- Ana María Gómez Ruiz was accused by Francisca Coleto Gutiérrez (widow of Miguel Gutiérrez) of being a communist and in the presence of right-wing prisoners, having called out loudly for their death. Sentenced to 30 years in prison.

Juana "La Flora" Pozuelo Expósito. [Causa General Case number 27,416/39, pre-trial hearing, Villanueva de Cordoba, 25 April 1940.] Sentenced to 20 years in prison.

- Juana "La Flora" Pozuelo Expósito, sister to the famous leader Nemesio Pozuelo, was accused of the following absurd charges of being a communist and great propagandist and of having lent her house as a prison for the widows and orphans of Guardia Civil, which was a monstrous lie. What had happened was that when the barracks were closed 24 July 1936 after the Republicans re-took the town from the insurgents, she offered her house as a shelter for the families of the Guardia. An altruistic action that the victors turned into an accusation, also alledging that she went into the fields and countryside looking for weapons. Sentenced to 20 years in prison. Obviously, both the allegations and charges were far-fetched nonsense, simply used to pad the file for a case whose resolution had already been decided.

APPENDIX IV

THE FRANCOIST DEATH RITUAL FIVE EYE-WITNESS DESCRIPTIONS OF THE RITUAL

Leading to the execution

<u>Ángel Horrillo</u>. OJUELOS ALTOS, FUENTEOBEJUNA. Description of the moments leading up to the execution by a survivor. Letter to Moreno Gómez from Peñarroya-Pueblonuevo, 1 July 1983.

- "When I returned to my village in May, even before I entered it I was surrounded by armed men and taken to the Falange. I could easily deny the first allegations, because when they met in their committee where they used to determine the charge, they came up with such a number of false accusations, with the sole purpose of eliminating me. I was tried by a summary court martial, with another nine men, and there were ten death sentences.

  There were some 80 of us in jail during 1939 and the beginning of 1940. From the patio, we could see the arrival of those who came to sign the list of those who would be executed that night. In this terrible situation we found ourselves at 8 or 9 at night and, arranged in circles, the jailor – *Don Manuel* he was called – made us sing *Cara al Sol*, once or twice. He then gave us five seconds for all to go through the 70-centimetre door, but before doing so, hit us left, right and centre.

  A little later, speaking very slowly, he would read out the list and, sarcastically, say 'To the chop' after each name. Four of my group were shot on four different nights: Antonio Ruiz, Luis Romero, Antonio Múñez and Juan Pedro Hidalgo, the last of whom was my uncle. He and his wife were kept in a separate room, but of the same lot of prisoners and when his name was called, she let out a terribly cry. I found it remarkable that I could not control either my heart or my nerves."

<u>**Eva Ruíz**</u>. SEVILLE. Granddaughter of Antonio Ruíz Quiles from Alcalá del Rio, Seville, executed following a saca from Seville prison 22 October 1936. Report presented by Cecilio Gordillo at the Meeting of the Historic Memory Association September 2006.

- "The night my grandfather was shot, a cousin of his or of my grandmother's, I am not sure which, and who worked with him at the power plant, was nearby. It was dawn and he heard voices next to one of the cemetery walls, and he recognized my grandfather's voice. My father tells me that, according to this relative, he recognized his voice shouting and begging not to be killed because he was the father of four."

Antonio Chaparro. VILLANUEVA DE CÓRDOBA. Eye witness account of the trip to the cemetery and the execution of three men 7 November 1940.

- "We were at Fuente Vieja when we heard Pedro Juan "El Chunga" Martínez shouting *Let's go to the bullfight!* We followed the truck and stood behind some walls close to the cemetery. There were a great many soldiers and Guardias Civiles. The condemned men got off the truck like sleepwalkers, white as sheets and, without a word, walked towards the wall. They stood with their backs to the firing squad. Corporal "Pepinillo" Moreno Sevilleno gave the signal with a white handkerchief, without saying a word. The shots rang out and suddenly, the head of one of the men with white hair and a ruddy complexion turned red, as if it had exploded. He and another man fell to the ground, but Pedro Juan jerked upwards, fell on his back, one leg bent at the knee and moving. Corporal Moreno approached him and administered the shot of mercy."

José Moreno Salazar. BUJALANCE. Eye witness to the execution of three young men from Bujalance, without due process of law, 22 November 1941. Reported from a position near the cemetery.

- "I witnessed the execution of those four companions [three, according to the Civil Registry records], friends of my brother's. They were shot at 9 a.m., against the cemetery wall, where the executions were carried out daily, at dawn. In the case of my brother's friends, they wanted to advertise the event and issue a word of terror, which is why they chose daylight. My father and I stood behind a nearby wall and we watched it all. The two brothers, Nievas and Joseíllo, stood with heads bent and said nothing before they died. However, one of them was a true anarchist, 19-year-old Alfonso Alharilla Morales, a close friend of mine, whose father and older brother had already been executed in the same place. He often went out with me to look for food for his mother and young brothers. He was a courageous person... It was a very clear day and you could see and hear everything perfectly. From my look-out point, I heard the fatal "Ready, Aim...!" The two brothers Nievas had Joseíllo dropped their heads but Alharilla, unbuttoning his shirt and presenting his chest to the firing squad, shouted: "Shoot, cowards! We anarchists do not fear death! Viva! the FAI!" I couldn't see anything else because my eyes filled with tears."

Antonio Gómez Tienda. BAENA. Description of the death of Manuel Cañete Tarifa, a young farmer, killed 11 November during the transfer of prisoners from one prison in town to another, the day following a saca of 10 victims 8 November.

- "Prisoners were being transferred in the town when the prison guard, an animal called Palomero, came in and began calling out names. One asked him whether he needed to take his backpack and he replied that he wouldn't need his backpack where he was going. This caused some concern among the prisoners who, nonetheless, were being tied together, two by two. Soon, they heard a shot.

    One of the prisoners, Cañete, who was tied to "El Mota", cut the rope with a shaving stick and ran away. Unfortunately, he was shot in the leg and they caught and finished him off in the Marbella arroyo.

    The prisoners who had remained inside refused to leave, believing that they would be killed in the street. They said that if they were going to kill them outside, they might as well do it indoors. The prison guard explained what had happened but they did not believe him. They had to bring the prisoners who were already out in the street, back in to the prison so that those who were inside could see for themselves that they were still alive.

    The transfer of prisoners was then accomplished without further difficulties. The prisoners were marched down the street forced to sing *Cara al Sol* on the way."